SO-AAZ-090

And Then I Met This Woman

Previously Married Women's Journeys into Lesbian Relationships

Barbee J. Cassingham, M.A.
Sally M. O'Neil, Ph.D.

Expanded Second Edition

Published by
Soaring Eagle Publishing
PO Box 578
Freeland, WA 98249

Copyright 1993, 1998 © by Barbee J. Cassingham and Sally M. O'Neil. All rights reserved. No part of this publication may be reproduced, stored in a retrieval system or transmitted in any form or by any means, electronic photocopying, recording or otherwise, without the prior written permission from the copyright holders, except for the inclusion of brief quotations in a review.

Third Printing: 2002
Library of Congress catalog card number 98-60940
ISBN 0-9658844-1-4

Cover and Book Design: Luci Goodman
Cover Illustration: Zapia Forest

Soaring Eagle Publishing
P O Box 578
Freeland, Washington 98249
Phone: 360-331-4412
Fax: 360-331-4523
email: oneilcas@whidbey.com

Dedication

This book is dedicated, with gratitude, to these
women who opened their lives to us.
Each courageous woman spoke out in order to assist
other women in their journeys.

Acknowledgments

We wish to express our deep appreciation to
Marsha Rule, Patricia Leahy, Sandra Hubert, and Pam West
for reviewing and editing the text
and for their heartening support of our work;
to
Luci Goodman for her continuing encouragement,
support and design assistance with our publishing projects;
and to
Betty who arranged the interviews in Texas.

Introduction

The first edition of *And Then I Met This Woman* was published in 1993 by Mother Courage Press. Since that publication we have had a continuous flow of comments from women about how that book spoke to them. Many could see their own journeys reflected in those stories. All spoke of the relief at knowing that they were not alone in this transition. Many spoke about how moved they were by these women's courage in telling their stories.

In this expanded second edition we have added more stories, included a photo album from those we could contact who wished to submit a photo, and redesigned the cover and book. The basic intent of this edition remains the same as the first: to convey, as much as each woman could impart, the joys and struggles in this very intimate journey.

These women range in age from 28 to 66, their ages at the time of their interview. Many are highly educated with Master's degrees and Ph.D.s and are engaged in diverse occupations. The interviews occurred in Texas, Washington, Oregon, North Carolina and Wisconsin. All stories are edited accounts from longer interviews. It is not our intention that this work be viewed as a research study in which we would present an analysis of our interviews, but rather to be seen as a collection of women telling their stories. We want each voice to be heard.

We were impressed with each woman's willingness and openness in telling her story. These women knew the book's purpose, and they wanted to share what they learned in order to help someone else who might be struggling through conflicts in discovering an attraction to another woman. While there are commonalities in these women's experiences, each negotiated this passage in her own unique way. Because the women spoke from a place in themselves of deep honesty, the telling of their stories was quite an emotional experience for them, often ranging from laughter and joy to deep sadness, pain and tears within each interview. Unfortunately, the printed work does not always reflect the intensity of the emotional experience of the storyteller. As a result, in some of the stories, the emotional content is very subtle.

These transitions are not simply a decision to become a lesbian but, rather, are a transforming commitment to own the authenticity of their feelings for another woman. It is set within a context of wanting to be congruent in all areas of their lives. As a result, they may be coming to terms with other realities that are common to all women. These can include the complexities inherent in loving their children, husbands, parents and friends, as well as struggles with unfulfilling marriages, addictions, and seeking meaningful work. And, for the women in this book, their lives were further complicated by their love for a woman and the issues that are intrinsic to coming out.

As you will see, these stories as a whole reflect all stages of the coming out process. For some, coming out is a very gradual emergence to family and friends. For others, coming out is an all-inclusive, immediate act. For some, it is redefining who they thought they were. For others, it is becoming more fully who they already know themselves to be.

The value of this work, as we see it, is twofold. First, we want to let women know that they are not alone in their attraction to other women. Many of the women interviewed told us that when they were wondering what to do with their feelings for women and with their lives, they had felt very alone and wished there had been a book like this; they wanted more information. We offer these stories to serve that purpose.

The second value of this work lies in the discovery that we are experiencing a change in our society. Even in the six years since the publication of the first edition, the cultural landscape has changed. We are in a time when women are more able to realize they can have a choice in their love relationships. They are finding the courage to follow their hearts, and are discovering the personal empowerment inherent in accepting this part of who they really are.

In offering this book, we are not suggesting that loving another woman is the only way to live authentically. It is simply part of living one's inner truth when part of that truth is love for another woman—as reflected in the paths of these 46 women.

We are touched that these women told us about their lives and their dreams. It is our hope that their dreams will be fulfilled.

Barbee Cassingham
Sally O'Neil
1999

Contents

Susan

We were married for 21 years. . . . Then
I fell in love with a woman!

When I met Tom I was 17 and a freshman in college, and we
went together from then on. We were engaged for five years and
got married. We were married for 21 years and had three children.
Then I fell in love with a woman!

Without naming it or thinking of what was going on, it just
happened. It was an intense friendship at first and then I started
to realize that there was something going on that was sexual, too.
It was exciting and it was scary. It was scary in that I didn't know
what was going to happen next, either in that relationship or in
my whole life with my husband and children.

Actually, Tom and I joined a group that Ann was leading.
Friends asked us if we would like to join them. We went and it was
a very good group.

There was just a special spark that went between Ann and
me. I felt very interested in having a friendship with her. She was
someone I had heard a lot about for some time before I met her.
At that point, it never occurred to me to have sexual thoughts
about another woman. I just thought that this was someone I really
wanted to be friends with.

After the group finished, she and I got together a couple of
times for coffee and later had a picnic with my youngest child. We
did a few things like that, then she went to Europe for the summer.
Her parents were living there. We had a little correspondence

while she was away and it was particularly intense. When she came back we spent a lot of time together. Very gradually it evolved into a sexual relationship.

I never had the feeling that I didn't want to be a lesbian. Before long I was able to name it. We both kind of looked at each other and said, "Do you know what this means?" It's not like we were pretending that we didn't know what we were doing. We were both 33, and neither one of us had ever been with a woman before.

I told Tom about our relationship—not knowing what his reaction was going to be—and he responded that maybe he needed to get to know Ann better, too. She had been spending a lot of time with all of us as a family. Then he spent some time with her on his own, and they started a sexual relationship. That was the way it was when we decided to live together. It was about six months after we had started to become close. We were not into being a threesome—in bed—or really any place else. We were a collection of couples. This was the craziest thing that I have ever done in my life.

I'm glad I did something totally crazy because it helps me relate to others who do crazy things. When we all look at it now, we say, "How could we have been so dumb or so naive to think we could make anything like that work?" It didn't. You know, the beauty of it was that we all managed to stay friends. After a few years, when we had all split up, Ann and I started to rebuild our friendship and now we are the very best of friends. Tom and Ann don't really see each other, although there is no hostility between them.

Tom and I are good friends. All the things that were good in our relationship survived the divorce. We always treated each other with respect. There still is a lot of affection there, and I consider him a part of my family. My kids are my closest family and I have one sister with whom I'm very close. I have a good relationship with them. I also have my close friends who are my chosen family.

I had one other relationship with a man after I had that relationship with Ann. And there were four relationships with women. The shortest one was 18 months. Every relationship with a woman has lasted at least that long, although I haven't lived with each one. One was a long distance relationship with a woman in California. She was an old P.E. teacher of mine with whom I got back in touch and we had a relationship going. We'd get together every six weeks or so and we'd take trips together but I knew that it was going absolutely nowhere.

I was working nights and I didn't see how I was ever going to meet anybody. I had no inroads into the lesbian community. I had finished school and then was working nights and had this long distance relationship going. I was looking at what I might do, including going to some Lesbian Resource Center groups. I knew I had to do something. It wasn't so much that I wanted an intimate relationship—I just needed to know some other lesbians. The only lesbians I knew were two former lovers and they didn't seem to be very interested in introducing me to any of their friends. Each one of those relationships had been pretty closeted and I never felt like I knew other lesbians.

Then one day I happened to pick up a copy of *The Weekly*, where the ads are, and there was a real cute ad that introduced me to the person with whom I had my next relationship. I did meet more people through her; she had more friends and was a little more into the community than I had ever been before.

I have never liked to go to bars to meet people. I like to do things in the outdoors. I like to go up in the mountains and go hiking. I love to go to the theater—plays, concerts, movies, and opera. I also like hanging out by myself and puttering around. I get in a bad way if I don't have enough time of my own. I spend time alone just being relaxed and refreshed.

I am currently in a relationship with Sharon. I met her in the hospital when I was taking care of her mother. She was a very interesting and attractive person. A friend of mine who is a social

3

worker told me that Sharon was a lesbian and had a partner. Sharon didn't know about me. People don't usually know that I'm a lesbian when they meet me.

So, I was looking on her as a lesbian. I remember wondering, "Why don't I get to meet people like this?" I could imagine meeting another nurse but a patient's family member—I had never thought of that as a possibility. I remember wishing I could have a friend like this in my life.I was thinking she was very attractive and about the right age. I was also very interested in what she was doing with her life. She was making a major career change and she talked about it in such an animated way. That was something I had done, too, and I could really relate to it. She had a lot of good energy and was very open and friendly. My feelings were just, "Gee! What a shame she was taken."

I had to call her the night I thought her mother was going to die to say that she should come to the hospital soon. I got her answering machine and I remember thinking afterwards that the message on the machine seemed as if only one person lived there. But people do have relationships where they don't live together.

Then I took a very unusual step for me; I reached out to her when she left that night, saying to her, "I think I'm going to see you again and that we may have more in common than you realize." That was a mysterious thing for me to say to her. I figured that she had no idea that I was a lesbian.

I knew I wouldn't call her, and I really didn't think she'd call me. I thought I might run into her sometime at some lesbian concert or something like that. That has happened to me where I have run into family members of patients in public places. There is this instant recognition of, "Oh my God, I didn't know you were one too." That's what I thought would happen with Sharon. I told people about her. I told my daughter that I had met this person who was neat but that was kind of the end of it. Then Sharon called me. She had figured out what I meant about "more in common than you realize." It went really rather quickly after that. She was not involved with anyone, and we started out by just doing some things together. But both of us were around 50 when we met, and we knew what kind of relationship we wanted. It became clear to both of us that this was it.

We moved very quickly into making plans for being together and we had our commitment ceremony after we had known each other a little over a year. We want to live together, but we won't do that until the house I have now is remodeled and she sells the house she is living in. We've known all along that that's what we were going to do. We both have a lot of confidence that this is going to be the relationship that we both go out on.

In many ways Sharon is just what I wanted and needed. I had had a lot of unsuccessful relationships that I got into for the wrong reasons and in the wrong way. I had, at that point, been in therapy and ended a relationship that I needed to end. For the first time ever I was single and was happy being single. I wasn't looking for a relationship at all. I also knew that if I ever did have another relationship, it was going to be the right one. I had a sense that this was the right one.

I found a journal the other day that I had written shortly after meeting Sharon and I saw where I was already thinking about having a ceremony. I thought then that this relationship was going to be the big one. I had never even wanted to live with any other woman with whom I had had a relationship. Fortunately, she was ready too.

I feel challenged by Sharon and that was one of the things I needed. She really wants to work on our relationship and our communication. She is honest and pushes me to be. We are different in a lot of ways. That's good, too. We complement each other. It's exciting. I would not get into another relationship again unless I felt that way. Being alone would be much, much better.

I was totally closeted during the early years. It was not difficult for me personally to be a lesbian, but I thought it was difficult socially. It was certainly complicated by the fact that I was married and had three small children. We may as well have been on the moon because we were not part of any community at all. What I was doing was beyond the pale because Tom, Ann and I were living together and we didn't feel safe exposing the nature of our relationship to anyone. Our attitude toward our children was that we would never lie to them but we didn't force any information on them either. They asked questions when they were ready.

I guess the only place where I'm not out now is at work. But I know my job would not be threatened if I came out there. There are a lot of gay nurses where I work, and there is no threat. I just haven't felt it was important to do. There is one person at work who knows. The rest have known me for six years and have never known this about me. I wouldn't mind if they knew, but I would feel strange making a grand announcement.

My daughter is a lesbian, and she and other young lesbians I know are very, very comfortable with being who they are and are supported in their work and social environments. I haven't ever seen that they have felt the kind of discrimination that older lesbians have. They have come out in a totally open and supportive environment. My daughter came out when she was in college and found it was wonderful to be a lesbian. There was no question about coming out. She continues to live her life pretty much that way, whereas for me, coming out to straight friends is a process that has taken me some time.

If I could live my life over again I wouldn't do it differently. I wouldn't have my children if I had done things differently and they are a very important part of my life. Not having them is unimaginable. From the point of view of my own fulfillment and my own self-development, I don't think I ever really felt like I knew myself or felt attractive before I knew I was a lesbian. I think that there was something that just wasn't quite right and I didn't know what it was for all those years. I like who I am now and I got here because of all the things that went before. I've had the best of two worlds.

I'm an oncology nurse now. I went back to school when I was in my forties. I have a B.S. in speech pathology and a master's degree in audiology. I used to be a speech pathologist, but I'd been out of the field for a very long time and I didn't have any passion for going back into it. I wanted to do something that I really had some passion about doing. I felt free to make a clean choice at that time and do what I wanted to do. So I went back to school and got a B.S. in nursing.

I've been a nurse for seven years and I like it. It is such hard work that I might decide that I've had enough of it. I'm not close to burning out, although it is physically and mentally demanding.

I look forward to the time when Sharon and I will have gone through some of the rough parts of living together. I think both of us feel that there will be a lot of adjusting to do. We are very strong people and kind of set in our ways. But we don't have any doubt that we will be able to work it out.

Being a lesbian means knowing who I am. It does not have to do with rejecting men nor does sexual activity have much of anything to do with it. I'm not politically active with gay and lesbian organizations, although I do write checks for some causes. I never go to lesbian bars.

To me, being a lesbian is freedom from being defined by relationships to other people—wife, mother, daughter, sister, etc. It's a statement that I value women, find my true self nurtured and stimulated by women, and am comfortable with women. I feel strong and whole in this identity.

I don't know whether I had a choice about being a lesbian, but I did choose to leave a traditional heterosexual life, to make a public commitment to Sharon, and to come out in all areas of my life, except with my patients. These have been powerful and validating choices.

When I came out, I soon realized that all my problems were not solved. Going to a lesbian singles potluck was no easier than going to a college mixer. Intimate relationships are no less challenging with a partner than with a husband. I carry my own issues with me wherever I go, but this is where I belong. I am at home. I am a lesbian.

Peggy

I feel compassion for both of my love affairs.
I feel I've gained wonderfully from both of them.
In that way they are both on an equal plain.

I've had two love affairs in my life, one with a man and one with a woman. The latter was the one that I would call a "love affair" in poetic terms. I would not want to belittle the hetero-sexual affair because it had elements that the other relationship did not have—and vice versa. The difference between the two of them for me was *freedom: physical freedom and lack of fear.* Throughout all my relationships with men (other than with gay men) fear has been a very big element. That doesn't mean fear of sex because I never particularly had that. It was a feeling of being.... victimized.... of being cajoled, of being made ready, of being courted with that one goal in mind. It was done gently but it never felt like an equal relationship.

Ewan MacColl (who wrote "The First Time Ever I Saw your Face" for me) was besotted with me. He was twenty years older than I and had been married twice. We were very, very compat-ible. We were more compatible than Irene (my current partner) and I are. We got on well *because* he was so besotted. Men (especially in middle and old age) seem to regard it as a feather in their cap when they have someone much younger. We were a good pair of opposites: I was woman and he was a man. I was North American and he was Scots-English. I was from the well-off intelligentsia and he was from the very poor working class. He had no "education" to speak of and I had had two years of college—

but I always reckoned he was smarter than I was. He was from the inner city (read slums) and I was from a Washington, D.C. suburb. I had a good musical education. I could read music and play five instruments. He could hardly read music and was hopeless on instruments; but, he could *sing*. Oh, he could sing! He was totally literate as far as words were concerned. He knew more words than you could believe.

It is strange that so many opposites worked. But, I wasn't in love with him the way I'm in love with Irene. Ewan's wife wouldn't give him a divorce so we couldn't marry. We married after twenty years after having three children out of wedlock. He once told me that he'd do anything for me—*even marry me.* (Mind you, he said that when he wasn't free to do so.) I didn't want to marry him. When somebody says, "I'll do anything for you, even marry you," it's hardly an incentive to go to the altar. We only married because of changes in the tax laws. It was a miserable day. Two of our children were at the ceremony helpless with laughter. We both got drunk and cried. It didn't change anything for us the way it seems to do for some people who live together for some time and then get married. Ours was a peaceful relationship but, now that I look back on it, quite controlling. But then I'm easy to dominate. People who want to be liked are in a very weak position and I always wanted to be liked. Irene controls me. She is a strong person. So was Ewan. I'm getting stronger now and able to stand up for myself, but I haven't been dominant in either of my relationships. At least not the most dominant of the two.

Ewan and I lived in England and in each other's pockets for thirty-two years. We worked together, slept together, ate together, traveled together, had children together. We were regarded as one of the main props of the British folksong revival—a duo that stayed together for three decades and did really seminal and innovative work. We argued very rarely. We lapsed very quickly from a passionate relationship into domesticity. This is something Irene and I haven't. We were very passionate and are not particularly domestically suited. My relationship with Ewan was damaged very early by the fact that after he came to live with me his wife had another child. I know the circumstances (verified by, of all people, his mother), so I forgave him because it all arose out of compassion and (I now realize) love for his wife. You see, he had a son when we met. Then he and I had a son. Then he and his wife had a daughter—it was the sex of that child that hurt me so much for I was my father's first daughter after four boys. I thought girls had a special place in their father's eyes and here *she* had provided this for him. I never got over that. For me, it colored our relationship. It broke its fineness. It put a crack in the china that was whole and unblemished before that. There was the whole bowl there before that happened. If his wife reads this book, she might be very happy about that—her daughter was her ace-in-the-hole. Then I had another boy. I had wanted a girl, but the minute I saw him, I wanted him, so there was no grief there. When that son was ten, we decided to have a third child. I studied up and this time we got a daughter. She was the apple of Ewan's eye (the last child always seems to be). Neither of us had favorites.

Of all the men that I dallied with (to put it blandly) none of them knew about proper foreplay. I mean *real foreplay*, not just the stuff that starts the juices flowing. None of them knew about continual courtship. I am sure that there are men who do know these things—it's just that I never met them. There is something in the make-up of so many men that makes them in a hurry both before and after. Of course, it may be part of their charm—and maybe we don't really want them around a lot. You know, come and move my piano and then go! With Irene, I discovered the glory of just lying in bed and just touching and just sitting across a table and just looking at each other. We felt that way for years. Sometimes we still do.

This is not to say that Ewan wasn't "romantic." He'd have liked to have been but I just wasn't enough in love with him. He was a poet and he wrote very beautifully about love. He would often turn up with some nice little present completely out of the blue. Or, he'd write a song—a love song—when I was least expecting it. But there was always that penis, that demanding, pleading, ever-present member. I don't think I could have a relationship with a man again. It's that penis; it has no conscience, as the saying goes. With a man, you lie down in bed, say, and you want to read. Or you want to go to sleep. Then you feel it rising, poking you, and unless you have a perfect relationship, you cannot say, "NO." Our relationship was good on almost every front but this one. I soon learned that there was a mood, a kind of *quiet* if I didn't say yes. So I learned to pretend. And pretending is not something that stops at the foreplay level. Unless you *really* feel like making love, you feel put upon. I use the word "victimized." It's a very oppressive word, I know, but I think that's what happens even with someone you love deeply and with whom you get along on every other level. It's as if the penis takes them to a level that cannot be socialized. That's why if I ever broke up with Irene (which I can't imagine) I doubt if I'd go to another man because I don't think I could deal with that again. Especially now that I am older and would probably take an older man. So much of their self-image is carried in that little appendage. Ewan was twenty years older than I, and when he began to loose his sexual powers it grieved him terribly. He became quite jealous of me even talking to other men for any prolonged amount of time or with any deep interest. Then, when he got ill with his heart problem, we were in trouble.

So I think of myself as a lesbian and I am. Years ago, if you asked me if I was heterosexual, I would have said, "Yes," without knowing any better. I'd like to say that love is love. I've written ten love songs for Irene and not one of them suggests it's between women because love is love.

Ewan got ill a lot. When I first knew him he always had some ailment or other. He was a man of extremes, including physical extremes. One moment he could be hale and hearty and the next

12

moment he would be bent with a slipped disc or holed up in bed with a hot water bottle and rum toddies. One minute he'd be walking out in the winter in shorts and a T-shirt and the next moment he'd be in bed with bronchitis gasping for breath. He was up and down, in and out of a sick bed—but he wasn't a hypochondriac.

In 1979, his heart problems began and he gave up smoking immediately. For me, it was the beginning of ten years of caregiving. He was very philosophical and, in many ways, very humorous about it. But our roles changed and I gradually became the dominant force. I was just watching very carefully what was going to happen to this man. By 1984, 1985, he was having attacks every few days; by 1988 they were daily. He had arrhythmia, diverticulitis, a hiatal hernia, arteriosclerosis, and I forget what else. He had various digestive problems. He had old Fateful, his ever-present slipped disc. There was always something wrong with him although his bronchitis had eased up once he quit smoking. He even had malaria symptoms every five years or so after receiving malaria shots in 1976 so that we could go to Australia.

I'm not a good caregiver and having to be in that role made me ripe for what happened in the winter of 1988. Every caregiver needs care and I wasn't getting it. I was so busy—taking care of two businesses, going out to sing, handling a household, as well as being a nurse and hand-holder. I only had one child left at home, Kitty. She was in her teens and we were in the usual standoff state that so many mothers and daughters seem to hit at that time. I have believed ever since that I was neglecting her in order to take care of Ewan. His state of health dictated everything despite the fact that Kitty had had serious asthma (and I do mean *serious*) since she was six weeks old. The whole focus of the house had simply shifted so that he was at its centre, the centre that had belonged to Kitty previous to 1979. Every time he got sick plans had to change.

It sounds heartless when I put it that way, but I did resent it. And I think Kitty did,too.

I have known Irene since 1963. I don't remember meeting her for the first time. She remembers though. Ewan and I went over to Belfast to sing at a benefit for Dave Kitson, who'd been arrested with Nelson Mandela. Irene was a part of the support act—we have a picture of her performing with Ewan listening. She remembers that all I talked about were my children. She is the sister of an artist who was a good friend of ours so we met her again in London. When one of our house-helpers left suddenly, Irene stepped into the breach. She has some funny stories about that. We lived in the same suburb. My first concrete memory of her is of a girl, with a whirlwind of red hair, running down the pavement in front of a house in Beckenham. She appeared on and off in our lives from the late sixties onward.

I first really began to remember Irene on a regular basis in about 1982, 1983. We were both members of an anti-nuclear power group and her ideas were always too daring, too advanced, for the rest of the group. I wasn't attracted to her physically but I kept seeking out her company although I never felt we were friends. Ewan disliked her strongly. This was very strange because Ewan did like women's company, but he definitely took against Irene. We didn't have a friendship then, Irene and I. That didn't really start until 1985 or so when occasionally Ewan would get too ill to perform. I'd go to the concert alone and so that the audience wouldn't have to listen to my voice all the way through, I would ask Irene if she would go along and sing with me. She was always amenable. She likes spontaneity. I don't know why I always asked her because I felt rather awkward with her. I don't know quite why. Perhaps, it's that when she looks at you she does more than look at you. Her gaze is remarkably steady. You sit in a restaurant with her and she LOOKS at people. It's almost a stare. One of these days somebody is going to punch her in the face. That "watching" kind of made me nervous. Like she saw through me. She wasn't like any woman I'd ever known. I found I couldn't charm her. She was always asking these awkward questions and saying awkward things. She always told you exactly what she thought. I knew she lived with a woman but it never occurred to me that it was a lesbian relationship.

In 1985, we were about to go into our group meeting and she said, "What do you think about me getting married?" I asked, "Who to?" for there was no man in her life to my knowledge. She said, "To Philip." He was her partner in the veterinary surgery where she worked. I said, "I didn't know you were in love with him." She replied that she was not, that it was going to be a business marriage so they could start their own veterinary surgery together. I said, "Why are you asking me?" She said her mother was in Australia and she had to ask somebody. The next thing I knew, she was married. I wasn't even invited. I assumed that she was properly married, physical and all. Turned out that it really *was* a business marriage. Nothing else. He's a nice man. I like him and regard him as a friend.

We toddled along in this kind of relationship. We were in political and singing groups—and all this time Ewan was getting more and more ill. By 1987 his attacks were so bad that I daily believed that I was losing him. This was an absolutely heart-rending time for me because I had been with him for 32 years. He was my mate. Every time he got an attack I would tell myself, "This is it. He's going to die today." I would just try and stay calm or I would take him down to the hospital. I would get his medicine and he would lie down. Half the time he was laughing or joking. He'd say, "I'm going now, Peg. If I go this time...." and then he'd give me some message for one of the kids or remind me of something that had to be done. That's the way he was. He was very good natured and brave. He was very afraid, too, but he loved me and much of his bravado was for my sake. By November of 1988, I was totally exhausted. I was bone-weary. We hadn't scaled down on much except for touring and whenever we went on holiday he'd be in hospital—once he had an attack at Gatwick and was lying on the floor. Kitty was standing holding our holiday bags. I think she got used to it quicker than I did.

Ewan and I had always been together. We hardly ever went out socially. He had given up his circle of friends when I came along. We were just—together. I didn't mind. We worked well together. We were very, very productive, much more so than I am now. We did radio shows, television shows, music for films, gave lectures and workshops. We were into every possible political issue because he was a lifelong activist and he burned with political commitment. That kept me going too. It was very, very exciting and I wouldn't have missed it for anything. Part of my problem in the late 80s was that I *did* miss it because his illness was curtailing so much of our life. We were home too much. He was in bed too much. He wanted to sit home and watch television or read. So that autumn of 1988 I started going out on my own, with Irene or with the women. He thought I was safe with the women . He'd ask me when I'd be home. I'd say 11:30. If I got home at 12 there was trouble. Moods. He would confront me about staying out; what I'd been doing. Of course, a lot of it was because he worried that I might have been in a traffic accident or something like that. We always worried when we missed connections like that. I rarely thought to phone and tell him I was going to be late. All this time I was writing feminist songs and talking feminist talk. Irene would tell me that I wasn't a feminist. I would say I was. She would say that I wasn't because I had to be home by 11:30. Of course, she was right. This particular aspect of my relationship with Ewan was very suffocating.

That autumn, Irene and I went off several times for hill walks, usually with members of the singing group. But one time, we went alone, the two of us. The weather was bitter cold—November, 1988. We had to drive north for four or five hours to find a place to stay. We ended up at a bed and breakfast and asked to see the rooms. There was a room with two single beds in it. I don't

16

to this day know why I did it, but I said that we would like two single rooms, please. It was, as they say, "cold as a witch's tit, cold as an Eskimo's tool." Anyway we both froze for two nights in the pitiful single rooms. Irene still teases me about it. Irene and I didn't know each other very well. We walked and talked. She told me she was going to Australia in a month to help her woman-friend get settled there. I still didn't suspect that that friend had been her lover for 20 years! I wasn't even curious about it. She was very, very low in spirits—depressed and talking about suicide. I didn't even understand why she was talking to me about this. She had never confided in me before.

You know, I always liked looking at the bodies of women. I've never been attracted by nude males. I had never seen Irene with nothing on. I rarely touched her. I'd never had women friends so I didn't know how to be a friend. Previously, I had gotten several commiserating hugs from her when I'd been in a state about Ewan's illness. Once I'd burst out crying about it and she held me in her arms in the front seat of the car for ten or fifteen minutes while I bawled and sobbed. His illness was just killing me. It was draining me. I was grieving before he was dead. But now, we were walking down from the pub above Miller's Dale and she told me that anytime I needed a hug just to tell her. I said that I needed one now. She just stopped in the middle of the road and gave me this wonderful long hug. Very, very comforting, just standing there in the road hugging. It felt more solid than the other hugs she'd given me. We came back and got in the car, went to eat and then went to our single beds. The concept of gaining emotional sustenance from a woman had never occurred to me. I didn't talk about my private life to anyone then. I do now—endlessly. Friends, both men and women, talk about their private lives to me. I especially like talking to women. It's as if I have entered a community that I didn't know existed, that I'd been excluded from because of my relationship with (and commitment to) a man. Many times, before I fell in love with Irene, I would come back from doing

17

something with her and Ewan would accuse me of having a lesbian relationship with her. Which I did not. I preferred her company to the other women and she was always ready to get up and go. He did not like my relationship with her. He did not like my being with her a lot. He'd have rather I went with Jackie, or Sue, or Barbara; anyone but Irene. But I preferred her company to the other women.

We had to come home the next day. We stopped for a cup of coffee at a welcoming little pub set way off in the middle of a bleak Derbyshire moorland. We have always enjoyed sitting over coffee together. Still do. It was cold, damp and grey, and there was a fire. I looked across the table and saw her lifting her coffee cup to her mouth. There's just this way that her mouth sometimes sets—and I thought, "Oh my God, I love this woman." I was swept with cold from head to foot. I sat there just watching while she drank her coffee. I don't know how long I sat there with my mouth open and my mind whirling. She doesn't remember it. I will never forget it. We got up and paid. She drove all the way back and I didn't say a word all the way. I had brought work with me that had a deadline assigned. I told her I was just trying to do my work. I couldn't have spoken. I couldn't even look at her.

I felt terrible about lying to Ewan, although I had lied about quite a number of little things during our life together. When you begin with the big lie, little lies follow easily in its wake. But this was another big lie. It made no matter that he lied to his wife for three years about us. He had left her for me. I now know that he lied to me about a number of things in his life—but I didn't know then. But a lot of poets and writers are...er...creative with the truth. They want to be seen as bigger than they are or wish to be perceived as they are not. But who was I to talk when I had spent most of my life wanting to be liked, wanting to be seen for what I was not?

All of December of 1988 I was in an erotic state. I liquified. I trembled. I shook with shame. All my preconceptions about lesbianism came to haunt me. But I took every opportunity to be with Irene, to watch her. I didn't say anything to her. I thought, "Yes, this is what's happening. I'm in love." And I drowned in it. I was being sucked out of my family, away from Ewan. I would sit at the table and I wouldn't know who was talking to me. I would have to tell myself to concentrate. "Peggy, you're here at the dinner table. Kitty is talking. Now listen to Kitty. Now you have to answer Kitty. Now you are passing the beans." My mind would wander and I'd haul it back forcefully. Short sentences helped. They concentrated my attention. Then I would retreat into that lovely dream world.

It's a long sweet story—no time to tell it all. She went to Australia for January, 1989, and I didn't think I would survive that month. My suffering was real, unending. My heartbeat woke me early in the morning and I thought of her last thing at night. I was terrified of talking in my sleep. I went away to a health farm for a week because I couldn't bear to be at home. When she finally came back I declared myself to her (in, of all places, the Sanctuary in London)...a prepared speech after which I fully expected her to forsake my company. She didn't. Several days later, she declared herself as well and we embarked upon the sweetest physical relationship of my life. It was the most delicious total relationship. We didn't hop into bed quickly. We courted in her bedroom but didn't sleep together for over three months—till we both agreed that it was time. And when it was time, it was as I understand love and lovemaking should be. No fear, no victimization. I gave myself completely for the first time in my life. We snatched bits and pieces of time away from our other lives. We melted together. That's my version of it.

Irene pulled me through a very bad time. When Ewan got really ill in the summer of 1989 I think that he knew that I was in love with somebody else and that gave him less will to live, for living was a struggle for him. We had been drawing apart over that year and I was incapable of being with him physically any more. He had told me any number of times that if I took another lover

19

he would want to die. I can now understand that. When I fell in love with Irene, I could understand that total commitment. You do anything to stay with this person and I have done *anything*. Irene and I have been through a very bad time these last two years and I'm still here. I think Ewan decided it was time to go. He knew what he was getting into with a woman twenty years younger... but who knows what they're getting into? Love is irrational. You can't do anything with it once it comes—it's just there. It's a blessing and a curse.

When Ewan died, I went into a tailspin of guilt and sorrow. I genuinely missed him. I had constant headaches and crying fits. I was no comfort to my daughter, about whom I felt so guilty. We hadn't been getting along terribly well recently anyway. It was a terrible, terrible time. Irene loved me deeply and she pulled me through those very bad years, probably at great cost to her other relationship. Our physical closeness was probably the main thing that pulled me through—that physical bonding with her was the closest I have ever come to feeling my mind, body and heart all totally working and responding together. We had a very bad period. Irene is a caregiver. She'll care for you even when you don't want her to. She'll watch over you. She'll see that you do things right. She's always trying to improve everything with which she comes in contact, be it a pudding, a lover or the earth. She pulled me through crisis after crisis. Her situation with Philip was still solid—he was probably better for her than I was. She and I didn't want to live together. Being in England reminded me always of Ewan. My house, the weather and the pollution of my suburb depressed me. I had always wanted to return to America to live even if just for awhile. So I left. I came to North Carolina with four musical instruments and six boxes of belongings. I think I probably broke her heart by coming to America. I wanted to come back and find out what I had been pre-Ewan. I wanted to come back to the music and the culture I was brought up with. I wanted bright autumn leaves and spacious skies and predictable weather.

I suppose I wanted independence. So I looked for a place I thought she would like, for I assumed that she would join me. I found Asheville, North Carolina, and liked it. It wasn't until she came over the first time that I found out how deeply she dislikes the American superculture. She doesn't really want to live here. She'll probably spend a lot of her time here because I'm here. She really wants to live in Australia or New Zealand and it looks like she'll get there. I don't have enough points to live there—and I don't want to anyway. It's too far from my kids. It's too far from the banjo and guitar music that I love.

I don't define myself by my sexuality. I'm a person who happens to love a woman. I hope I've been a good lover to her. Our last couple of years have been rocky but we're trying to work our way through it. I think we have something very strong if we can work out the kinks. We don't live well together in close quarters. She is a perfectionist and I definitely am not. I'm getting absent-minded now (even more absentminded than I used to be) and I have a career that takes me away from home. Two years ago her husband decided that he wanted to leave. He is ten years younger that she. They get along beautifully. Best marriage I've ever seen —platonic and cheerful and sharing. They were total friends. They were also both perfectionists! Together they had a home and a veterinary surgery business and now everything was having to be split up. It's been emotionally harrowing for her. Her life has been turned upside down in the last two years and she's trying to rebuild it. My falling in love with her put a wedge into things. Who knows, it all might have collapsed anyhow. She's not blaming me for it in any way but now she's having to find something she really wants to do. She is fifty-one and I am sixty-three. Now I'm finding myself in the same situation that Ewan (74) and I (54) were in a decade ago. That is, I am very conscious of getting older more quickly than my partner.

My father ruled our household, albeit with a velvet glove. He was gentle and my mother was energetic and always doing things.

But my father was the one who really set the pace for the household. I went from that father to a surrogate one, Ewan, to whom I practically apprenticed myself from the age of 21. Ewan was always on the move with ideas and projects and I was quick to follow. To *follow*. Now I'm looking at this household that Irene and I have (when she is in Asheville). I really have to stand up for myself so as to not be in that "following" position. We always seem to choose our opposites. I've heard it said that every middle-class person should partner with a working-class one, every active person with a passive one, in order to keep the partnership alive and interesting. I have chosen a second love very much like my first love. My relationship with Irene fascinates me, although at present, it is causing me some grief, for at this point I don't know what I give her or what she wants from me. I know what I *used* to give her but she is in such a state now that my role seems confusing to me. I don't know why she sticks with me. Maybe the time has come for her to move on.

Irene has a different world view from me. I get an enormous number of ideas for songs from her. She is the best critic of my work that I have ever had. She has insights into people and things that evade me entirely. On the other hand, I grew up with the ability to learn skills in music which she wants but cannot seem to master. She has a lovely singing voice but lacks the incentive to make herself "a singer". We sang together for four years, but it didn't quite work out. I am better as a solo artist. I grew up being happy with what I am in terms of my musical skills and I am able to live within my limitations. She wants to be everything and she wants me to be beyond what I do, more than I am. I don't know if I will be enough for her or if she will be enough for herself. That's very hard.

For a long time I didn't talk to friends about my relationship with Irene. I got in such a state after Ewan died that I had a constant headache or crying fit. My head was killing me and my beloved daughter, Kitty, and I were at each other's throats. She has been the treasure of my life; an asthmatic child with whom I bonded from the moment she was born. After Ewan died, there were so many things I couldn't deal with, including her, that I just wanted to be out of this world. Not dead—just out of my head. I decided to put myself on sedation for six weeks. Just before I went on it, I got the kids together and I confessed to being deeply in love with Irene. My oldest son almost started laughing, "You think we don't *know* that?" Kitty was very angry. She got in the car and drove away—she stayed away for three or four hours. She and Irene don't take to each other and I don't know if they ever will. My sons like her, though. But, nonetheless, I was very ill and Irene and Kitty handled my sedation at home together. Coming out to my kids? It wasn't such a big deal when I finally faced up to it. I don't know how I thought they didn't know. Kids are so smart these days, although maybe I wasn't good at concealment. It must have been obvious to an awful lot of people.

In 1994, the BBC decided to do five half-hour programs on my life. I suspected they chiefly wanted to know about my life with Ewan. So I talked and talked and the producer edited it down. It was very well received. It got the Sony Silver Award for that year. I asked the producer if I could have a sixth program because I felt there was someone else in my life to whom I hadn't paid tribute. He agreed and I did a program in which I talked about Irene and my debt to her. The morning after the broadcast, *The Daily Mirror* (one of our tabloids) featured a centre spread containing a photo of me looking sad and pensive, a terrible photo of Irene and a photo of Ewan looking glum. I could never believe that Camilla Parker-Bowles looked as dreadful as those pictures that came out when Diana and Charles were splitting up. The papers choose and print what they want. The headline was bold: WOMAN TO WHOM "FIRST TIME EVER" WAS WRITTEN HAS GAY LOVER. Other papers phoned me. I got hate letters. I also got letters of thanks and congratulations. The BBC phoned me and I went on *Woman's Hour*—it was quite a public outing. It was necessary because I felt I was a sham unless I credited Irene for supporting me and pulling me out of a state that was spiritually life-threatening. Both she and Philip agreed to my action.

Sometimes when your partner is female, it is almost like being an old person, a person in a wheelchair, or a child. People talk past you or above your head. Your lovelife is invisible. You ask them about their (heterosexual, of course) partner and they don't ask back. For a long time none of my kids ever asked me how Irene was faring. I would ask about *their* wives, partners, friends—only in the last four or five years have they asked, "How's Irene?" or said, "Give my love to Irene," irrespective of whether I have asked after their partners first. It especially touches me when Kitty asks.

When I was with Ewan I saw the world based on a heterosexual norm. I remember once being interviewed by a lovely young woman. The subject was feminism. It was a very skillful interview. She asked all the right questions and she was very compassionate and knowledgeable. She asked me how I felt about lesbians, for none of my feminist songs were about homosexuality. I replied that I didn't really feel at home with lesbians. (This was stupid for a start for I didn't know any.) She asked why. "I really don't know," said I. She asked, "Do you feel they are after your body?" I told her, "No." I told her that I was a heterosexual woman and that I felt at home with heterosexual women. Then, she asked me what I thought lesbians were like? I told her what I thought—how ignorant I was! I described the stereotype lesbian so beloved of homophobics—something that was totally different from her. Then she said calmly, "I'm a lesbian."

Having a lesbian relationship has helped me to see heterosexual women where they are because I've been there, done that. I notice how many women there are who have left their husbands, or whose husbands have left them, especially in my age group. Of those who have moved on to lesbian relationships.... the stories they have to tell about their marriages, oh my! It has made me

24

much more cynical about marriage as an institution; not about heterosexuality, but about marriage. And it has made me much more compassionate for where we are as women. We are internally colonized, as much colonized as people of color. Our virtues and strengths have been marginalized, put down, discouraged. Our deep connections with the earth, with nature, have been scorned. Etc., etc., etc. This is a big subject and I won't get into it here. It's my hobby horse. But I think the next millennium is going to be the women's millennium. We're going to forge ahead and take our share of leadership and do things that are absolutely going to stun that other gender and I hope we can all share and develop and be excited about it—for there is a hard time coming.

It's now possible to come out as you couldn't do when I first fell in love with Irene. Within this last decade, being a lesbian has become socially acceptable in large sections of the population. There is so much talk and theorizing about it. You read about lesbians in the papers and there are so many well-known women who have come out. I don't want to make a thing of it, though. I don't want to be defined by my sexuality even if it *is* a political declaration as well as an emotional one. How do I want to be defined? I'm a singer, a political person, a good lover, a (good?) mother, a human who has been fortunate to love deeply.

I feel compassion for both of my love affairs. I feel I've gained wonderfully from both of them. In that way they are both on an equal plain. Ewan was besotted with me and I am besotted with Irene. I don't think Irene is besotted with me. I know she loves me very dearly, but I don't think she has that same compulsion, the same physical needs that I have. It is something I don't want to discuss too much or turn into something cerebral. Ewan always knew that he loved me "more" than I loved him. We both talked about it. We had to because our staying together depended on understanding that discrepancy in devotion. His love made him a better person. It made him willing to fight his temperament and to put up with my immaturity and my eccentricity. He hardly ever lost his temper with me. He hit me once and, by God, I deserved it. He was so horrified by what he had done that he burst into tears. He never hit me again. There have been occasions on which I have been sorely tempted to hit Irene. I am not a violent person, but I recognize that being besotted and frustrated beyond your limit can make you lose control. I'm afraid of that. I can't imagine how *two* people besotted and frustrated would manage....

If ever I broke up with Irene, I'd be rudderless. I thought for the last three years we were breaking up. I didn't know where she was in her head. She is not a person who tells me where she is. I have to guess, for she goes quiet for hours on end. Sometimes days.

Ewan and I never went for long without sorting out a modus operandi for day-to-day existence. Neither of us had moods. But Irene pulls back into herself and I have no idea where she is. I get frantic and tell myself that she doesn't love me any more, then I make her life difficult by my reactions. Laughable, isn't it?.

I haven't written any songs about lesbians. I've written Irene buckets of love poetry (some quite obviously lesbian) but all my dozen or so love songs to her give no clue as to the gender of either of us. I should write about lesbianism; maybe I will sometime. It's been quite an eye-opener to come out, to become part of the women's community and have so many women couples as friends. The biggest eye-opener was the Womyn's Festival in Michigan in 1992 where the butch-and-femme scene was in full play. We both found it very upsetting to see women with their heads shaved, dressed in leather and looking for all the world like men, sitting with their legs splayed and their femmes sitting on their laps in lipstick, high heels and little skirts. It seemed as if we were just passing on the power structure that we'd inherited from the heterosexual world. I know that oppressed peoples often take on the manifestations of the oppressor as part of their defense. But now I know that there are many different kinds of lesbians, that there are women whom you would never *guess* are lesbians. I've been told that I am one such. I used to think you could tell a lesbian at a hundred yards.

I don't want to live my life out only among lesbians or women any more than I want to live it totally within any homogeneous group. I like a good mix. There are a lot of men I really like being with. Years ago if you had asked me if I were heterosexual, I'd have said, "Yes, of course," without knowing any better. I didn't know then how easily things change. I'd like to say that love is love no matter at whom it is directed. Mine's been directed at Irene for nearly ten years now and it doesn't look like it's going to abate.

Cathryn

Coming out to God is one of the first things Christian people do. But, coming out to God is huge. As if God doesn't know!

My name is Cathryn Cummings-Bond. I was born in Pendleton, Oregon, and grew up in Walla Walla, Washington. I am an ordained minister, a hospice chaplain, an inspirational speaker, and the pastor of Spirit of the Sound. As a speaker, I talk about women from history—Helen Keller, Eleanor Roosevelt, Sojourner Truth, and Harriet Tubman. They have been the best role models for me in my coming out and in finding the courage to do what I needed to do, and to live truth with integrity. In Spirit of the Sound, I'm trying to create a community of faith and a nest for gay and lesbian Christians.

My family is a loving Christian family. I was raised in the United Church of Christ which is where I am now. I was ordained in the Presbyterian Church. I am the youngest of four children. For me, the truth of the matter is that I never gave it any thought or even considered the possibility of loving a woman. I am a very people-oriented person. I love people passionately—men and women. I was a pleaser; I wanted to please people.

I fell in love in high school, at least I think I fell in love. I know he was my best friend. He was a wonderful man. Seven years later we were married. We grew up together in terms of faith and a lot of things. We went off to seminary together and then did powerful ministry together. We had two beautiful children. We had a good relationship and were married for seventeen years.

I still care about my husband, but he doesn't speak to me today. This is still very hard because I work at keeping my heart supple and forgiving. I hope that there will be reconciliation. I know that is what I want and I know that is what God wants. I think that life is about relationships. Divorce is hard whether it has the gay component or not. If you can focus on the relationship once the marriage is over, that is the important thing. I preach that and I try to live it. But, it is hard when the other person refuses to speak to you. Many times a year, I ask him if we can have a conversation and he refuses. So, unfortunately, it puts the children in the middle, which makes me so sad. It's a horrible place for a child to be. He is a pastor and therapist! The children are with him half the time. I'm the one who had to fight for shared custody because I'm the one who's gay.

At thirty-seven years old, I fell in love with a woman. I fell in love—bonkers. I know that this is a very common story—women in mid-life falling in love with women, particularly among women of faith. I am deeply committed as a person. So when I fell in love with her, it wasn't going to be a passing thing. One time, my five-year old daughter and I were walking down the street and she said, "Mom, do you love Daddy or Connie more?" I just about choked and nearly fell off the curb. I said, "Of course, your daddy."

Connie's and my love is a different kind of love than I had ever experienced. It has been very hard because of my children, my ordination, and society. At one point, I remember it was as though I were on a teeter-totter. At one end was all my education, my degree, my profession, the children, everyone I had known in my life, and all that I had made of my life thus far. On the other side was this one little woman whom I loved.

It just took one person to say, "If you choose this woman, I will stand with you." It allowed me to follow my heart, to live with integrity, speaking the truth in love. I must say that I have worked so hard at being loving, regardless of how I've been treated by the church and by past friends. I've worked at not being a victim, although I can still fall into that.

A friend from a church I served in California, a woman who is older than I and my dearest friend said, "I heard that your marriage is in trouble." She and her husband came immediately to be with us. She said, "If you choose Connie, I will stand with you." It certainly was the road less traveled. It was the more difficult path and I knew it. It was a love that took courage. That's why Sojourner Truth and Harriet Tubman are my role models and I believe the underground railroad of today is gay and lesbian people, particularly in the church. That's why I'm working in Spirit of the Sound to let people know that it is not an oxymoron to be a gay or lesbian, bisexual or trans-sexual Christian.

It's still so painful. It is still so painful because I never wanted to hurt anybody. So much of the pain is because there has been such a lack of reconciliation with my kids' father. I refuse to call him my ex. I think our culture has a problem in that we think you have to hate your previous spouse. How could you ever hate the person you loved and had children with? It's immature.

Like most people in the gay community, I had gone to a therapist. We all know about therapy. I went to a woman who was a Jewish angel, a woman who respected my faith. She said, "I will not tell you what to do, but I will help you reach down inside yourself and know what it is that you want to do." I had lost about 25 pounds. I wanted to know how I could be faithful, be a good mother, do it all, and still get to love this person that my heart said I love.

In my first session I told her that I was in love with someone other than my husband. I just broke into tears and said that it was much more complicated, that she lived in another state. I cried the whole session. She told me not to tell my husband yet, because I had a lot of work to do. Later, when he found that out, he saw it as a betrayal and he got very angry. I don't want to say that I'm blameless here. I was an adulterer.

I told my parents that I was going to get a divorce and that I was going to spend the rest of my life with Connie. They were flabbergasted. I had given the impression that my husband and I had the best marriage in the world. I was a great actress.

I have a closer relationship with my dad than with my mom, and I asked my dad to go see *Fried Green Tomatoes*. He went the next day. He is a very wise man in his eighties. When I asked him what he thought, he said, "Well, not everyone thinks they were lesbians."" I said," Are you conducting a survey?" He said, "That's exactly what I am doing. I've been asking strangers in the grocery store if they saw the movie and if they thought they were lesbians. My world is all turned upside down, dear." So, I said, "What do you think?" He said, "I think they were upstanding citizens, strong members of their community, and, yes, I think they were lesbians." Then he said, "Now I have a question for you. How did you get Hollywood to make this movie during this time in your life?" My dad's been stellar. My mom has come around. She came around at Connie's and my wedding four years ago. My dad and sister have led and my brother and mother have come around.

But those months of deciding were hell! My friend who said she would stand by me also said, "Most people find out who their friends are when they die; you got to find out earlier." It certainly did help me to find out who my real friends are. Many folks in the church have been deafeningly silent. I don't think it is out of anger or disapproval; it is out of not knowing what to do. When there's a divorce, people don't know what to do so they don't do or say anything. But, my previous husband was getting all kinds of letters of support. I was glad he was getting that support, but I needed it too.

In retrospect, I believe this has been the greatest blessing in my kids' lives. It's also been one of the hardest things, because they have had to deal with homophobia. We live in a suburban area, and our son, at thirteen or fourteen, said, "Mom, we *are* the diversity in this community."

I was well known in the Presbyterian Church, and they didn't know what to do with me, once they knew I was gay. So, I was drawn back to the United Church of Christ. The UCC ordains gay and lesbian people. It was a very difficult process getting my ordination changed. I went to a very well-known seminary and have all the necessary degrees, but I am one of the first people to come through the chute from another denomination. They have barely enough jobs for their own pastors. What are they going to do with all of us as we come from Methodist, Presbyterian, Lutheran, Episcopalian, and Baptist traditions? At one point, the Presbyterian Church sent me a letter—one paragraph—that said I was defrocked after 20 years of ordination. I just sat there in the kitchen and cried. It was the wrong place and time to be gay. So, I called the man on the committee who was an advocate for me. He told the committee that he would give up his ordination if they took mine away. He put everything on the line for me. He said, "If they are going to take away your ordination, I am ready to walk with you." There are many in the Presbyterian Church who feel committed with us and feel so frustrated with the hard line taken by the church. So, it took years for me to finally get my ordination changed. The people in the United Church of Christ had to go through their process also.

I began a community of faith reaching out to gay and lesbian people. It is happening much more slowly than I would have thought. The gay community is not eager to get into the church. We've been through enough without asking for more. It's slow but it is so meaningful to those who have come. We meet twice a month, once in Seattle and once in Federal Way. We'll probably add a third service in Tacoma soon. To sit in our community of faith is like sitting with freed slaves. A person, in the process of being transgendered stood up and shared that he had just had a mastectomy and he was thrilled, and the congregation applauded. In how many churches would that happen? He finally got the body that I think God intended him to have. We have just had four weddings. They are not legal, but they are so powerful. We have people in our community of faith who haven't taken communion for 30 years, because they thought God would strike them dead if they were gay and took communion. I have no question that this is the most important ministry I have ever done. It is hard, though, and it's really a tough way to make a living. That's why I have four jobs.

Our wedding was phenomenal. We had it in our backyard, because no church would let us be married. (My church, the United Church of Christ, would have let us but there was a conflict with the date.) The other churches said, "No." I've performed hundreds of weddings. We had people of marginal faith all the time being married in the church. Here, we had a preacher's daughter and a pastor wanting to get married, and they wouldn't let us. People came from all over the country to stand with us. The custody battle and divorce were over by then.

I had always thought of myself as a pastor and a mother, and, when I came out, both of those were up for grabs. I had to fight like the dickens to keep my ordination and to be a mother. I got a straight, white male lawyer who was tough as nails. There was a guardian ad litum, and the guardian met Connie and me and loved us. For two years I lived in Seattle and only saw the kids every other weekend. I cried all the time. The kids were with their dad during the custody battle. I drove one and a half hours to volunteer at my kids' school once a week. When I found out we could share custody, Connie and I moved into the kids' community. Their dad was furious.

The children live in two worlds. They live in a conservative, fundamentalist home, and a lesbian, Christian home. These homes are only one and a half miles apart, but are totally different worlds. It has summoned them to muster all their maturity and composure to do this. I'm so proud of how they have done. Their dad has remarried. I have a better working relationship with her than him. She will talk to me on the phone. The children are now sixteen and thirteen. Grethe Cammermeyer said to me one time,

"I've never known a lesbian who lost her relationship with her children." She was so compassionate and loving. My children have no abandonment issues. They love and respect both me and Connie. They know that what we have done has been very hard. When Susie` was very little, she stood between her dad and me, with her hands on her hips, and said to her dad, "When you treat Mom like that it hurts me!"

The truth is that I set out to have integrity, to be loving, and to follow my heart. I'm sorry that people have gotten hurt. Hurt comes when relationships change. But if I have learned anything, it is to just reach out to those coming out, and to those going through divorce. Be there for them. Connie says that I came out more in six weeks than she had in twenty years. The kids' dad was outing me all over the country anyway, so I just told everyone. I won't keep secrets because they make us crazy. I've walked many people away from retaliation and actions out of anger. How do we model reconciliation and kindness when we are given hatred, exclusion and shame?

It just takes forever to educate people about homophobia. The condescension is palpable. I get it all the time. I work in a hospital, and when some of the nurses found out I was gay, they changed toward me. So, I work hard daily at reconciliation and coach others in how to do that. We have to live what we believe. Otherwise, we are not doing anyone any good.

I couldn't say the word lesbian for several years, and I've learned that that's part of the process. I think God gives the gift to the people who can take it and to people that he needs as trailblazers. I feel that I'm a trailblazer. I thought it was about being a woman minister. Twenty years ago I was fighting for women's rights in ministry, and now I'm fighting for gay rights. Sometimes I get frustrated with the lesbian community, with our pettiness. Sometimes I'm so proud. I'm very comfortable being called gay. I have no problem saying I'm a lesbian now. People ask me what my husband does, and I reply, "Well, that's a very good question. I am married but I don't have a husband; I'm married to a wonderful woman." My experience has been that if I'm okay with it, they are okay with it.

This community of faith which I lead is so dynamic, so exciting, and so powerful. We're small, around a hundred, but it's just so powerful. There is one woman in our congregation who is straight, and when people ask her, "Now, are you gay?" She looks at them and she says, "Well, I'm flattered, but no." When people know there is a group of gay and lesbian Christians to support them, they can do anything. They come out to their family and to their church. It is so empowering. They know that we're there with them, we'll catch and hold them. Coming out to God is one of the first things Christian people do. They come out to themselves, then to God, then to their family and friends. But, coming out to God is huge. As if God doesn't know! I wear a button that says, *If God didn't create homosexuals, there wouldn't be any.*

Randi

When I recognized my lesbianism, it felt like a liberation.
It felt great! It was the natural thing. I'm out to everyone.

A year and a half ago in 1996, I was first diagnosed with breast cancer. This finding was the result of a routine annual checkup and mammogram. My doctors said, "You have some interesting little specks on your film, and although we're sure they are nothing, we just want to take a closer look." Great! We were planning to move; I was just starting to get some momentum going in my new career in real estate; we had hired a builder and found financing to build our dream home in the woods; and now this! "Not me—not now! Hey, wait a minute! This doesn't even run in my family," I exclaimed in angry disbelief. Well, the big C isn't all that particular it seems. So, we did the biopsy. Then, eight months later, I lost both my "hood ornaments," as I like to say jokingly to people who seem to look at me as if they can see death standing over my shoulder when I tell them. All of this has certainly given me an opportunity to look back at my life....

I was married right out of high school. It was really wild. I came from a very abusive father and a chaotic family life, and all I could see was getting the hell out of the house.

I met this guy; we had a kind of camaraderie. At that point, that was all I could understand. I didn't know there was anything more to it than that. As soon as I turned 18, I'd had it with living at home and I moved in with him. We never had a marriage ceremony; it was a common-law marriage. I found out what the rules were and started using his name. I wanted his name because I could go into the honky-tonks that way. I had aspirations of being a musician in those days. We both played music and we played together in some of the bars.

We lived together for several years. But after about six months, I wanted out of Texas. I told him that I wanted to go to Colorado. I'd seen pictures, I'd heard about it, and I wanted to go. He was very reluctant.

The marriage was kind of weird. I was the boss of things. He couldn't keep a job; he was very unstable. He was a good musician, but very flaky. I kept pressuring him to go. Finally, I came home with a '46 Chevy panel truck. I picked it up for $250, and said, "I'm goin', Baby. You can come with me, or not." He said, "Okay, okay," and we just took off for Denver. I was only there for three weeks when I realized I hated it. I wanted to be in those mountains; I wanted to live up there in the snow. So, we got a place in the mountains above Boulder. I was just happy as hell.

Within no time, I knew that I didn't need this marriage to get along. It was kind of a security thing, and I had had no experience of being alone. I didn't know any girls my age who would take off like that. I was pretty functional, but he was pretty dysfunctional. As soon as I had my feet on the ground, I started drifting away. He was really jealous and had fits about it all.

We lived in a hippie-type community. This was about 1971–72. There were cabins, and we would go to each other's cabins at night, playing music and smoking pot. I didn't know a whole lot of people up there.

One night my truck died and I hitchhiked down to Boulder to play some music and make some money, and it started snowing. I thought, "Oh shit, I better leave." So, I started hitchin' home, and this guy in an old pickup picked me up. We were going up the mountain, and it was really snowing, and he was trying to make small talk. It was really a blizzard. As we were going along, all of a sudden I saw this woman. She had long blond hair sticking out of her ski cap. She put up her thumb and I yelled, "Pull over." I didn't know her or anything, but as soon as I opened the door this light went on in my head. It was like instant recognition. She looked at me and said, "Thanks for pulling over," and I said, "Thank him; it's his truck." She figured out that I was hitchin', too.

As we drove on, we found out that we were both heading for the same neighborhood. We found out that we both played music and that we both lived in the same rural community. So, we agreed that we'd get together soon—and that's how I met her.

That was my first lesbian experience. It turned out that she wasn't even a lesbian. She had just come out of a relationship with a guy and had never been with a woman before. It was kind of like love at first sight for both of us. I was 19 then.

It turned out that she was bisexual. I was the spark; I was the one who instigated the sex and stuff. You could tell she was really interested but not into the whole idea. We never lived together; she was a traveler. She had a chance to crew on a boat and she took off for Fiji. She was gone for awhile, and when she came back, we were together. Next, she took off for New Zealand. That was the way it went.

In the meantime, I realized I was really into this. That's where my head was. I started finding women . . . going to the lesbian bar. I've had four long-term relationships.

When I met the woman traveler, I decided I wanted my name back. I also wanted to get away from my husband, so I lived in a tent for three months. I was given a bad time about that because we were considered married. I had to get a legal divorce. I did it through legal aid, and it cost me $100. He met a woman about then and moved to New Hampshire for a year with her. I went to Europe for a year with a friend of mine.

Then I met this woman, Laura. We were more like a partnership than a relationship. There was very little sex, but we were just really good friends and we lived together very well. We decided that we were both ready to leave Colorado; that was in 1979. We bought a station wagon. I had a dog and she had four cats. We got a trailer and we moved to Seattle together. I was with her for another couple of years.

The thing is that ever since I was very young all my crushes were on my girlfriends. I never really understood that. No one did. When girls started dating the boys, I wanted to go with girls. When we were about 14 and going to the dances, I wanted to dance with the girls. When girls were going steady with boys, I wasn't interested. If a girl decided she didn't want to be my friend anymore, that would break my heart. All through high school I would have very close relationships with my girl friends.

When I was 16, I had this really close friendship with Stephanie, and we spent the night together; we would just hold each other. I just loved it. We got in trouble together; we did something wild and her parents decided I was the bad influence. They banned her from me and I cried for a week.

When I recognized my lesbianism, it felt like a liberation. It felt great. It was the natural thing. I'm out with everyone.

My parents were divorced when I came out. My mother's first reaction was, "I don't need to know that! Just do what you have to do and don't give me any details!" I didn't even bother telling my dad; I knew she would. They still see each other from time to time.

Mom has totally adjusted now. She had started college before she met my father, then bam, bam, bam . . . six kids. Twenty years later, she wanted to go back to school. So, she divorced him, and finally got her master's degree. She is an art therapist. She subscribes to a lot of women's magazines and has come quite a ways. She is now able to deal with my lesbianism and I feel she accepts me as I am.

There were three boys and three girls in my family. They all know. I am number three in the group of six. Only my oldest sister and I are on speaking terms and we have a very good relationship.

She is a psych major and teaches women's studies at a university. She has always been very liberal minded. My sexuality doesn't faze her a bit. The rest don't like me because I'm a lesbian. My youngest sister was a Catholic and has now turned Baptist. I can't even sleep in her house. The other brothers and sisters think I'm really sick.

I have no children. I had a four-year relationship with a woman who had a nine-year-old boy, and I was sort of a father figure for a while.

I've had my current relationship for seven years, and it's wonderful. It's the best part of my life. Living with Jean is a gift.

Right now, I have to admit that I feel like a spiritual zero. That is, if one were to qualify spirituality as something tangible, something substantive. I am not actively engaged in any particular spiritual practice. Spirituality for me now consists of gazing deeply into my lover's eyes until I feel we connect. My heart does a little flip, like the first time we kissed, and I know I am still a breathing being in this universe. I realize this may sound irreverent or heretical to some who spend hours each day meditating, studying their religion or reading self-help books but that's what things have boiled down to for me in the last couple of years. I did that once. Now, spirituality is taking one second at a time.

Spirituality means going out to our land—the five acres we bought for that dream house we still want to build—and being with the trees, the creek, and the wildlife. I love to watch my lover work our land—tilling the soil, weeding, and watering her hundreds of plants. I feel my heart slow down, my breath deepen, my eyesight clear. I begin to feel the ground under my feet again, and my eyes become less afraid to see.

In the city, driving around a lot for my job, listening to people's gripes and solving problems, I don't even realize it when my ears begin not to hear, my eyes not to see, and my feet can't even tell me where I am. Sometimes, I just come home in the middle of the day, make a snack lunch, and head for our land. It brings me back to myself and to my partner again.

Jean

I feel that I made the right choice. It feels very solid.
Now, the thought of living with a man is alien to me.

My first marriage was in 1966 and I was 20 years old. I was just a child, and so was he. It lasted four and a half years and was very difficult.

I think we each came from two dysfunctional families and had no concept of what it was like to live with another person. We had no skills in communication. I was so blocked up with my family's lack of openness about sexuality that we couldn't even consummate the marriage in the beginning. There was no affection or warmth shared in my family. I didn't know what it was like to be affectionate or sexual with a person. Sexual things were difficult throughout the marriage. Anyway, I put him through a seminary, and then we split up. I got a divorce in 1970.

I married again in 1974. The biological clock was ticking and I married because I wanted to have children. I met my husband while I was a teller at a bank, and there was this very cute person with little twinkly eyes. He was adorable.

That marriage lasted nine years. Our son, Nile, was born in 1978, and we divorced in 1981. He was from Mexico, a different culture and very rigid. He had a set view of what women did. I learned that he didn't like me when I was myself, and that was a very big lesson. I wondered what I was doing in a relationship when I was not encouraged to be who I was. What I was supposed to do was to support him and, literally, take care of him. I was a

41

housewife and a mother at that time, but I also had my own business in tiles and I was the bookkeeper for his insulation business. I was doing a lot.

When our child was tiny, my husband was a good father; but as the child got older, we had some big conflicts in parenting. He didn't want to set limits or give the child responsibility; I wanted to be consistent. That was a real clash on top of our already strained relationship. I finally told my husband that we needed some changes and asked him to go to counseling with me. He said, and I can almost quote it, "There will be no changes, and I will not go to counseling." The next week I told him there would be a divorce.

After I had filed for divorce, Nile became ill. He was ill before we realized it, and, by the time his illness was evident, he had a stroke because of blood clots forming in his heart. He died when he was four and a half.

After Nile's death and the divorce, I worked for awhile and then got into school. I changed my major from art to psychology, finished my B.A. and started looking for a graduate school. I needed a very strong focus because I didn't feel like living. I wanted to go back into psychology because I really liked it and, in counseling, I felt I could offer something of my experience to parents who lose children. There wasn't a lot of help back then; that was in 1982.

During my first marriage, I had met a woman named Judith and we became very good friends. A couple of years after we met she told me that she had had a sexy dream about me. I was just horrified! It never crossed my mind. I sort of pushed her away. At that time I didn't want her to touch me. It was really scary. I thought I was plugging along as a confirmed heterosexual, but Judith prompted me to begin my introspection.

In the beginning, I was worried about my sexuality. But as I worked through it, I didn't feel bad about it anymore and came to see it as a gift. By then, 10 years later, I thought I was bisexual and that felt natural. Then I thought, "This is wonderful!" I was still married while I was working through all that. Judith and I shared those feelings through the years and still do.

In 1986, I was going with a man, and I might have married him, but then, I met a woman who I got a definite crush on. I told the man about my ambivalence, and a year later the relationship with him ended and I became involved with this woman. That was my first relationship with a woman. I think I was still working through my family-of-origin issues with her, and so was she, because it was a very difficult relationship. I was with her a year and a half.

Randi and I have been together over seven years now. It feels great! I feel that I made the right choice. It feels very solid. I match her on levels I hadn't matched anyone before. It's about spirituality and our feelings about personal growth, our goals, and our values. It's been a good seven years, though ragged in places. Randi's illness was a terror. From the first suspicious mammogram in November of 1996, the biopsy and later radical surgery in September, 1997, it was very difficult. There are so many layers. And, having watched my mom die of breast cancer in 1993 made Randi's diagnosis hard to take. Supporting Randi stirred up a range of feelings including some anger. I've had to do too much of this—my son Nile, Dad and Mom. Fearing the loss of Randi was enormous. There was also real joy watching her take charge of her recovery. Now, knowing she is well and hoping she stays that way is prominent in my life. Facing life-threatening illness changes a person. It makes life more precious, more immediate, and for me, more about spiritual tasks. These are important. We really are friends. I feel very comfortable with her, and she has converted me. I am a lesbian now; I wasn't before.

My mother knew about my lesbianism. Her reaction was, "Oh my God!"

I am out at work and pretty much to everybody. I do have a couple of friends with whom I haven't talked in a few years. A lot of my relatives don't know. I have two brothers and they know.

One is being supportive now, but in the beginning he was horrified. The other brother was supportive at first and now he is horrified, so it has balanced out!

Through all our heavy experiences, I have treasured being with someone who accepts all of me right where I am. When I feel like a challenge to live with, she is there for me. When she is busy and distracted, I may have to wait for a time we can talk. But I know I can ask for her support, and it is mine. Our relationship is anchoring for me. It has a base of trust that I find comforting and secure in a crazy time.

Having differences or disagreements is not terrible. We are both creative problem solvers; I know we can work out whatever it is. I have that much faith in us. Our humor and laughter are buoyant and sustaining. Our relationship provides a place in which I can wrestle with my issues, moan and mellow into menopause, and deepen further into my own sense of spirituality.

For me, spirituality is about healing. It is about feeling deeply from my core that place of quiet knowing and integrity. It is about walking in harmony with the earth, and all beings. It is about learning, loving, and sharing what I can, helping where I can. It is about touching and connecting with others from a level of respect and compassion. I cherish my own process of learning to be more fully who I am.

My advice to women who are thinking of leaving a marriage and are questioning their sexual preference would be to get a supportive female therapist, and then find supportive people. Then, give yourself time to work through it all. Be kind to yourself. I met Randi in Tae Kwon Do, and I certainly didn't expect to find her there!

Sarah

My advice for women who are in a marriage and thinking about getting out, is get out! Just do it. It isn't that hard to meet other lesbians.

When I was 16, I ran away from home to New York where I lived with gay men. There were a lot of runaway girls that lived with gay men; it was a cover for us, and they protected us. They fed us, clothed us, and they kept us off the streets. They were wonderful.

I was there about two years and then I got very ill. My parents, who were Christian Scientists, got hold of me again. They told me that I had two choices: I could marry this nice boy they had picked out for me or I could go out to St. Elizabeth's Psychiatric Hospital for a while. People had the power to do that to you in those days.

I had slept with girls, but I had never identified with women. We were very careful to sleep with one boy every six months, to keep a bisexual label to it. I did a lot of drugs and I was really in bad shape.

I just didn't have any resistance to my parents or their plan, and he was all right. So I was first married in 1968 when I was 19.

We went immediately to the Orient. He was in the service and we would see each other every six months; it was great. I had a woman I was sleeping with while I was there, and it was marvelous.

Then, when we came back here, people expected us to be married, including our parents. It was just horrible and the marriage started coming apart. We had only slept together maybe three times when we were married; we didn't even know

45

each other. But now, there were all of those pressures to conform to—such as having kids. It got really nasty and we got to hate each other. So, we finally just stopped. That was in the mid-seventies. I tried to join women's groups, but they were all heterosexual and they didn't help much.

My second husband was a man who worked with me and he was kind and gentle. I thought then that I wasn't really gay, but I had just been married to the wrong man the first time. This man and I had been very good friends at work for a long time. I thought that he was going to deep-six my lesbianism, and it was all going to be all right.

After we married, we got along together and had fun and we really loved each other, but sex was a terrible thing. He also tried to influence me emotionally to make me feel that I couldn't make it on my own. I worked off and on during my marriage, so that didn't always carry much weight. Then, when that didn't work, he would say that it would destroy him if I left.

As time went on and things got worse, I got very depressed. As a result, I stayed at home a lot. Every time I met a woman I liked, I'd run back in the house again. This just seemed like it was going on forever, and then I started getting physically sick.

Finally, after the fourth minor operation in a row, a gay friend brought me the book, *Another Mother Tongue*, and just said, "Read it." I read it and it was the first time I could say, "Oh, this is okay." But that's as far as it went. I was scared to death. I started insisting to my husband that we go out, and we went to the gay male bars. He was really good about it, as he didn't have any problem with gay men. I went to all the gay bars, but it was different this time. I was trying to find connections.

I didn't much like gay men anymore. I felt that the more I was trying to come out, the less supportive they were. I gave support to the guys when they were coming out for years, but when I was trying to come out they said, "How can you do this to your husband?" They were horrible! They told me that I couldn't possibly be a lesbian, and all this ridiculous stuff.

Then I started going to a woman's bookstore across the bay. I'd sneak into the lending library section, and if anyone would come in, I'd throw down the book! I couldn't bring any of them into the house. This went on for about three months. Then I got to thinking, "Now where do you meet lesbians?" The boys were no help. I thought I should go to an organization who works for women. So I went to work for National Action Against Rape.

You should have seen me the first night. I had hair down to my waist, and my make-up was perfect, and I had little suede booties, right? Everyone there was a lesbian and wore lumberjack shirts and hiking boots. It was the perfect place to be—very militant women. This was in 1984, and there were still a lot of militant lesbians around. This was the heart of political lesbian land.

At this point, I was afraid of hurting my husband. I loved him a lot and we had been together a long time. If any of the women tried to touch me, it was all over. A couple of my lesbian friends had to literally drag me into Amelia's—a lesbian bar—I was so afraid.

I finally signed up for a poetry class, and the women I met there had been out since the fifties. They were not very supportive and it was a pretty hostile environment. However, one of the women there was my age. She was Israeli and had just gotten a divorce and really knew. She was my hero; I followed her everywhere.

She was the one who finally got me into bars. She went out with my husband and me and she would stand up to him. She was incredible. Slowly but surely, I was crawling along. One night, they dared me to go to Amelia's alone. For one thing, it was in a scary district of town. I had never gone to the grocery store without my husband at night. Anyway, I went to the bar and met this wonderful woman. We danced together and she drove me home and kissed me goodnight in front of my husband's door. She also understood that I was in no way ready for anything else.

It turned out she had a long-term lover. I began going to their house a lot and they double-dated with my husband and me. They helped me to get up enough nerve to walk out the door. My husband was getting very angry—and very violent. If I had gotten interested in a guy, it would have been much better. His next illusion was that we could do a menage-a-trois with one of the women I knew. When he got violent the second time, I threw what I could into a plastic bag and walked out of the door and I never went back. That was 1985.

At this point, I was working again and was making real money. I got a little apartment of my own, for the first time in my life. I signed up at City College in the Gay and Lesbian Studies division, and I got interested in writing. In the meantime, I was seeing too much of my best friends. They were having a lot of problems, and one of them and I became very close. She was coming over to the city to stay with me. One thing led to another and . . . we both felt just terrible.

The day after this happened we were all supposed to go to the parade together. We couldn't keep our hands off each other and the other woman picked up on this. It was really miserable. Finally, these two good friends stopped speaking to me. My Israeli friend had left the country, and my husband, who wielded a lot of power, was making life miserable for me.

Eventually, my friends decided the solution was for the three of us to sleep together. We went through that for three months. It turned out to be very healing for their relationship—and very destructive for me. I stopped meeting other people and going anywhere where I was likely to meet other women.

Then I wrote letters to a teacher at City College. He encouraged me to write. We would write back and forth and it was good therapy for me. It got me started writing, and I ended up writing a novel! I got into a lesbian relationships group which helped me to sort through what I wanted. It helped me think about what it meant to be a lesbian. I cut off all my hair and got with the flannel shirts.

At that point, I stopped sleeping with men, and I went through a series of different women. I really didn't want to get very involved again. A year later, I went to class and Betty showed up, sitting next to me. She had just moved to San Francisco, and I was living in a collective at that point and we had an extra room. I talked to the women who ran the place, and Betty moved in.

We were friends first, and little by little, things evolved. I was very afraid of commitment. The first couple of years we were together, we didn't declare monogamy; we gave each other a lot of space. Finally, we gave up other women, and now we have been together six years.

We are very much married. We have done all the legal paper-work that makes us as married as you can get. We own the house together. We started light and let it develop. Neither of us had had a serious lesbian relationship before.

We moved to this city eight months ago and I'm out to everyone. I have had work done on the house and I hire only lesbians or gays. We are in activities where we meet other lesbians. I don't go to the bars because I have a problem with smoke. I have a very serious heart problem for which I had surgery a year ago. I think a lot of my physical problems stemmed from the early drug abuse.

I am pretty happy the way I am. I am studying accounting, because I want to get a good job in that field. I'd love to get my book published. We are very happy; I hope that we'll be together forever.

Jackie

I knew at seven that I wanted nothing to do with men.

I was married in 1951 because it was the thing that was expected. All my friends were getting married and everybody was looking at me. I wasn't in love, but he was a nice fellow from a nice family, and I was a nice girl from a nice family, and everybody thought we were just perfect. We were married 11 years and had two boys during that time. One is now 38 and the other is 33.

I was an Army wife during the Korean situation. I got pregnant within the first year and my family wanted me to come home as they thought they could do more for me. John, meanwhile, was accepted into Officers' Candidate School. The marriage could have been fine, but I wasn't in love with him and I drank a lot.

I tried to conform to the Army's way of doing things and I was not good at it. He hung in and I think he loved me. I tried my hardest to make him think that I loved him. We were sent to Japan and I was pregnant again. Next, we went to Okinawa. The men were busy and the wives played cards and such. I was most unhappy. I didn't participate too well as an Army wife.

I made a grand mess of the whole marriage during those three years on that island. When we got back to the States, I think both of us knew that the marriage was over. When he came to get me and the kids for the next move, I just said, "I'm sorry. I have had it." I could not pretend any longer.

I look back now and I think I was pretty brave. Many of my

friends are still in marriages they hate. They are still there because they have a nice home in a good area and all that. My father and my mother had been divorced for many years and my father lived in Detroit, so I decided to go there. But it was too damned cold in Detroit! I don't know . . . there was something wrong with me. I was just trying to find me. I got divorced while I was there and then, I couldn't stay there either. So, I came back to Houston. My kids were here with my mother.

The first lesbian I met was a friend of my mother's. She was a female doctor. We took one look at each other and that was it. The problem was that everybody in Houston knew that she was gay. My mother and everybody else knew. It was the talk of Houston. I was disgracing the family by going with this woman. That was in 1962.

This doctor and I were together for quite a while and my mother wanted to die. She knew, in spite of the doctor's reputation, that I wasn't like that. The doctor was gay but I wasn't, according to my mother. The doctor and my mother were friends and she would come over to visit. My mother noticed that we were going out an awful lot. This just killed my mother. It became such a big deal to everybody that we just decided to forget it. Except we couldn't forget it. So, we would sneak off and see each other from time to time. That was the first time I had had a lesbian experience.

I knew at seven that I wanted nothing to do with men. I just knew. I didn't know what to call myself except a tomboy. With the doctor, I found a release at last. The weight of the world just fell off my shoulders. We didn't live together; we just saw each other. Actually everything was going pretty well and one day I had to do something and she told me to take her car. Black Houston at that time was very close knit. Everybody knew everything. Here's Jackie in the doctor's car. The people weren't as dumb as we thought. We were together about two years, but there was so much pressure I was about to go out of my mind. I had to leave her. We both decided we just couldn't do it.

My mother found a psychiatrist for me. I talked to him until I got tired of him. I told my mother she was wasting her money because he was telling me, "Well, you have a mother complex and you're not really a gay." I listened to that and he was charging about $50 dollars an hour—that was a lot of money in those days.

My current partner, Sue, and I just celebrated our twenty-first anniversary. When I first went to work in the English department, I had seen her and I knew that she was a lesbian. I knew a guy in the department and he asked me if I had ever read Sue's thesis and I said, "No." He said, "It's just beautiful, but all the poems are to women." At graduation, Sue asked me if I'd like to go over to a bar. We went and got pretty high. Then she said why didn't I go home with her. So I went with her and that was the beginning of that.

About three weeks ago, my mother had this big gumbo party with people from the school. I said to my mother that since we had entertained all these people, I want to do something for my special friends. So my mother, who is 80 years old, said, "I understand you have a different lifestyle." It like to killed me. All these damn years I've wasted trying to keep it from her. We had the party and everybody thought it was just wonderful.

My mother could not stand Sue at first. She thought it was all Sue's fault. Somebody else is taking me and I'm not like that. Sue hung in there and eventually they became friends. I think my oldest son understands this whole thing. My youngest son—I don't think it has ever dawned on him. Both of them have known Sue most of their lives, and I think both of them love her. My grandkids love her. My children grew up with my mother. Both sons are very successful and I'm very proud of them. I don't think this relationship has hurt them in any way.

I am also out at work. I know everybody knows. We were the talk of the department for about a week. Then we just settled in. My department head knows about it and she appointed me to be her assistant. I guess it doesn't bother her.

My advice for other women who are thinking about a change in their sexual orientation is to go for it. Now there are so many opportunities. Twenty-one years ago we were very isolated. We didn't know there were organizations—and there weren't many. But, now, we have many opportunities for support.

Mari Ann

I didn't decide to be a lesbian; I think I just gave in to it.

I was first married in 1981. I was just eighteen. I think I got married to get out of the house. I wanted to be on my own. I wanted to have a home of my own. I wanted to get on with things, and I thought that was the only way. I thought that was what you were supposed to do.

We were married for almost five years. He was slightly older than I and had an alcohol problem. He was mentally abusive. He almost had me convinced that it was my fault that he had the drinking problem. Then he slept with a friend of mine, and that ended it for me. I initiated the divorce. I'm sure glad I found that out, or maybe it would have gone on longer.

My second marriage was in 1986. I married a wonderful, kind person that I didn't know for very long. We had both gone through a lot in our first marriages and came together because we were lonely and we were a comfort to each other. We finally realized that we didn't have a whole lot in common. He was also unfaithful, so I initiated a second divorce. That marriage ended in 1989. I'm still in contact with him. He's married to a nice woman. I had no children from either marriage.

I didn't decide to be lesbian; I think I just gave into it. I always knew that I wasn't very attracted to men. I didn't much like them, either. I still don't, though I can think of a few that I think are okay people.

I grew up in a small suburb, a really closed-minded little area and I never knew any gay people. But, I've always been attracted to women and finally found gay friends when I changed my job and went into the flower business.

When I met these people I thought, "That's the lifestyle I'd like to lead." I started reading *The Weekly*--the personals. Gosh, there were gay women who wanted to meet other women in that paper. I thought, "Why not?"

I answered one ad and got my mail order bride. She's wonderful. She was exactly what I would have described as my ideal. It's amazing that it happened that way. She had answered many ads herself before she put an ad in. She went on lots of dates, but darned if she didn't pick me. It just worked out so well. I've had other affairs, but I've never really been in love until her. We are monogamous.

It felt so right to have my love interest be a woman. It was so normal. It was like I'd finally found the right thing to do.

I came out to everybody in the world. I called my Mom and told her, and my family and my friends, and everybody at work. It felt very right.

I was rejected by only two people. One was a good friend who was very active in her church. She and I still correspond but we are much more distant than we were, and that's kind of sad.

My brother had a hard time with it. He didn't want to invite me to family events. He couldn't understand how I could be such a different person. This brother is 11 years older than I. This Christmas I called and said, "Is it just my imagination or are we not having Christmas? Tell me what's going on." I have always been the initiator of these family things. It turned out that nobody had done anything. At the last function, he said, "Please come, but don't let anybody know about what you're doing." It was okay for my partner to come as long as we didn't say what was going on. I told him I couldn't do that. I felt it was being untrue to myself.

Anyway, we worked it out for Christmas, and he was almost getting used to the idea when his wife's brother told the family that in addition to being gay, he had AIDS! The whole family is in shock.

I talked to my brother a couple of days ago, and he said that he really wasn't an Archie Bunker and that he had begun to view things a lot differently. I said, "Yeah, you are . . . but you're doing a lot better." They are helping the brother and supporting him.

My mom still thinks I'm going to change my mind. The thing is, she just loves Joan and they've accepted us. However, the other day she said, "But you're so feminine." I said, "It's okay, Mom; don't worry about it. You didn't do it."

My father just says, "Don't say anything to anybody." Everybody is so concerned about how it makes them look. My mom says, "Don't tell our side of the family until I'm dead." The thing is, I would like to tell those people I am close to. It would be natural to tell.

I'm out at work. My boss is a wonderful guy. I don't think I said directly to him what was going on, but he picked it up. One day when we were alone, he said, "I'm sure glad you got that sexuality thing worked out." He said I was so much happier. I've been there five years. He saw me go through my divorce; he's been so supportive.

My partner is not out at all. Her mom came to stay recently and it was real straighten-up time. Hide the newspapers and don't call her "Honey." Her family is all in Idaho, so it's easy to be in the old closet.

She practices being out with my friends and family. I finally realized that's what she was doing! I have been in therapy for 17 years, and I finally realized with my shrink's help that it wasn't so much that I wanted her to tell her family. . . . I wanted her to act like she was a part of our partnership. Now she is. It's very much like we're a family. That was very important to me. We have been together a year and a half.

56

Maggie

I think men may sense that their wives could be involved with other women, but that becomes okay because it takes some of the pressure off them.

I actually didn't have any doubt about being a lesbian. I knew that I was, and had been all my life, but I was raised in an environment in which that was totally unacceptable. I was born in West Texas but I grew up in Dallas. I was a young adult in a pretty oppressive time.

The first time I was ever madly in love with another female was when I was fourteen. Then, all through high school and college I had a double life. I was dating men and actually enjoying it. I wasn't really wildly in love with these guys, but I liked their company. At that time, if you wanted to socialize, that's how you did it. Also, I didn't want to be thought of as queer. I really enjoyed dating, but I never went steady and I always saw several different fellows at the same time because I didn't want to get too intense with anybody. Of course, the pressure was always on. There was something about my personality that egged these guys on. I didn't fall all over them, so they tended to fall all over me.

When I was a junior in college, I got engaged. Partly I was caving in to expectations, and partly I figured this was the best of the guys I had gone with. It was during the Korean war, which made relationships so romantic. He went into the Army as a lieutenant right after graduation and was shipped overseas. In April of the next year he came back and "the chips were down." I broke off the engagement in June because, by that time, it was really clear to me that I didn't want to get married. I actually loved him too much as a person to marry him. I realized that my roommate from college, who had also been my lover for awhile, was perfect for him. She was just the kind of girl he was looking for, and she wasn't truly gay. She really wanted to be married, have a family, be traditional, and settle down. So, in the next few months, I successfully managed to get them interested in each other. They got married about a year later and are still married after forty-some years. I'm still so happy for them. They both wanted a regular life, and my participation in supporting that dream has been very gratifying over the years. They still live in the same house, in the same town, with the same friends. I would have been bored to tears with that. He spent his whole career in aerospace with the same company. They are stability personified.

I went to work after college. Three years later I went to graduate school in another state. All this time I was involved with women. It was serial monogamy. In the late 60's, I ended up living in California in a relationship with a woman I cared about very much. We kind of came apart at the seams because I did some really stupid things. We were too caught up in a lifestyle that wasn't really who we were. There was a lot of drinking and loose living in the 60's. It was a difficult time because we were so oppressed in our workplace and general society, and we were really underground. Neither one of us liked spending much time that way and we had a lot of straight friends. However, both of us were developing a drinking problem because we weren't mature enough to withstand the pressure. When I look back on it now, in the light of a more mature view of life, I think it could have been avoided. But, at the time, it all seemed impossible. We had been together five years when we broke up and I took a job in another city.

In the new city, in the course of my work, I met a man I really liked and he liked me a lot. He was a widower and a good deal older than I and very different from most of the men I had known in my life. He was totally supportive and didn't come on with "women should do this or do that." We really got a kick out of each other and had tons of things in common. He was a very successful businessman, absolutely unpretentious and easy to get along with. It came as quite a surprise to have the window of his life open to me. When it became evident that he cared more about me than I did him, I was pretty resistant. He had kids who were pretty much grown and they liked me, too. But I wanted to stay just friends. Over time, I began to ask myself whether getting married would work as the gay life had been consistently heart-breaking. So I decided that I would go into therapy. Bear in mind that this was in the sixties. Ironically, I had a male therapist who thought my life would certainly be better with a man. (Now, I think, "Gee, was I nuts?") Somehow, between the therapist and this wonderful man who was courting me, and my need to escape, I succumbed and decided that I would get married. "Hey, it might work!" I wasn't without experience with men—not a separatist or anything like that. I always enjoyed being around men and this particular one was a gentle soul.

So, we got married. For a few years we had a really good time. We traveled a lot. We had financial projects that we did together. We built a vacation house with our own labor. It was a pretty good life, but it felt essentially empty for me at the emotional level when compared to the way that women can be together with real intimacy, sharing, and emotion. He was not able to do that and had his reasons for it. He had his story of being a kind of semi-abandoned child. I could understand where his defenses came from but they just didn't allow the kind of relationship that I wanted.

Then, a strange thing happened. I was very active in an organization and this woman seemed to be pursuing me. I wondered what there was about me that made her think I was pursuable. I thought I had my smoke screen really down pat. This went on for months and I didn't let on that I could understand her feelings. Finally, her pursuit and my willingness to be pursued

59

came together and I let her know that I could be interested. This developed into a personal relationship which went on for a long time. She was also married. We were pretty much together for about fifteen years.

I think that men may sense that their wives may be involved with other women, but it becomes okay because it takes some of the pressure off them. I think there were a lot of things that my husband and hers didn't really want to do, in the way of activities and travel and they said to themselves, "Oh, let the girls do that." My conclusion is that a lot of marriages are held together by a second relationship because, without it, the woman couldn't stand being married to that man. The second relationship provides some substance and satisfaction.

There came a point in our marriage when, by mutual agreement, sex just stopped. We had fought about my wanting more acknowledgment from him—that our relationship was more important than his business and civic stuff. It really had to do with my place in the hierarchy of his life, and I told him that I felt as if I were number three. He didn't exactly deny it; he just defended it. He indicated that these commitments were all going on before we got married and that it was just who he was. (True, but inflexible.)

I was his second wife and I knew enough about his first one to know that she was very compliant and more or less in the background. I, on the other hand, had been independent all these years before the marriage. I was supporting myself, had my own professional and civic identity, and I had expected to be in an equal relationship. I used to tell his daughter that "his train was on the track and, as far as I could see, I was invited to hook on." I finally realized that I had to get my own train. So I did! And, he didn't seem to mind all that much. He could do whatever he wanted to do and he had my companionship in the household. So things went on.

Years went by and, finally, my friend of many years just gave up on me. She finally got a divorce, but I wasn't willing to do the same at that time.

What I came to realize about my relationship with these two people was that the balance of power was very important because where one was weaker the other exceeded, and vice versa. I felt incomplete with either person exclusively. The woman I had chosen to be with was too emotional—too focused on me. She was, by definition, co-dependent. That riveting attention was too hard to live with. And, there was Mr. Detached with "I think you're wonderful and I love you. Good-bye." If I got too much from one, I'd go to the other. I realized that it was quite a management problem. On the other hand, considering that it was built piecemeal, it seemed to work pretty well. Anyway, when she ended up getting a divorce, it was clear that I wasn't going to fall into her life full time. So she gave up on me. I went through a couple of years when I wasn't with anybody. I was licking my wounds and feeling sorry for myself.

I finally decided to talk to my husband about this, as he was now retired and home all of the time. So I came out to him. I told him that I had been meaning to talk to him about this for a long time. I just said a few sentences to him. I was reading a book on lesbianism at the time and I said, "See what I'm reading here? This book is about me." I explained a few more things about it and he was very phlegmatic and he didn't seem very surprised. He didn't act like anything very dramatic was going on. He said he hadn't really known but that he thought perhaps that was the case. I asked him how he felt about that and he said it was okay and that he still loved me. So I said, "Okay."

He is a good deal older than I am. We had had this sex truce for about sixteen years, so it wasn't as though we were wrenching apart a passionate relationship. Even so, I thought his reaction was amazing. I didn't really want to get a divorce. I loved his kids and we have grandchildren. I didn't want to lose this family. Also, we had put a lot of time and effort into properties and other ventures. Neither one of us wanted to disassemble what we had built. I wondered, "What next?" It seemed that the next step in this process was to convey to him that I probably would be doing some things with women—lesbian activities.

It was hilarious that summer. I signed up for Arthur Murray dance lessons with a group of lesbians, went to concerts, and showed my face in the gay community after 20 years of invisibility. I really didn't know the culture anymore, but was so pleased with the changes!

Then, in 1991, I decided that if I was going to find someone I really wanted, I would have to "materialize" this person. I started writing down the characteristics I was looking for and finally placed my own personal ad. It was a long one and covered a lot of ground (with no reference to sunsets and walks on the beach). Qualities and interests were what I was looking for. I got quite a lot of responses. One day I got this amazing letter. It just jumped off the page. This woman said that she was the person I was looking for and she wanted to meet me *right away*. She wanted me to call her the day I got her letter and set up an appointment because she "didn't want anybody else to get ahead of her". I couldn't believe it.

I spoke to her on the phone on a Saturday morning and we met that afternoon. She lived in another town and we met at a coffee shop in my city. It was a strangely mesmerizing experience. I told her right away that I was married and had no plans to divorce my husband but that I was looking for a serious relationship. It sounds crazy to me as I say it, but that's what I said. I explained that my marital situation was entirely my doing and that my husband had done nothing to deserve rejection. Because he was older and pretty much retired, if I threw him out, he would have to start his life over alone. I told her that he knew I was gay and was going to be seeing women and that it was okay—it wasn't like he was going to come apart about this. I told her that I just couldn't bear to feel as if I were throwing him away. She replied that she thought that was the most beautiful thing she had ever heard. Then, she told me about herself.

About five years before, she had been in an automobile accident and was left with a head injury. She had made a substantial recovery but still had some difficulties. She was an artist and was highly intolerant of a lot of noise, light, and stimulation. She was earning her living by doing a paper route in the mornings when it was dark and quiet. She also had a house and rented out rooms. I initially thought her lifestyle was rather unorthodox for me, a person with a master's degree and a lot of professional experiences. We were an odd couple, but we really hit it off. She was a very different person from me—very open, very candid. All the facades she had were gone, which I found very refreshing. There wasn't a game in sight.

That week I went ahead and saw other people with whom I had made engagements, but we got back together a week later and we went to a concert. After it was over, we were sitting in the car talking. I liked her a lot and I just reached over and took her hand in mine. We talked a little while and went down to a coffee shop and hung out for a little while. After that, we didn't see each other for a couple of weeks because I was going out of town. But I wrote her a letter and gave her three choices. (This was my little litmus test) Let's meet and go hiking, or we can meet here in my town, or, if you like, I can drive to visit you. She called and said that I must come to her place. I thought then that she liked me. That's how it all started.

I went down to visit her and we started spending long hours together. About the fourth time we saw each other we decided we wanted to live together. I was astounded! I hadn't contemplated that I was going to be in that situation. At my age, I was surprised that I *could* be in that situation. It was startling, yet pretty romantic and exciting. I was trying to figure out what would be a good way to approach this.

I invited her to come and visit my husband and me, and

they hit it off great. He is also an artist by avocation. The next thing that happened was that we had a holiday weekend coming up on July 4th, and I planned for the three of us to go up to our cabin for the weekend. I also invited another friend to come along as a kind of buffer—another energy field. So off we went for four days to the cabin and that seemed to go reasonably well.

A few days later, I told my husband that she wanted to come and live with us. Actually, I left him a letter as I was on my way to spend the night at her place. I told him that Susan and I wanted to be together, and that I realized he was going to be affected by this. I told him that he should think about how he wanted to respond and that I would call on Saturday to see if he wanted to talk about it. Off I went. I called him on Saturday and asked if he had read the letter. He didn't have a lot to say. Then, I told him that we were thinking about coming up for dinner with him and asked what he thought about that. He said to come on. He thought that was great and said we'd talk about it.

Over the next few days, when he and I discussed the situation, practically nothing happened. It was like a strange black hole. I believe he had weighed the alternatives and said to himself that he could live with these dynamic, loving, interesting people or he could be by himself. He was just taciturn about the whole thing and showed relatively little emotion. I was sure that he'd been through an internal process. However when he first asked me to marry him and I wouldn't, he half jokingly had told me that if I didn't want to get married, he would be glad to adopt me or we could just live together. That was his way of saying that he wanted to be with me and I was to name the terms. I always felt that was endearing. Now, I gave him a choice as well. There wasn't room in our condo for all of us. If we were going to live together, then we all needed our own space. So, we decided to buy a house.

There is a lot more to the tale. I don't want you to think it was a Cinderella story. After we all got lodged under the same roof there were problems. One of them was that a lot of things that I routinely did were viewed by Susan as "being with him." In my opinion, I was just being me. For example, I used to sit and read the newspaper in the evening in the living room, but he might have also been in the living room looking at the newspaper and watching the news on TV. So Susan viewed this as a joint activity. It didn't feel like that to me. This was just what I did. Other things were somewhat territorial. I wasn't used to sharing my kitchen and domestic routines with another woman and neither was she! There were also noise and space issues—who could walk through whose space and for what reason—and communication patterns. There is no question that my husband also had all kinds of systems in place that appeared immutable.

Susan had a hard time articulating her needs, which was part of her head injury . If something wasn't the way she wanted it, or she wanted somebody to act differently, she could not just come out and say that she would really like it better if I did such and such. That kind of direct communication wasn't within her capability at that time. So we would both get the anger, the sulking, the retribution and all those negative responses that people go through. I had so many years of being right about so many things that I was pretty awful in this situation. Because I'd been with somebody who just liked *me*, I hadn't had all these complaints. It seemed at the time that some things were so petty. It was just amazing to me that we had to work so hard on so many issues and our process wasn't very good.

Susan had been through two marriages that hadn't worked out for her, and she was rather surprised to find herself with me because she was originally reading the ads to meet a man. This is not as simple as it seems because she had also had a relationship with a woman. I think it was soon after she moved in with us that she started to wonder if she had made a terrible mistake. It wasn't that she didn't love me—but this God-awful household! Three people trying to circle around each other. My husband's male ego was definitely doing its thing—a little passive-aggressive behavior.

There was also a little covert competition going on. It was very difficult.

After several years, Susan moved out. We didn't officially break up, but we went into a pretty traumatized state for a long time. By that time she and I were working together in a professional practice, so we had this double-barreled, tension-producing situation. Working together is hard enough even if you are just good friends.

Everything kind of went to hell in a handbasket. So this idealistic concept didn't work out. We had set out to design our own unique life and instead designed a nightmare. That's really what it was—just terrible. The great experiment was completely falling apart. We had been living together about three years.

My perception of myself was that I was extremely supportive of her while she was recovering from her head injury. I facilitated her getting back into a professional role and into a situation that reflected her intellectual ability and her ability to work with people. The other side of that coin was that I had expectations, such as wanting her to show up for work every day. She wanted more autonomy and flexibility to do her art. Obviously, we had commitments to our clients and other tasks that we needed to do. Since I had assumed responsibility for administrative duties, and was carrying financial obligations, if she were anybody else I would have fired her. But, basically, I wanted her to succeed.

Susan is beautifully creative and makes wonderful contributions to our professional practice, but isn't into routines, deadlines, etc. She produced a fantastic video for us, among other things. I'm retardedly accepting the reality of not judging her performance by my own ingrained concepts of structure.

My husband has recently had a stroke and is in a care facility for people with dementia. He probably won't live long now. He's delighted to see me every time I visit, though some days he can't remember the details of who I am. All of his defenses have evaporated, and we talk real feelings and thoughts. We are both so sad that "his brain got hurt," but maintain our warm friendship every day.

Susan and I have agreed that we should sell the house; each of us is one-third owner. She has a house near the center where we work and I'm going to move in with her. We are going to see if we can function in a relationship (without a third party). We need to identify space needs, not only physical space but emotional space. How will we function with friends who are individually ours or mutually ours? She also has grown kids. It will be interesting; it will be the first time in our seven-year relationship that there will be just the two of us. We are still willing to make the effort. Amazing! Both of us have mentally left this relationship many times, but we keep coming back. One of the ways she has been really good for me is that she's so supportive of who I am. She supports my gayness and reminds me that I don't need to hide behind marriage as a screen. She supports me to come on out. The only place I'm not out is at work. We have joined a church together and we're totally out. Everybody there sees us as a couple. We're out to all of our kids .

Anyway, it's a wild life I lead. Sometimes I can't believe it myself. Ever since I was a little kid my interests were always extremely eclectic. I was a musician, I was an artist and I was also the biggest little butch tomboy you ever saw. I was the wilderness camper and also the introspective poet and writer. I could be with my husband and discuss politics, social change, business, history, and world affairs. He was in the power structure of the city. He was a giver of himself. It was a fascinating life. I loved that part of our relationship—but that wasn't enough. Then with Susan there is another kind of relationship that goes inside where your heart and private thoughts are. I realized that that was what was missing my whole life.

Susan and I are in the process of healing our relationship. We both have done a lot of work on that, including testing our priorities and acknowledging the necessity for compromise. We see each other every day and spends nights together often. We both attend to spiritual growth, health, art, and satisfying work. We're not sure whether living together just yet is right, but we are seeking that answer in the messages of the heart and soul. That's where we're connected!

Janet

*Coming to terms with being a lesbian took a long time.
All the rules for social interaction, as I knew them,
were out the window.*

I was married in March of 1967. I was sixteen and pregnant and married to a man whose mother opposed the marriage. She was very high up in the Selective Service at that time, and her response was to see that he was drafted! He was shipped out pretty quickly to Vietnam.

He came back in 1969 and was in pretty bad shape. He hadn't actually done combat, but he had been traumatized by being over there. We were ill-matched to begin with and, in the interval, I had grown in a different direction. We stayed together for another year because I had a commitment to helping him adjust back into the world. I did that and then we separated.

I was the one who filed for divorce. We would probably have stayed together longer, but he was gambling a lot at that time and also womanizing. There were limits to what I would endure. So, I ended that marriage in 1970.

After that, I entered a long-term relationship with my employer, who was a male veterinarian. We were romantically involved for sometime, and then we started living together in 1971. We stayed together until I got in touch with my sexual preference in 1977.

For me, it was the lack of a fulfilling sexual relationship that ended it. We were in counseling at that time, and I was just really waking up. Looking back now, I feel that I was coming out of a fog.

I had been reacting to things all of my life. I began becoming more pro-active. I was a late bloomer. I had never had an orgasm with him or with any man. I discovered that I really was a lesbian and that ended the relationship.

I was teaching photography at that time and I had a friendship with a number of people involved with the local camera store. The strongest friendship was with a woman there. The time with her was quality time. We did a lot of things together and one night she suggested that we all go into San Francisco for the evening. There was a police officer and his wife and the two of us. So, we went and we ended up at Peg's Place, which is a lesbian bar.

I hadn't the foggiest idea what I had landed in. I was really shocked, and totally unprepared. I had no idea this was where we were going to go. I was trying to be cool and cope and be appropriate. The next thing I knew, I was on the dance floor dancing with my friend, Karen!

She seduced me that night, and it wasn't terribly difficult. We spent almost the entire night together and ended up going home before dawn. That just turned my whole world upside down and was really hard for me. I had an incredible amount of internalized homophobia. I hadn't even come into my feminism yet. I was very male-identified. I was a good wife, a good partner, coming from the 50's . . . Betty Crocker—the whole thing. I could hardly say "lesbian" without gagging.

Coming to terms with being a lesbian took a long time. All the rules for social interaction, as I knew them, were out the window. It was all very confusing.

I was now in a new culture, and within that, more subcultures. At Peg's I met women who ironed their white shirts on Friday night. They had their black slacks, and their high collars, and they would go out just so. They had a certain way about them that I just loved to watch, and they'd play pool and do all these things. But that wasn't my identity.

Now I really enjoy those women, but it still is a different

subculture from my own. At the time, I had no idea; I thought that that was what I was going to be. The tough women at the bar—I felt like I was running a gauntlet when I went in there. I felt the lack of any guidelines for how to negotiate all this.

My friend was amused more than anything else. She wasn't terribly helpful in understanding all of this. She was incredibly powerful in my life at that time, but she really wasn't there to help.

There was a rap group I'd heard about in the neighborhood, but the first time I went I couldn't even go in. I drove up and I sat in front and I couldn't get out of the car. Then I left.

The next time I went, I almost made it to the door. Then someone came along and sort of swept me in. That was really the beginning of being helped. There was a very diverse group in the room and I got a sense of different possibilities. There were lots of different bars in Marin and I found where I was comfortable.

This first woman and I had a very wonderful, hot, passionate affair which ended the relationship with the man I had been with. He and I continued to work together and have remained friends. He took it pretty well, all things considered. I did tell him what was going on. His response was to become involved with a succession of very young, very pretty women. That was fine with me.

My woman friend and I carried on for quite a while. Then I found out that her roommate was not really her roommate but was really a woman that she had a committed relationship with. I felt very betrayed and hurt and angry. She hadn't told me that. It was months before she told me. We still carried on after that but I felt uncomfortable. That wasn't what I wanted.

Even after that when I would have a photography show, she would come and, for me, the whole room would stop and there would be nothing but her. She had that much of a hold over me. Eventually I told her that I couldn't continue doing that.

There were many subsequent relationships with women. I got a sense of what dating was and I wouldn't want to do that again. Dating is difficult. I eventually dated a number of Karen's ex-lovers and we discovered that all we had to talk about was Karen!

I am currently in a relationship with Hannah and we will soon be together seven years. It's going wonderfully. I met her at my job. We became friends those first six months. I was in two other relationships during that time; then Hannah and I got together. We went to a poetry reading by Adriene Rich and during the trip down and back it became clear to me that I wanted to be with her. So now it's seven years, and it gets better and deeper—and it's wonderful.

I've always been out, but there is a huge fundamentalist Christian community where I live now. So, I'm out to only some of the community. I'm out to my immediate friends and to women's groups in the area. I helped organize the lesbian community here.

My father is dead. He died two years after I came out. My mother is alive and living in California. When I first came out to them it was okay; they weren't particularly upset. But after my Dad died, my mother had a fit about me being a lesbian. She said she was containing her feelings because of my dad's health. We didn't talk for a few years. Now, she accepts my lifestyle, although she doesn't agree with it.

I am out to my brother and sister. My sister fluctuates between being supportive and not. Mostly, she is accepting. My brother is fine about it.

I did have a child from my marriage, but we gave him up for adoption at birth. I just found him this last spring. It's a pretty powerful thing in my life. He is now 24 and is pretty amazing. He was raised in Tennessee to be a very Southern working class good ol' boy. He's very bigoted, very racist. But, I came out to him in the second conversation we had and he has been extremely accepting. We call every so often. He's not into writing. He considers Hannah his stepmother, and considers her family. It really is amazing. Hannah and I are planning on having a child, and he is totally involved in that. Hannah will be the biological mother.

It's very difficult not being out to everyone. I'm accustomed to being out and, since moving to this rural area, it's been very difficult. I don't like hiding; I don't like the power that one gives away. I don't like not being able to be myself and having to be on guard all the time.

I've made a decision to put serious roots down here. I've invested a lot of time and energy in starting my massage practice here. I intend to continue that. I'm sure my partner and I will grow old together.

I would like to tell other women that I know how hard it is to make that change. At least it was for me. I think it helps if one already has a feminist orientation to begin with. If I had been female-identified, I wouldn't have bought into so many of the male ideas.

You should just be kind to yourself. You should believe what your gut and heart say. I believed what my clit said and went with that—even when the rational stuff was at odds with what I was feeling.

You should know that if it's right for you, you'll be able to move through the difficulties.

Eve

It was a huge relief to change my sexual orientation.
It wasn't so much a change as a discovery!

I moved in with John when I was 16 years old and was with him for eight years. We didn't actually get married until two years later. We moved in together with a really strong commitment and the intention to be married. My mother had a fit because she didn't want me to marry him. The moving in didn't thrill her, but her concern was that I not marry him. She's pretty liberal, but it was hard on her that I moved out of her home.

It was an okay marriage in lots of ways, but not a terrific one. We had an ongoing discrepancy about what the word "love" meant. He didn't want to tell me that he loved me and said it was because he wasn't head-over-heels crazy about me all the time. I claimed that nobody ever is. You have disagreements and stuff. It took me eight years to get to this conversation where I would say, "Do you love me?" and he would say, "Yes" and I would say, "Yes, what?" and he would say, "I do." Finally, I would get him to say "I love you" altogether.

The other big issue for me in the marriage was feminism. I was a feminist and my mother was a feminist. She had always told me to have money of my own and to take care of myself in the ways of education and a separate bank account and things like that. He didn't mind that stuff. I suppose that's why I was with him. He was fairly progressive, but not really progressive enough for me. We had a lot of fights about who would do the dishes.

The dishes thing sort of culminated with a very sincere conversation we had one night where I was trying for the millionth time to reach some kind of compromise. Finally he said, "When I come home from work, I just want to sit and space out for awhile because I've had a hard day. And then I want to eat, so I don't really want to cook. Then after dinner, frankly, I have better things to do." I was speechless and I looked at him and told him that I had better things to do, too. Anyway, I took money from our joint checking account and bought a dishwasher.

That was the story of my marriage. It was about housework. At that time, I was a full-time student working on my art degree and, at times, I was up nights doing labor support for women who were giving birth. I was busy, too. I did more than half of the work, and I also lived in an absolute pigsty for a long period of time out of pure stubbornness because I was damned if I was going to do more than half.

Another issue in our marriage was fat phobia. At the time I first was with John, I was not particularly fat; however, I got fatter and fatter during the course of our marriage. My weight fluctuated a lot at that time. At any rate, he was never satisfied with my body. He never thought it was small enough. He always had criticism about the food I chose to eat, and yet he ate like a pig! He was thin as a rail all the time. Anyhow, this was a big deal for us.

Sex became an issue, too. We did have a good sex life for quite a long time. Eventually it kind of faded out, and we had sex once a month—which wasn't often enough for me. I always felt like a tramp because I wanted to have sex and he didn't. It was compounded by the fact that I didn't feel that he was attracted to me, and it turned out that I had reason to think that.

On the bright side of the marriage, he let me do my own thing. He didn't hassle me. I could have friends of the sort that I wanted, and that was okay. He was an inventor, and what he really liked to do was to come home and go down to the basement and make stuff. I liked to go to my friend's house and go dancing and things like that. He didn't have a problem with that, so I pretty much had my own life. I carried on a couple of flirtations during the course of our relationship. We had a non-monogamy agreement in which we'd have to ask each other first. I broke that agreement to be with a woman. I was seventeen and a freshman in college. I went to an out-of-state college even though it meant living away from John. My brother was friends with this woman, and she came over to visit, and she and I pretty much fell in love at first sight. I thought she had the most beautiful hands in the world. I didn't know what I was feeling or what I was doing or anything. I just knew that I thought she was the best. We got to know each other gradually and wrote love letters to each other. She came over to visit me sometimes. It didn't really feel like a romance to me but I do remember having a big, big crush on her.

One day she came to the school where I was and told me that she had dropped out of school and was going home because her parents needed her. She asked if I wanted to come along from Indiana to Colorado. I said, "Sure."

I took homework with me and we read *King Lear* in the car. The plan was that we were going to drive to Colorado, then she would drive me back to school for my finals, and then drive back to Colorado.

On the trip to Colorado, we identified what we were doing as love—not as lesbianism. Sue was one year older than I was. I think she was a little more on top of the lesbian issue, although she was not out at that time. So we took this trip, and we slept in the same bed, and there was all this sexual tension. After awhile, the car broke down and her parents wouldn't help us. We ended up calling my mom, and she bought us both plane tickets back to Indiana so I could be there for my finals. Sue and I spent finals week back in my dorm room and we spent a lot of time hugging and kissing.

At some point, it dawned on me that I had told John I wouldn't do that. I was sorry about it and was somewhat guilt-ridden—but not guilt-ridden enough to stop kissing her. I did confess over the telephone, though. He said that he suspected as much. He wasn't too upset about it until he came to where I was, and he told me that I had to choose between the two of them. It was clear to me that I would choose him as I had this established relationship with him. I barely knew her, and she was doing different stuff with her life.

I transferred schools to be with John. Sue came to visit and went to classes with me. It seemed that we couldn't be together without being hot for each other. I guess this is reasonable when you think about thwarted love at 17. Anyway, there we were.

She got involved with a woman shortly after that for a couple of years, and then with another woman for a couple of years after that. I got married, and Sue was the maid of honor at my wedding. I'm not particularly proud of that. She'd come to visit me every year or so all during the years of my marriage. We discovered that we didn't have much to talk about, but we were still intensely attracted to one another. We would be reminiscing and talking and laughing and all of a sudden there would be all this sexual tension.

It wasn't like I was trying to be so true to John, but more that I was trying to stay out of a relationship with Sue. I did not even consider the issue of lesbianism. By then, Sue had come out as a lesbian, so I had heard the word and I knew the concept. She and I had talked about it.

I knew I had been in love with her. I had sort of forgotten the significance of that somewhere along the line. I'm a great one at forgetting significant events. I knew we had kissed and all that stuff, but I didn't really remember that we had been in love.

Anyway, years later, we were having a phone conversation and I told her that I was moving to another city to go to midwifery school. She thought that was a great idea, that I was moving and leaving John. I moved to where I didn't know a soul and got involved right away in the lesbian community. A few weeks later,

I came out as a lesbian! Sue sent me a dozen roses for a housewarming and a coming-out gift. That was October—and darned if she wasn't there at Halloween!

We weren't together for more than three hours before we were in bed together. She and I were sexually involved for a few months, and then we broke up. This relationship with Sue has gone on and off for 12 years.

My coming out happened like this. I had only been in this city a few weeks. I had gotten away from everything—my mother, my husband, my family, my friends and all my support group. I had never been in a situation like this before where I was completely independent and completely alone. I was staying at the house of a couple of lesbians. I am a Quaker, and I had attended some meetings and asked if anyone had some housing; these two women had offered to let me stay there for a couple of weeks. I was enamored with the idea of lesbianism, but I couldn't be a lesbian because I thought I wasn't attracted to women. I had forgotten all the women that I had been attracted to in my life. I had even forgotten that Sue and I had been in love. I had forgotten all this stuff, and here I was in this lesbian household with no ties to my old reality at all.

As a part of my feminism when I was married, I wanted so badly to be a lesbian but didn't think I could be because I wasn't attracted to women. I wanted to be a lesbian because I loved women and I completely identified with women. All my friends were women; I had lots of lesbian friends.

Here, I didn't have the old ties and I regained a lot of memory. I remembered going to bed with a girl when I was eight years old and we had this sexual relationship. We had it for a couple of years and we were orgasmic. I decided that if I could do this when I was eight, I could do it now!

So, I sat down to dinner with the women I was staying with and told them I was confused. They asked me what I was confused about and I told them I was really confused about my sexuality.

They suggested that I go to the lesbian center and get in a group. I went to a Lesbians-in-Transition group. I felt like I had been coming out for the last four years. I discovered I was just happy to be a dyke. In my group, I met a couple of women I really liked and they are friends to this day.

I just started coming out to people. Some of my classmates are born-again Christians, so that was quite an ordeal. I just came out in a big, big way, and I did it before I had sex with a woman.

It was a huge relief to change my sexual orientation. It wasn't so much a change as a discovery! It was good. When I changed my sexual orientation I saw a lot of privileges slip away . . . things like not being able to hold hands or kiss in public and like getting married. It was always kind of a cover for me to have a husband. I could do anything I wanted.

I have had a couple of relationships with women since Sue. All my female relationships beat my marriage. One of my relationships lasted for two years. It occurred while I was in midwifery school. We challenged each other a lot in that relationship, and it was very growth producing for me. She was just out of a 10-year marriage and I was her first lesbian lover. That was a major relationship in my life. That woman is now my closest friend. I had a brief affair with another woman, and then I went through a celibacy period—not because I wanted to be single, but because I wanted to be alone. That was good for me. I did a lot of emotional healing and took care of a lot of childhood stuff.

After that, I moved to a more rural location. Out here in the boondocks, it's not that easy to participate in a same-sex relationship. I was alone for eight months in the country and got lonesome. So, I got a housemate and, while it was never our intention to become lovers, that's what happened. That's been going now for a year. No relationship is perfect, but this is very good. We are able to talk. It feels like a very successful relationship to me. It's the best relationship I've had.

I consider myself out. I don't announce it, but even here in the country, I would answer truthfully if I were asked. I don't talk about my personal life with my clients. I just take care of their healthcare needs. I am out to my co-workers even here in the country. I don't hold hands with my lover on the streets.

My husband knows, my parents know and my sisters know. I have no children. I have not come out to my boss. When I told my husband, he said it was about time and he wasn't surprised. He didn't see me as any different person.

I told my mom, and she burst into tears. She told me that it broke her heart that I always had to do things the hard way. She was brokenhearted to think that people would ridicule me on the streets. She said that homophobia was a real thing. She wasn't delighted, but she wasn't horrified either. My father died when I was six, and my stepfather was present at this conversation. He has never said anything to me about it. Now, my mom is a great advocate of gay rights. She has marched in a parade with me.

My parents just met my current partner six months ago. They like her a lot. She is younger than I am and they thought it was great that I wasn't involved with someone older.

Now I want to settle down and have a baby. I want to build a house with my own hands. I want to have a stable job in a place I like living.

Such a small part of being a lesbian is having sex with women. It is more about a feminist belief system. It's a life orientation, not just a sexual one. Sex with women is much more interesting because there's much more give and take. There is much more intimacy. Having sex with a man for me was fun, but it was not nearly as much fun as with a woman.

You just have to follow your heart. Lots of women are afraid to come out because they are afraid they'll be ridiculed or they're going to be shunned by their families. Not coming out is not going to prevent you from becoming a lesbian. You have to be who you are.

Binnie

What worked for me in this change of sexual orientation was keeping an open heart and mind.

I wasn't quite 14 when I left home. My mother was an alcoholic and has been married five times. It was a very abusive home life. By that time my mother was on her fourth marriage, and the abuse from that stepfather was horrendous. I told my mother that it was either him or me; so I left home.

I moved up to Vancouver at that point and lived there for several years. I was on my own. I got myself through school and I was a topless dancer. That's where I met my husband, Steve. He was from the States and came up with some friends. He came to the club where I was dancing. We were married for roughly seven years. The last two years it was kind of on and off.

On the whole, our marriage was a kind of healing process for me more than anything else. He was six years older than I was. He was kind and gentle; I was pretty calloused. It was hard for me to show affection or to be trusting. Steve had the capability of working through some things with me.

To this day, I look back and see that he was a wonderful man. We kind of just grew apart. He had dreams and ideas. He wanted children and that was not my cup of tea. By the time I was in my mid-twenties I was not going the same direction he was. We parted friends. I saw him up until four or five years ago. He had remarried and had twin boys, and that was good for him.

My mother had a relationship with a woman when I was

young. That time was probably one of the best times for me and my brother. Things were serene, and for a change, I wanted to go home. I remember wondering in the back of my mind what this bond was between them. I wondered how things could be so calm in my mother's chaotic life.

Shortly after Steve and I actually split up, I was still living here on the island and tending bar. I knew a lot of lesbians around here. I was never intimidated, shy, or afraid to say, "Hello." I couldn't have cared less. If they said "Hi" back, that was great.

I started playing sports, and for the first time in my life I had a lot of intimate, close women friends. I think a lot of women were intimidated by me before. I had always been bold and outspoken. I definitely have opinions and I'm not afraid to speak out. It was always hard for me to get close to women. I think I always wanted that, but I didn't know how to go about it.

Suddenly, I found myself with all these women. They would call and say, "We are going down to Maxwelton and play softball. Why don't you come down?" I was suddenly accepted and was very content with the bonding and sharing that women have. That is kind of how it all got started. I think I was 25. In the midst of these gals, there was Cheryl. She hadn't had a relationship in quite a few years and she was a good friend of my present partner. The next thing I knew we were together. We shared about a year together, but we each had our own home.

It was during that time that Marty, another friend, was going through some problems with her partner. I don't know what really transpired between Marty and me, but Marty used to come into the bar where I worked.

Now, this was a bar for retired types—a lot of retired gentlemen who had known me since I moved here when I was in my late teens. They kind of saw me grow up. And Marty would come in and would bring me flowers and sit at the end of the bar and just court me. Anyway, after about a year, Cheryl and I broke up. I had to tell her that we had a wonderful friendship, but I wasn't in love. That's what I was looking for at the time. We split up but are still very good friends.

I don't know how I can explain how I really feel about this. When I fell in love with Marty, it was like something I had never experienced in my life. She charmed the socks right off of me. Eight years later I still love her to pieces. In fact, Marty and I didn't have a physical relationship for six months. Other than kissing, we just thought we would take it nice and slow. The whole time we spent—those six months—I never thought of her as being male or female. I never thought of her as being a sex. I just knew that I loved her. I knew that I had to be with her.

Anyway, I can remember the first time my parents met Marty. It was on Thanksgiving at their home. I hadn't told my folks that Marty and I were planning on moving in together. I just said that I was bringing a friend over. Before the evening ended, my stepdad whispered to me, "I don't think I've ever seen so much love that happens between two people as between the two of you."

We are both very fortunate in that we have families that love both of us and accept both of us. Marty is part of our family and I'm a part of hers. They are totally aware of the relationship. I have one brother who is three years younger than I. He is kind of shy and doesn't say a lot, but the first time he met Marty he absolutely adored her and they became good friends.

Marty is a California girl. She found out early that she was a lesbian and socialized with no one but lesbian friends. She has a total of seven other brothers and sisters. They just accept that that is Marty.

I am out to all the people I work or worked with. I've been a beautician for seven years. I love it. I even have clients who asked me why I don't have a boyfriend. And I say, "Did you ask me because you really want to know?" And they'll say, "Yeah," and I tell them. I've very seldom had somebody, at least while they are in my chair, get up and leave or anything. In fact, this one gal who was in my chair not long ago says, "Okay, you've been doing my hair for years and I want to know what it is with you and Marty." I replied that we had been living together for eight years. I said, "Yes, we are together." She says, "Hot damn! I'm glad you told me that. It's been on my mind for a long time."

I have, however, lost clients that have found out through the community. I had a mother and daughter who had been coming to me for about five years. In fact, they followed me to this shop. Someone told them I was lesbian, and the daughter called me on the phone and told me that she could no longer come to me. Every time that happens it hurts.

I have this dream that Marty and I are old and sitting on our front porch rocking in chairs. Marty will be finished with school. She has one more year. It's been a rough year with only one income. But we're getting through it okay. We are definitely going to be building something on our property. We also talk about having a child. We'll probably adopt. We'll probably get a black child as Marty's parents adopted two black children and she was very close to them.

We have also raised two children. When I first met Marty, she had her 13-year-old brother with her. He was sent up here because he was incorrigible. He was failing school and into drugs and a dropout. We raised him from 13 until he graduated high school with honors. He is now in his third year of college. We didn't baby him; we just gave him rules that he had to abide by. We told him he was responsible for getting up to go to school. I don't know why it worked, it just worked.

I also have a godson who is going to be 21 soon. I have had him off and on from when he was nine until he was 17. There were several years that overlapped that we had both kids in our home. Pretty wild!

We have great fun together. We love camping. We ride bicycles. We are really into our animals. We have a dog that we take to the beaches. Sometimes we go to Seattle and walk around Pike Place Market. We both like to cook. I'm kind of a social butterfly and I love to entertain. I play music a little bit. Marty and I sing some; she has a beautiful voice.

What worked for me in this change of sexual orientation was keeping an open heart and mind. I think honesty is very important. It certainly isn't easy. It can be very lonely living a double standard of life. I think that without honesty both lives aren't full. You are not living to the potential of who you could be.

It would have been a lot lonelier if I hadn't been committed to honesty. I'm not lonely and I know that I can pick up the phone and call my mother. If I'm just feeling blue about something, I can share that with her.

I have a lot of people I can call upon. I think that's really important. We all need that.

Darlene

My youngest daughter knew that I had had this near-death experience and thought I was going to be a changed person. She thought I was going to become "normal."

I married to have a home—a place to live—and was married for 34 years. My parents died when I was young and I lived with a guardian and was switched back and forth between a brother and sister. I really didn't have a home. I was fifteen and Bill was eighteen when we married. I had known Bill six weeks when I married him, and I'd have to say that it was a pretty good marriage. He raised me. It was like a parent-child thing because he was so much older mentally than I was. We belonged to a very straight and narrow church. We had rocky times as well as good times. Making a living was very difficult because neither he nor I had much education. He always did the best he could to take care of the family. He was very proud of the fact that, no matter what, we were always able to make it. I had my first child when I was sixteen. Every two years there came another one until we had four. I found out what caused it and had a hysterectomy.

Bill drove a truck and was gone a lot. I had a job with responsibility and I also had the responsibility of the house. But when he came home, he expected me to turn back into this clinging vine that couldn't do anything any more. He thought that my assertive personality was okay for work or for anywhere else, but he didn't want it brought home. Whenever some of the guys from work called to tell me they weren't going to work or that something had gone wrong, Bill saw no reason why those men should be calling me at home. It really tore me apart emotionally because I was having to act as if I were two or three different people. I used to go camping with my friend, Marianne. We had raised our children together and had become, and still are, good friends. She is like my sister. She always encouraged me to be myself and to do what I wanted to do.

At the moment, I am in my third relationship with a woman. It all started at work when I became attached to this woman named Jane. I simply wanted to be where she was—a very strange feeling! In a way, I was kind of embarrassed to be seen with her because she was pretty obviously different. Yet, I picked her up for a drive one Saturday morning and I began to voice my feelings toward her. I didn't really understand what was going on. I was hoping that we wouldn't see anyone I knew because I felt that this wasn't any different than if I had been with a man other than Bill. But still, these feelings were definitely different than any I had felt before. I just wanted to be with her. She was a person who had a few problems, and I guess I thought I could help her. I was just very much drawn to her. I could look into her eyes and that was where I wanted to be.

When my youngest daughter got married, I felt all alone. There was no longer a buffer between Bill and me. Meanwhile, Bill had been having some long-term health problems. He thought his trucking was causing them, but he would not go to a doctor. One morning he left for work, and I put all my clothes in the car and I left, too. There was never any discussion about it. He was totally surprised that I was gone and was very hurt. He loved me very much. Finally, he asked me to come back and I did. He went to the doctor and found out that he was allergic to his medication. All this time, we hadn't gone anywhere or done anything together because of his health, and he could have done something about it. Instead of being sympathetic like I should have been, I left for good after being back only a week. This time I was afraid to talk to him because I was afraid he would drag me back home. In addition,

I felt so guilty about it all that I refused to talk with him for years.

My leaving was very hard on my family—and on me, too. I came out to my children when I left because I had always been very close to them. My son was devastated! He simply couldn't understand why his mother would do this. He was 30, and didn't have much to do with me for a couple of years. I felt so hurt by this. Finally, he told me that I was his mom and that the important thing was for me to be happy. If I was happy then he was happy. My girls were supportive of me because they were all married to husbands who were of this new supportive generation and were not domineering. I felt that it was my turn to have a life. I had done my part. I had raised my kids. After we were divorced for five years, Bill met a very nice lady and got married. It took a while longer but gradually I started talking to him. Now I consider him a very good friend and I'm very glad that he is here. The most important thing I want for him is to be happy. I want him around for support for the kids. We talk often and he is support for me, too. It took me some years to be comfortable enough with me that I could talk to him. I needed to get rid of that guilt. When he married, I found that I could be friends with him again.

When I left, I stayed with my friend, Marianne, for a month and then Jane and I got an apartment. We were together for about a year. Our relationship was wonderful at first because I had someone that I could do things with. She cared about me and made me feel good. Life was fun! Yet, it also had a serious side. She had gambling and drinking problems which made our time together difficult.

Then, Paula, a very self-assured woman, came on the scene and wanted to be helpful. She felt the relationship I was in was destructive for me and that I was being taken advantage of. Again, here was this person who was very attractive to me—exciting to be around. Between the two of them and trying to sort out my life, I had a nervous breakdown. I was in the middle of my divorce; I was in a relationship with Jane; and Paula was on the scene. I just wasn't handling my life very well. All I wanted to do was run away. So, I just ran away from everything into a nervous breakdown. I ended up in the psychiatric ward at the local hospital for a couple of weeks. I was very depressed, wanting to commit suicide, because I felt that I didn't have any control over my life. I was being pulled in so many different directions at once, I didn't know which way to go and wanted to please everybody. That's the way I'd spent my life. I thought if I pleased everybody, I would have a place to stay —I would have a home.

Finally, I broke off my relationship with Jane and went into a relationship with Paula. That relationship was wonderful. We were always doing things, and it certainly was never boring. At the same time, I was very naive and not really understanding how the gay community worked. Paula was still best friends with the person she had had a relationship with. To me, coming from the heterosexual community, this was a foreign idea. I couldn't understand it at the time, and it was a big problem for me. So, after five years, I broke up the relationship and moved back in with my friend, Marianne. I still saw Paula for about a year on weekends.

After I broke up with Paula, I began searching for something spiritually. There was a woman at work, Joanna, who had given me some information on a church, and she asked me if I would go with her. I did, and we became friends. At the same time, ten of us from our company were being sent to India on a job. I planned to stop in Hawaii on my way back for a vacation with Joanna who had decided to meet me there.

During our stay in India I got very sick with a serious gastrointestinal illness. I became completely dehydrated. When they got me to a hospital, the sanitary conditions were so bad there wasn't enough bedding so my co-workers got bedding for me from the hotel. I was so weak I could hardly talk. I felt like I was yelling but it came out as a whisper. Finally, I left my body and I walked into this light that was indescribable! I felt that I had never been so loved. This light I was going through was a kind of radiance.

I walked up into this light and I felt welcomed with open arms. I always had a fear of dying and not being ready to go. But I got there and God knew all about me. I was told that in Heaven we are known not as male nor female but as spirits. I was told that I had things to do and I couldn't stay. I had to go back. So, I went back down into my body. It was a shock to be back in my hospital bed, and I didn't want to be there. I didn't say anything about this experience to anyone. My team leader felt he had to get me out of India because they were losing me. He managed to get me on a plane and when we got to Hawaii he turned me over to Joanna. She said I really looked awful.

From the minute I got to Hawaii, I started getting better. It is really and truly a healing place. Joanna told me that when I left my body, she went psychically looking for me and all she found was a thin thread of energy. She grabbed hold of it and told me I wasn't leaving yet. So I came back. I don't know whether it's her fault that I came back or not.

When I got home, Marianne and my whole family met me at the airport. I hadn't called Marianne while I was away and she felt left out. When we got to her house, I wanted to tell her about all that had happened but she was too hurt and angry to listen. Joanna didn't have her own car there and was planning to spend the night but felt she couldn't with Marianne being so angry. So I told Marianne that I was taking Joanna home and I'd be back in the morning. A month later I moved in with Joanna. When I was sick and she was taking care of me, I fell in love with her. We had such a deep spiritual bond to build upon.

Joanna and I had a ceremony and my children were there. It was a good beginning. My youngest daughter knew about my near-death experience and thought I was going to be a changed person. She thought I was going to become "normal." Then one day, she made the comment that Joanna was so normal. That was her statement of acceptance, and she has continued to be very supportive of Joanna and me.

When I returned from Hawaii, I called my oldest daughter and told her that I needed to talk to her. I started telling her all about my experiences. Four hours later I shut up. She had said very little(usually she doesn't let me get a word in edgewise). Then, she said that I was a changed woman—that I had gone to India as a lamb and came back as a lion.

I apologized to my children because I didn't know how to love them. I'm amazed that my children love me so much. They've turned out to be wonderful people.

Joanna and I have a good, comfortable relationship. She's very active in the Unity Church. Recently she told our pastor that she was gay, and it has made no difference. We have acquired a good base of friends in the gay community. One of our very best friends is Joanna's former partner.

I'm still friends with Paula. I have come to understand that just because you are not in a relationship with someone doesn't mean they are out of your life. I finally realized that I can still be good friends with those who were very important to me. I was talking with Paula recently and she told me that she had felt that I was ashamed to be seen with her. I said that she was probably right; I wasn't comfortable with *me*.

At Christmas time I had the whole family over—Bill, his wife, and all the children. Everyone enjoyed themselves and they all accept Joanna as part of our family. My girls want to know that if anything happens to me that Joanna will be taken care of. There is so much comfort in all of this.

Eleanor

I felt that I had come home. It was an "A-Ha!" experience.

I remember when I was young that I wished I could figure out a way to have children without men.

As long as I can remember I wanted to be a mother. I had four children in less than five years. Not so great, let me tell you! I was married two weeks after I graduated from junior college. It was in 1958, and I was twenty years old. We moved to New York City where I was teaching in a nursery school. My husband was an apprentice to become a funeral director. We lived in New York City for four years. During that time, I had three babies. Seven months after we got married I got pregnant. From then on, it was babies.

My marriage was mostly raising a family. I worked very little outside of the home. My husband was an alcoholic and that was probably the biggest problem in our marriage. We were very much in love when we got married and very close, but when the alcohol started interfering with the relationship, it just started crumbling. I think I've realized that I should have left that marriage after ten years, but I was afraid of being on my own. I didn't feel that I could support myself and the children, and I wanted the marriage to work.

I wanted to be married. I didn't want to be single. We had visions of all these wonderful things we were going to do when the children were grown and he was retired. I didn't want out until it got so bad that I realized that's what I had to do. That was about twenty years into the marriage. Our children were 14 to 19.

I had a problem with alcohol during the marriage, too, because I would go along with it. Then one day I looked pretty seriously at myself. I heard about a hypnotist who was conducting a group for those wanting to quit smoking. I was curious about it, so I went. When he hypnotized us, I substituted drinking for smoking. After that session I didn't drink for four years. I had no more desire. After that, I drank only very moderately.

Finally, I went to a lawyer and got a legal separation, thinking that it would straighten him out and I would go back to him. It didn't take me too long to figure out that we don't straighten people out; we can only take care of ourselves. We were separated for two years but still very married. Neither one of us dated anyone else. We would take vacations and do things together. I had moved into an apartment with my youngest daughter. The other children chose to stay with their father. They realized that if they lived with me it was going to be a greater responsibility for them as they would have to contribute to the household.

I felt like I was in the mire—I wasn't married and I wasn't not married. I got no support from my husband except for $35-a-week child support. I ended up working two jobs. I had a lot of anger and resentment. Between the two jobs I was working seven days a week.

I filed for divorce about two years later. One reason I waited so long was because of his insurance. There was a certain amount of security in still being legally married. I think I was afraid of letting go completely. Then, one day, I just said, "I'm going to do it."

It was quite a few years later, actually, that I realized that I was interested in women. I didn't think I had any feelings for women. I had quite a few gay men friends. They would kid around with me saying, "When are you going to change over?" Even some younger female friends came right out and asked me, "Are you a lesbian?"

And I'd say, "Well, I don't think I am." I was confused, I really was. I still had some interest in men. I dated a little bit, but not very much. I can't say that I really enjoyed it that much. I realized that my friends were all women or gay men. I really never had friendships with heterosexual men.

Then about four years ago, it finally happened. I was working in a restaurant where one of the owners was gay, and he knew that I was leaning towards women. Some people were having a birthday party, and everyone who worked at the restaurant was invited to the party. When I got to the party, there was a young woman there named June. She was the lover of the daughter of one of my closest friends. I happened to know her, and as the party was progressing, one of the guys said to me, "June is in love with you." I said, "I have known June for 10 years. She loves me and I love her, but she is young enough to be my daughter."

I really didn't think any more about it. Then I was sitting in a chair, and she came over and sat in my lap and put her arms around me. She asked me if I would go out to lunch with her sometime and I said, "Sure."

I was living with a woman at the time; it was a platonic friendship. She asked me when I was going to call June and have lunch with her. I said, "I will get around to it one of these days." I finally did call her and then we got together. It really didn't last very long because every time we started getting close she would run away. She was scared to death of the whole thing. But that was my initiation into lesbianism.

I felt that I had come home. It was an "A-Ha!' experience. I wanted to put it in the *Chronicle* or the *Post*. I called a local TV station which aired women's stuff and told them I had just come home. I called my ex-husband and told him. He told me that he wasn't surprised, that he had felt that from me for a long time because of my friends. I hung around a lot of women who were closeted lesbians. I was attracted to them and he knew it.

Now I am with Pat. When we got together, we just knew that

we were supposed to be together. Our first date was in November 1990 and we moved in together in January 1991. I met her at a group of lesbians over the age of fifty; the meeting was held in a church. Now, I tell people I met her at church. She just cracks up. It was my second meeting with the group; I'm very glad I went.

I am out to my kids. When I told my oldest daughter, Sandy, it was as if she had opened up the door for that conversation to come through.

I went over to her apartment after work one night, and I was very nervous. I thought how am I going to say this and then she just said, "How can I help you, Mom?" She said, "Now, Mom. We've got to find a man for you." And I said, "Sandy, I need to tell you something." "You don't want a man do you? You want a woman," she said. She was at that birthday party and she knew something about what was going on there. I told her that was true, and that I was very attracted to June. She said, "I've known about this for a long time." I asked, "How long?' and she said, "About 15 years."

At that time, when she was about 13 years old, I had be-friended a young woman. She was about 21. Her younger brother was working for me and I met her through him. Now I had this husband who was falling out drunk by 10 o'clock at night. He wasn't a violent drunk. He just drank until he dropped.

So, from 10 o'clock, I was free to do what I wanted. She and I got very close. I never had any sexual feelings for her—I guess I suppressed them. I remember that whenever I would see her, I would just light up. We would go out and ride bikes in the summer time until two o'clock in the morning. I had a lot of energy, too, the kind we get when we fall in love. I could be up late and get up in the morning and be a mother.

This was what my daughter was referring to while I was coming out to her. It seemed at the time that Sandy was okay about my change in lifestyle. She hugged me and said, "Mom, I'm real happy for you." But, as things went on, she changed. At this point, she does not speak to me. She has since become religious and she no longer accepts my sexual preference. Her feeling is that I have replaced her father with a woman.

My youngest daughter was a little bit surprised when I told her but seemed to be accepting of it. She has always been very close to me. She did go through a period when Pat and I first got together when she felt that she was losing me to this other person and she was very jealous.

We talked about it a lot. She tried her darnedest to be as nasty to Pat as she could. She would say to me, "Mom, do you have to spend every night with her?" I told her that I chose to. It was hard for her, but still, there was a certain level of acceptance from the beginning. On the other hand, she was very closeted about it as far as telling other people. God forbid that her boyfriend should find out.

I have a son who lives in New York with his father, and I told him a year later. I was waiting to tell him in person, but when Pat and I moved in together last January, I called him on the phone. I really thought there would be problems, but he just said, "Well, Mom, that's all right. You're still the same person and I still love you." He's 28. Pat and I went up to New York to see him and it was like he had known her all of his life.

We took him out to dinner, and he started asking her questions about college. And we met his fiancé, who was also fine about it. She has a son who calls me "Gramma". He kept asking me if Pat was my friend, and I said, "Yes, she's my best friend."As a matter of fact, this past Christmas they came down here and stayed with us.

I am not out in my new job. I don't know yet whether or not my job would really be threatened or not if I came out. It is difficult for me not being out. I don't understand how people manage not being out. I was out where I worked before—in the restaurant.

For women who are contemplating a change in their sexual orientation, my advice is to go for it! Some people suppress their desires consciously; but, for me, it was not a conscious thing. If you want to do it, go for it. If you feel you need counseling, go for that, too. Do whatever you need to do to make that transition.

Pat

I did the perfunctory things like trying to have a boyfriend.
Really, that just bored me to tears.

I just came out eight years ago at the age of 55. I was married twice.

The first time I was married for five years and my husband died. Then I was single about a year and a half and now have been legally married for something like 28 years. At the time I came out, my mother was living with us and we didn't want to split up housekeeping. It's been five years now, and my mother still lives there with him. I didn't see any sense in forcing any kind of change.

One of the reasons I stayed with him so long is that he is a very nice person. My lover and I spend holidays with him. I have an adopted daughter which he has also unofficially adopted. There are no problems. He feels pretty comfortable being in the same room with us. He knows I'm a lesbian. He was the first person I told.

I wrote him this long letter saying that all of our problems, of which we had plenty, were just as much my doing as his. I told him that I had decided for sure that I was a lesbian. I then talked to him and he got up from the table and put his arm around me and asked me how he could help me. It's kind of hard to hate somebody who is so supportive.

My daughter has always been very supportive, and, in fact, she had a friend in high school who was a lesbian. It wasn't any big deal to her. She is grown now with children of her own.

I probably always knew I was a lesbian. I remember myself as a small child and growing up. I did the perfunctory things like trying to have a boy friend. Really, that just bored me to tears. I wasn't very successful at it, either. I really didn't understand how all these girls were getting all that excited over these stupid guys. I was the perennial tomboy and played sandlot softball and all that. My mother made me quit at the appropriate age.

When I went away to college, I thought I would find out about all this. I read all the time so I knew something about homosexuals. The high school library books had told me that homosexuals were sick people and that they had to be cured. So I said, "Not for me!" I went to college at a girls' school—it is jokingly referred to now as "the dyke factory of Texas." I totally avoided women who I knew were homosexuals. I set myself up with straight people.

Then it became unbearable, and I began drinking. My folks were pillars of the community and the Methodist Church. My mother was very much the Southern belle and my father was the son of Yankees who'd moved to Texas. He was a Union man—so he was a little more radical. I was heavily into doing what my parents approved of. I felt they would be disappointed if I turned out to be one of those homosexuals. I never felt that I could talk to them. That first year of college was 1947. If I'd been less inclined to get information from books, I'd have probably been better off. I continued drinking to keep a lid on it until five years ago, when I stopped drinking and came out.

The reason I eventually made the decision to come out was because I visited an old high school friend whom I was crazy about. We exchanged confidences about our lives and I told her how miserable I was. She told me that she thought I ought to see a psychologist. I saw that she had received good help from the feminist psychologist that she recommended, so I went into therapy with her for six months and decided to quit drinking and to come out.

My first experience with a woman was with that high school friend. It was a very brief and not a very satisfactory sort of thing that wasn't terribly wonderful, but it certainly didn't discourage me. I launched on with a vengeance. I proceeded to try to get into every social group I could in order to meet people. I had four or five partners prior to my present partner. I thought of each in terms of a long-term relationship. I was raised that way and I agree with it.

I finally got to the point of coming out to my husband and my mother. My mother is the sort of person who doesn't deal with things. I told her that I was a lesbian and I was moving out. She stayed with my husband and that was that.

Moving out and being around other gays was an important decision for me. I got a little job working two hours a day at the Gay Political Caucus. Even though this was mostly gay men, I felt I could identify with them certainly more than I had even been able to identify with straight men. They would say little things about when they were children that I could understand. I gradually began to meet more and more women. I didn't join a lesbian group until a little later. I thought they were just a bunch of old women and I didn't want to get into that. I was probably more afraid of them because I did a lot of chasing of young women. That was to give myself more confidence, but it was remarkably unsuccessful!

I am out with two of my former co-workers—only with people I feel comfortable with. For all I know everybody at work already knows. I'm fairly well-known politically. I don't know that they don't know, but I don't feel threatened in this job. I did not go back into teaching because I wanted to be out and I didn't want to have to deal with parents. In a few years, I hope to have a private practice in drug and alcohol abuse or hold some elective office, if I have the stamina to do it. I would be an openly gay candidate.

I think women contemplating a change in lifestyle related to sexual preference should evaluate their feelings very carefully.

They should read all they can and talk with others about lesbian lifestyles. They should look at themselves and see what would make them happiest. Go with their feelings. Also if they are doing any drinking or drugging, they ought to quit it because they can't understand their own feelings unless they are sober.

I came out when I was 55 years old and I'm almost 60 now. I can say that these past five years have been the happiest years of my life. They haven't always been the easiest and I've had a lot of problems establishing a long-term relationship. I had some wonderful counseling and help along the way.

This was the best decision of my life!

ANNEE

*When I married my second husband, I already knew I had a
real interest in women. But I thought it was all fantasy stuff
and it would go away.*

In 1969, I married a man from Colombia, South America. I
knew him only three months when I went with him to live there.
The marriage was an escape from my parents' house. I was living
in Louisiana, and we eloped and drove into Texas and got married.
Then we took off for South America.

I was very unhappy and emotionally sick there. There was the
language barrier and I was very isolated. I had a lot of expectations
about what marriage was supposed to be, and there were a lot of
disappointments. He didn't want children and I did. We lived
with his family, who were very vocal, and very passionate. In my
home, we had to be very quiet around my father, so I wasn't used
to all the hubbub. I got depressed and didn't do very well. I felt
like a possession of his, and I didn't appreciate that. I felt that my
only purpose was to provide a sexual outlet for him.

I finally started attending a women's organization and I found
out there was an underground system for American women who
lived in Colombia. If you had children there, you couldn't leave
the country without your husband's permission. I didn't have any
kids, so that wasn't an issue, but my husband didn't want me to
leave. After about two and a half years, I told him I wanted to go
home and visit my parents and if he wouldn't let me, I'd go
underground. He bought me a round-trip ticket. I came back here
and got a job. I sent him money for a few months and then sent
back the other half of the ticket.

There were really no repercussions from him. He called a lot, and finally threatened that he would get involved with drugs and be an addict. In the meantime, I got involved with drugs. I got a divorce about ten years later. I was just too occupied with doing whatever I wanted to do. Eventually, he gave me a divorce without any contest.

The second time I married was in 1982. When I married my second husband, I already knew that I had a real interest in women, but I thought maybe it was just fantasy stuff and it would go away.

I met him the night I decided to go and find where women were. I was feeling thwarted because I couldn't find the women's bar that I was looking for. I couldn't find the address and I was walking up and down the street and finally decided to go home. He sat down beside me on the bus, and we just started talking. Then we started spending more time together. It was a whirlwind relationship, and we just decided to get married.

He was eight years younger than I and he was easily controlled and manipulated. There was a power imbalance, and I had more than he did. It wasn't good ultimately, but it was the first relationship where I had some power. I thought that he would be a ticket for me to have children. I had had a hysterectomy, but I still wanted to have kids.

Before we got married, we talked about adoption. Within a month after we got married, he said to me, "Let's go to the doctor and get you fixed so you can have kids." I got out a medical book and sat down with him and explained to him why I couldn't have kids. When he realized I could not have children, it became a real issue. He wanted kids of his own. I still wanted kids, but he wouldn't adopt. About this time, I started having affairs with women. We weren't married three months when I started going to the Lesbian Resource Center for their weekly rap groups.

I had done some experimentation with girls in high school. I had a real crush on one girl who the other students called a "lesbian," as if it were a dirty word. It sounded pretty interesting to me, and just served to intensify my crush. Then, in the early '70s, I started having affairs with women. There was a man/woman couple that I knew and they asked if I wanted to have a menage with them and I thought, "This is unique. Sure, I'll try this." But, I soon realized I didn't want to have anything to do with him—I was having a great time with her. She and I were sexual a couple more times, but it was awkward because her husband didn't want to be left out.

Then, shortly after my second husband and I were married, I really fell in love with a woman. And I finally knew that my real feelings belonged with women. It was wonderful! That relationship lasted for a year. It turned out that she was a heterosexual who was experimenting with me, all the while I'm telling her I love her. It was really heartbreaking for me. Of course, here I was married!

My husband worked weekend nights, so it was relatively easy for me to be out and about the women's community. And I would fabricate car breakdowns and other excuses to be away as much as possible. It ended because she got tired of waiting for me to end my marriage, and when I finally did, she was ready to move on. While she was not the love of my life, she was a stepping stone for me. That relationship made my preference very clear.

My husband and I divorced five years to the day we were married, but for two-and-a-half years we were separated. It was a real battle between heterosexual orientation and homosexuality at first. It was hard because I felt like I was straddling the fence. I felt like I really didn't belong in the women's community because I was married. I felt like I didn't belong with my husband because I really wanted to be with women. It was very difficult, also, because sometimes women didn't want to have anything to do with me because I was married, and I felt ostracized. On the other hand, a lot of the women were really friendly and made a beeline for the coming-out woman.

It was increasingly uncomfortable for me to be married, and

I started reading the books that were available. The way my husband found out was that he found these books. We worked different shifts, and I would read at night and put the books under my mattress. I would sneak the books out and take them to work with me and read them at lunch.

Then one day, I was in a hurry and I left the books out. He found the books and wanted to know what that was all about. I had been struggling with this issue of ending our marriage and trying to decide if I was really a lesbian. So, I just sat him down and said, "Well, look! It's not working out. I really want to get a divorce. We aren't making each other happy. I'm really a lesbian and I need to get where I feel comfortable." But he did so much crying that I ended up saying, "Okay, we won't get a divorce; I'll try to work it through."

That lasted a year and then I just couldn't do it anymore. It finally became a battle all the time. Every time I walked out of the door he wanted to know where I was going and what I was doing. He didn't trust me and I didn't feel good about myself. I was very uncomfortable.

I am not currently in a relationship with a woman. I've had a couple of relationships which I felt were heart connections; but to me, there are a lot of things that are really hard. A lot of us women in the community have so many family-of-origin issues. I think that keeps a lot of us from connecting emotionally. You do get involved with someone and they have so many issues to work through, it makes it really hard to have a relationship. I think it's very easy to say, "It's too much trouble and it's too hard."

I haven't found many long-term relationships. That's one of my greatest disappointments in the lesbian community, although it may be a universal thing and not just with lesbians. I do, however, find that my friendships are so fulfilling. I'm most grateful for the friends I have made in the women's community. I am not a separatist, but, I find it better to stay in the women's community. We share so many social occasions and have many things in common. I think that that's the greatest gift I could have ever received.

I'm out to my mother and my two sisters and my brother, but not to my father. My sisters said they were not surprised. One sister is very loving and is just a non-judgmental person. She just loves me for whoever I am. The other sister thinks this is a phase. I've always had conflicts with this sister because we see the world through different eyes. My brother was very loving and just said that he wanted me to be happy.

I didn't tell my father. My father's sister is a lesbian, and she came out and left her husband to be with a woman when I was 11. She's had two partners in these years. She's my role model. My dad doesn't have a lot to do with her. He doesn't approve of it. I don't tell him because of what went on with his sister and, also, because he has leukemia. He doesn't have that long to live and it's one less stress to be between us for as long as he lives.

My mother is a jewel. When I came out to my mom I brought her some books. When we talked, it was truly the most heart-to-heart conversation we'd ever had. I told her that I didn't want to be isolated from her and not share who I was, and that I didn't want to have to be careful with what I said to her. I didn't want a wall between us. I said, "Mama, I'm a lot like Aunt Nell." I think mama already knew.

My mother is a Christian, and her major concern was whether I might not get into heaven with her. I told her that she had instilled good morals, standards, and ethics, and through those values I'd get through the gates of heaven. It would not rest on whether I was a lesbian or not. That was a really good conversation, and then we got into whether I thought parents had any influence on kids. It was wonderful.

The next day, she was really angry. It came out in ways like old history being brought up. Then, a little while later, she told me some of the family were talking about the queers, and she didn't know what to do with that. All of a sudden "queer" became personal. It really hurt her feelings a lot. She didn't know what to do with it.

I talked to her about it and told her she needed to share with her family so she would have someone to support her. She said she couldn't do that. I suggested her minister, and she said she couldn't share with him. She felt very isolated. I told her I felt so much lighter having shared with her and she said, "I'm glad you feel better; now I have to carry the burden." She started to cry and yell more about the burden. I screamed, "Mama, put the burden down!" There was quiet—and then I heard this little chuckle on the side. Since then she has been really close to me.

Lauren

I consider Bonnie to be someone I happened to fall in love with.
I don't necessarily consider myself a lesbian.

I was married in 1971, and it lasted for six years. I met my husband in college in California where we were in the same music classes. I knew him for about a year and though we didn't plan to get married, I got pregnant. It was a surprise to both of us. I came to Oregon to go to school and was registered and everything, and then found out I was pregnant. I went back to Palm Springs and we got married in November of that year.

I knew when we were getting married that I shouldn't because I didn't love him. His parents were very rich, and they bought us a house, two cars and put $5,000 into a checking account.

Meanwhile, my mother wanted me to get an abortion. But every time I was supposed to sign something, I kept crying. My doctor thought that was a sign I really didn't want to have an abortion, and he was right. I knew that this would be the only child I would ever have, and I knew she would be a girl, and I even knew on what day she would be born.

The night I brought the baby home, Al was in college and he was going to have a test the next day, so he spent that night with his parents. He said it was too noisy to be around me and the baby. It made me feel awful and I felt very deserted. He didn't know how to be a husband. We were both 20.

Our daughter will be 20 this year. While I was married, I put myself through school. I was able to apply for grants on my own.

I didn't own anything that we had.

Through most of our marriage, we were good friends; we're still good friends. We finally got divorced because I was just too unhappy. I didn't want to be married anymore. I didn't want to live with him anymore.

I have never found the term "lesbian" comfortable, but I know by other people's descriptions that that's what I would be. It is important for me to be thought of as a heterosexual because I am a teacher. I consider Bonnie to be someone I happened to meet and fall in love with—and want to share my life with. But I don't necessarily consider myself a lesbian. I met her at my friend Kate's when I went to visit. Bonnie was there all the time and I could hardly talk to Kate alone. It turned out that they were in a relationship.

During this time in my life, I was very unaware of my own sexuality. When I found out a woman could have an orgasm, I went immediately to Kate and told her. I thought she couldn't possibly know that, and she was very kind and listened. I had taken a class called Preorgasmic Women and had started reading books about women having relationships with each other. I felt very compelled to teach Bonnie and Kate about these experiences that they could have!

I thought the home they created together was so cozy and warm. It didn't occur to me that this could be a way I could live. As Bonnie and I became closer, Kate began a relationship with another woman, and she moved in there, too. Before long I moved in with them and the four of us lived together for a year. Then Kate and her friend split up and Kate moved to Portland to be closer to her job, and Bonnie and I have been together ever since.

When I was first separated and moved out, Al was determined that Kate was the reason we split up. One day, he came to pick up our daughter at my apartment. I wasn't home and he went upstairs and got my journal where I had hidden it. I had written a lot about dreams and about Kate because she was someone I could talk to.

He was going to take me to court for custody of our daughter. He was looking for evidence that I was an unfit mother. That was a big deal and a lot of trust I had with Al was destroyed at that time. The journal got in the hands of lawyers and finally the agreement was that he would pay no more child support. I think today he still thinks that Kate is the cause of our divorce.

After I was divorced, I was a counselor in a teen parent program. I was the person the teens would come to when they first found out they were pregnant, and I would help them with their options. After that, I got a job as a teacher and have been a teacher ever since.

When I started living with Bonnie it was very easy. I felt very open and it was much more calming to change into this life. It was everything I ever thought living with a person should be. I have not had other relationships with women. I was never in counseling for my change in sexual orientation. Bonnie and I have been together since 1978.

I am not out to anyone except a few close lesbian friends. I have told my daughter that some people would call the relationship Bonnie and I have "lesbian" or "homosexual", but that I don't consider that to be the case. That's honest.

My daughter lived with us and went to school, so that added a whole different component to the relationship. Now, I think that she thinks that Bonnie and I are the very best of friends, and that we would do anything for each other.

It is not hard to maintain my secrecy. We are not demonstrative in public. My daughter doesn't live with us anymore, but she feels very free about popping into the school where Bonnie works at anytime and seeing her.

My mother is living and my father has been dead for 17 years. I'm a survivor of incest from my father. I've just remembered this in the past few years. It's a source of fear to remember those times. I've decided to tell my mom because she was there. I don't know whether or not she remembers it.

110

Mom doesn't like Bonnie much. She feels that my allegiance to my family has changed to Bonnie's family. A lot of that is true because my relationship with my mother is very awkward. Last year I finally asked her if she liked me, and she said that she loved me but she never liked me as a child and as a teenager, and that she feels uncomfortable around me now.

My advice for women who are thinking of changing their sexual orientation is if they think they are a lesbian, they probably are. There are lots of things at stake when you are in a marriage with children. A person has to be happy with herself and where she is or it doesn't matter if you have kids or anything. I would advise her to talk to a counselor—one who is neutral about sexuality.

Gayle

*It wasn't so much women. . . . It was this
particular woman!*

I was married in 1978 for seven years, although we were
separated for the last two. I met Mack as I was finishing college and
he was finishing up the last two years of his Ph.D. in electrical
engineering. We were very good friends and we had a lot of
things we wanted to do together and we had a lot of fun. In the
beginning of our marriage, we were very compatible. We argued
a lot, but we were never mean to each other. There was a lot of
respect. I think it was a nice marriage for what I knew and needed
then. But, as all things go, my life got complicated.

Shortly after I was married, I fell in love with Sue, who shared
an office with me at work. Both of us denied that it was anything
more than a friendship, and neither of us wanted it to be anything
more than a friendship. But in our hearts we knew. That went on
for years. I would call it more sensuality than sexuality. It wasn't
very sexual; it was mostly an affair of the heart. I just felt that I had
finally fallen in love. As much as I loved Mack, I really questioned
whether I'd ever fallen in love with him. It just was not the same.
I never felt that I'd really *fallen* in love with the guy. That really tore
me up.

Finally, I realized that I needed to make a change. It was
obvious that I was not in the right place. But I loved my house and
I loved my neighborhood. I had wonderful friends within walking
distance all around me. A bunch of us had all bought old farm

houses at the same time and we were all fixing them up. There was a great sense of community.

Even so, I knew that I was living a lie. It wasn't so much women. . . . it was this particular woman! Maybe that made it easier for me. I didn't want to be a lesbian; I knew that much. I would have just as soon have been heterosexual. Now I have matured!

At the time, I really wanted to be this good girl. I'd graduated from a good university and married a very successful man. Maybe down the road we'd have some lovely children. I bought into that whole fairy tale, but it was unravelling. It was a mess, and I really wanted to pursue this relationship with Sue. So, I separated from Mack.

I know now that my relationship with Sue was pretty classically dysfunctional and co-dependent. There was push-pull game playing going on. Her control was around sex; I was very willing to be sexual and she was not. I was so in love with her that I didn't care. But, as soon as I got out of my marriage, the relationship with Sue didn't work. She backed off and didn't want to have anything to do with it.

To this day, she hasn't done many long-term relationships. I don't know that she has ever lived with anyone in a committed relationship. She does not consider herself a lesbian. The last time I talked to her, she said she was "omnisexual." She doesn't like labels. We went through a period of time when we didn't see each other because it just became so very horrible. Then, about two years ago, we happened to run into each other and got together again and tried to work on the friendship and that just didn't work either.

When I first realized I was interested in women, I went to see a counselor. I was so torn I couldn't tell the truth about it. I had this life that sort of worked, and I just didn't want to throw it all away. A part of me knew I had to. It would have been good if Sue had said she wanted to be with me, or gave me a clear message about it. She told me flat out that she wasn't gay. I was very confused; it was awful.

I didn't really see myself as lesbian; I thought I could go on either side of the fence. I'm one of these people for whom sexuality is kind of an option. I felt I had crushes on both men and women. Now, I think it would be hard to be with a man again. I don't rule it out. I have wonderful friendships with men, but I'm just not driven to be with men. My former husband wasn't a bad fellow. He did not mistreat me. He was my biggest fan. He was wonderful. He was kind.

I have been in my present relationship six years. I'm really happy. Our hardest time was when I tried to re-establish that friendship with Sue. Actually, I ended up feeling like I was falling back in love with her. I don't regret doing it because, for me, it finalized things. It certainly was the hardest challenge that Jo and I will ever have and, because we were able to deal with it together, it took our relationship to a deeper level.

I met Jo as a part of a basketball team. Then, mutual friends of ours had a party and we got together. It was pretty obvious that there was a lot of attraction between us. She was partnered with a woman at the time, but that relationship had been falling apart for awhile. She had tried to make it work, but it was really over. I was the vehicle for making it really over. Once I met her, I just put everything else aside. I had had this short-term relationship with a 19-year-old who was a wonderful person. But, as soon as I met Jo, I just tidied up things. I broke with the woman and finalized my divorce.

I'm not out at work, except to certain people. I struggle a lot about coming out there. I think, "Who are you going to come out to—the whole hospital?" Since I move around all over the hospital, I just made my own little rules. If I decide that I'm going to see any of the people I work with outside of work, I come out to them. I figure if they are on the planet and I talk about my partner, then they either get it or they don't. I don't have a lot invested in most of the people I work with. I don't want to know about their personal lives so why should I spill my beans?

My ex-husband knows. We actually spent part of my last vacation together with mutual friends on their boat. I think for him it is an easy way to explain why he and I are not together. He never seemed to have any problem with it. I never got any sense that he thought it was disgusting or anything negative. He is really great.

I come from a family of five. I'm a twin and we're the youngest. My twin sister and I are very close, and we live very different lifestyles. She is very comfortable with my lifestyle, and she likes my partner. She told me she has had a few brief affairs with women and she understands the attraction to women. It makes sense to her when she thinks of me. She is an alcoholic and she has a relationship with a man that is sort of on-again, off-again. She lived with one guy who was put in jail twice for beating her up. We've had more separation in the past 10 years than before, and I feel it's because of who she has been with and her chaotic lifestyle. Even though I'm gay, I feel I live a very conservative lifestyle compared to her. I've been in the same job for five years. I come home at night. I own my own home. I'm very typical. I don't think my being with women has been a problem at all.

I have not come out to either of my brothers. My brother who lives in Georgia converted to Mormonism in his early twenties. He graduated from Brigham Young in police science, and he is very red necked. I don't see too much of him. I wouldn't be surprised if he knows. I have damn near said that I'm gay to my brother in San Diego. I think he knows, but he sometimes likes to think it's not real.

I came out to my other sister. I knew she had a hard time with it, but I really feel that she has come around. My mother knew, as mothers know, as soon as Jo moved in with me. Now, she openly talks about my being gay. She talks to her pastor about it. She includes Jo's name on cards.

Jo comes with me to every holiday family gathering. They are a lot less prejudiced than they used to be. I come from a family where four out of five children are divorced, and my mom is happy to see one of her kids settled. As for my father, I have never discussed it with him, and I don't know if my mother has. I think he knows. He would have to be an idiot, which he is not. I don't feel like I'm living much of a secret life.

I am enjoying my life. For fun, I like to go boating, scuba diving and walking the beach. In summers, we go up north for skiing, hiking and backpacking. I like the out of doors. My dream is to build a house all by myself on the 10 acres of land that we own.

Julia

I consider myself out, but it took 60 years!

I was married in 1945 and it lasted for 34 years. For 20 of those years I had a relationship with a woman. That is the crux of it!

I met this other married woman through the Junior League. After about seven years, my husband was transferred to Philadelphia. By this time, of course, she and I were very involved and we spent the next 13 years with her coming to Philadelphia and me spending the summers with her in Chicago. My children would always be at camp each summer, and she didn't have any kids.

In those 13 years we wrote every day and we called once a week. Looking back, I think we were living a fantasy. When we finally did get together, it busted up. The sexual part of the relationship sort of waned and that may have been part of the problem. We lost it from all of the stress we were under and there was a lot of homophobia in both of us. And, also, she had a wandering eye and had affairs with women which I closed my eyes to. But, in reality, I was very ambivalent.

Six weeks after I called it quits, she was in another affair. In order to win her back, I got a divorce. It was a very hard thing for me to do. You see, I married a peach of a guy. He just thought I was swell. He was easy. He would have stuck with me—he didn't care what I did. I think he knew all along what was going on. He wanted peace at any price and he didn't want the stigma of divorce and he did not want to be abandoned. He would have hung in there, but it was my guilt that was killing me.

So, I finally got a divorce to be with my friend. Then, when that didn't work, I felt that I had sacrificed a tremendous amount. In essence, I thought, "Look what I have given up for you. Now it is your turn to take care of me." But, this was not owning my own ambivalence.

As a result of the breakup, I've had a lot of therapy to determine what was going on with me. As I look back, I think it was that I couldn't handle the closeness. She wasn't perfect, but she was pretty great.

It has been a terrible three years. I have never experienced being abandoned before. She was everything to me, and I had a lot of pain. But, I'm feeling much better. I'm wiser and smarter. I'm out of my fantasy world. I had a lot to learn about being on my own. It's taken me a long time to let go of that relationship.

I have three daughters. My oldest is very supportive of me and my lifestyle. You see, I spent my life hiding it. My oldest daughter said she knew there were secrets in the house and she did not want any secrets. She, too, has three daughters and she didn't want her daughters to grow up with these secrets. So here I was—the most homophobic individual--and I was placed in a spot. After the split-up, I told all my daughters. My middle daughter will not discuss it. She and I have a lousy relationship. My youngest daughter doesn't say much about it. We get along fine, but we don't discuss it.

My oldest daughter asked me to tell my grandchildren. It was the most difficult thing to do, but it worked out fine. They say to others, "What's the matter with a gay person?" It's neat. I think they just look at me as Grandma. My ex-husband moved to Florida and remarried a few years ago. I told him, too. Now he thinks he is better than I am and is stuffy as can be. I see him about every other year when he comes to see the children and we get along fine.

When the break-up happened, I thought, "Now that's all behind me. I'll go back to the straight world." I'm a bridge player, and I have the Baptist Church. Between the church and my bridge, I thought I would meet people. I planned to close the door on the gay world. Well, it was very lonely. Life was pretty dull and pretty awful. I do have some church members that I still see and I still play bridge, but I find myself doing it less and less. I am much happier being who I really am and being part of a lesbian group. I consider myself out, but it took about sixty years!

After this breakup, I just climbed into the wine bottle—night after night. Then I went to a treatment center. They told me they thought I was alcoholic and that I ought to stay off booze. I joined Alcoholics Anonymous and that has been very positive for me. I go to both gay and straight meetings. I made friends through AA and they are the people I do things with. I hope that some meaningful person comes into my life.

To be honest, I think everybody looks for a companion. I think I could be responsible in a relationship now. I was so ambivalent before. I was torn between the woman and the tapes of my mother in my head that said I should be married. I knew in my heart what I really wanted, but I felt so pulled.

For the woman who is thinking about changing I would say, "Stop torturing yourself." I tried to go back to the straight world and it didn't work. I lost my relationship because I was so full of ambivalence. Make up your mind and go one way or the other. We all know people who deny their lesbianism and are miserable. I'm learning to enjoy people and to not be so afraid of life.

Nancy

I made a decision to become a lesbian based on the fact that I was in the fifth generation of very strong women.

I was married five years to the day: November of 1968 to November of 1973.

I married my high school sweetheart and I also put him through college, where he got two degrees in architecture. His name was Jerry and we were very kindred spirits—very entrepreneurial. We were both natives of Dallas and both from very wealthy families. We went to a city where we had no attachments to see what we were made of, and both of us became successes in our respective businesses.

Then, on the day of our anniversary, I learned that he wanted a divorce. I left that day and we were divorced two days later. I was devastated. He had given me no clues at all. I loved the marriage and I was very relationship oriented. I never wanted children and we didn't have any. What I see during this last 17 years since I was married is that Jerry wanted to see what he could do without a strong woman. His mother was a very strong woman and I am too. I think he wanted to see what he could do on his own. Now our relationship is friendly—but very perfunctory. We celebrated our high school reunion together and I see him periodically. He remarried six years ago and that marriage has just ended.

I consider myself very much a lesbian now. In 1978, I was very promiscuous with men, but I would still fantasize about women. I had a lot of close friends who were lesbians.

In 1980, I made a decision to become a lesbian based on the fact that I was in the fifth generation of very strong women and I was in a female business. I always worked very well with women. Many people have challenged me on that decision. I have had to deal with a lot of shame about being a lesbian. Once I made the decision, I became celibate. I traveled for two years around the world by myself to think about whether or not this was a good decision for me.

It was a good decision. When I came back home, I asked my lesbian friend to support me in getting into the lesbian community and to introduce me to a lesbian I had heard about for years. As a result, I met this woman whom I had never met before, and we became lovers for the next eight years. I was enthralled with the mystique of it. There was the thrill of that which was taboo.

Then reality set in. I thought something was wrong with me because I was gay. This was a very serious change that I had made. I abandoned all my straight friends. I felt that I was not in a position to go to them and tell them about my lifestyle change. The more I became committed in this relationship, the more I realized the shame.

Three years into the relationship I went into therapy and programs for alcoholism and compulsive overeating. I was a very compulsive person and I would go on some binges now and again.

When I made the decision to go into Alcoholics Anonymous, I could finally look at all that. I had tremendous difficulty dealing with the shame of those early years. The therapy and groups helped greatly. As a result of my AA work, I went to my straight friends and told them how wrong I was to cut them out of my life. I told them I was gay, and of course, they knew. I still had a lot of guilt about it. My relationship ended in May of 1988 when she left me for our best friend who was a woman 20 years younger than I. I was devastated!

To help me with the depression from this breakup, I went into a treatment center in Arizona for a 22-day program. Mostly, I needed an arena from which to tell my family. It was the first time I had been in a lot of pain and I felt I couldn't go to my sisters and my brother. I felt very sad about my dishonesty. When I talked with them, the response was excellent. They were very supportive and very nurturing, and they have never discussed it since!

My family makes constant homosexual jokes, and I guess it is unrealistic to have them accept my homosexuality. The fact that they have not accepted it is just not my problem. They didn't cut me off. If I got in trouble, I know I could turn to my family. I am the youngest of four children with stepbrothers and stepsisters. I am the least outgoing of the four. It's a strong group. I am my parents' favorite child. I was very relieved to get that secret out.

Somewhere around three years ago I finally made peace with being gay. I am out to just about everyone who is important to me in my life. I do not broadcast it, but if there is a need to tell someone in the course of a friendship, I tell. It is very easy.

I had this eight-year relationship in which I was monogamous. When she left, I had relationships with four women in a three-month period of time. I have been with a total of seven women, but for about four years I have had no relationships. I am seeing that there is greater need for me to be alone and to learn to be alone. I am now some 60 pounds overweight, and that is just another indication that I'm not ready to be in a relationship. I'm covering up too much. That's my suit of armor. I'm pretty much at peace, but, on the whole, I loved being in a relationship. I would hope that I'd soon be in another one. Finally, after three years, I'm letting go of that eight-year relationship that I had. I have found out how to nurture myself.

My advice to women contemplating a change is look at the consequences of what you are doing. It is a major change. There is a tremendous responsibility that comes with that. There is being out, and there is outing others. I have far more respect for lesbians' confidentiality now than when I was straight. Secondly, just do what is right for you. I have been fortunate that I finally learned to accept my homosexuality. It took a lot of dollars and a lot of pain to accept myself.

Now, I find my serenity and my contentment in a small world with a close support group. I do hope it's with a partner, and yet, I'm content to not have a partner if that seems to be the right course for me.

The
Family
Album

Peggy (L) & *Irene*

Photo by Marc Marnie

Carroll

Ginny

Karen

Jan

Cathryn (L) *& Connie*
Children: Rob & Susie

Denise

Diane

Randi (L) *& Jean*

Barbara (L) & *Jeanne*

Susan

Betty

J.C.

Audrey

128

Annie

If I had it to do over again . . . I wouldn't let my lover leave
while I stayed home with my husband and children.

I have been married 28 years. I am considering divorce now.
It's been an okay marriage—nothing exceptional. We don't fight,
we don't shout; I've never been abused. I'm getting out of it
because I know I've been a lesbian for 16 years and it's been
very hard having to live a lie.

I had a relationship with a woman for six and a half years. That
was my first and only lesbian relationship. It broke up because she
got a job out of state and I made a decision not to go with her. At
the time my kids were teenagers, and I had to agonize over what
to do. It was just an awful, awful decision. In the end, I decided
that being a teenager was hard enough without my leaving. So, I
made the decision to stay with them—to stay in the marriage for
their sake. They are now 27 and 24, so I no longer have that same
obligation to them.

My husband knows. His response is, "That's fine." He is an
engineer. My marriage was boring, but peaceful. After I told my
husband, it's been pretty much the same as it's always been. We
have been celibate for years. My husband suffers from clinical
depression. Because of that, and the medications he has been on,
his libido has diminished. Sex is not a big deal for him. He is
emotionally tied to me and he doesn't want me to leave the
marriage. He is happy for me to go and do what I have to do, but he
doesn't want me to leave. I'm not sure if he has ever been in love

with me. He is one of these people who never demonstrates any affection.

My lesbian relationship occurred when I was going to the university, back in the seventies. I got to know this woman who I thought was wonderful and I really enjoyed her. We were both political activists and she was out as a lesbian. At first it was nothing sexual. It was just a good friendship. I had known her for three years and then one afternoon something happened and I became incredibly sexually attracted to her. It was just an amazing feeling. I had never felt that for anyone before. We arranged to meet the following day and we ended up in bed. We spent most of the day in bed. It was wonderful! I discovered what sex was all about.

We knew each other for six and a half years. All this time my husband didn't know. It sounds strange, but actually it was very easy not to let him know. I would cross the bridge and go to school and be with her, and then in the evening, I would put on the other hat and cross over and be a mom. It was easy, but I was really two different people. It was easy because my life was so compartmentalized.

I didn't seek counseling because I was too happy. My happiness outweighed any feelings of confusion I might have had. I was very busy with my relationship and school and just doing so many political things. I didn't have an awful lot of time to think about it. Then she got a job in Illinois and moved.

I'm now at the stage where I'm trying to see how to go about this change; to see what steps to take to leave my marriage. My counselor's advice is to go very slowly and to be sure of every step.

I'm out selectively at work; five or six people know. Most of those people are lesbians and are really good friends. I used to have a circle of lesbian friends, but I really cut myself off from the community when my lover left. So, in the past year, I've been picking up the pieces a bit and making new contacts and new friendships. I've gone to the local lesbian center to an Over Forties Group. I met a few people through that and I joined another

130

lesbian group for professional women.

I have a mother in England. I don't get on with her at all so I have no desire to tell her about my sexuality. I was abused by her as a child, verbally and emotionally. It was only about ten years ago that I realized what had happened to me. I'm working through an awful lot of anger. I'll probably never see my mother again. The only reason I would tell her would be out of spite and I don't want to use it like that. I feel too joyful, it shouldn't be something used in spite or rage.

I am not out to my children yet. It's the next thing that I'll be doing. I haven't told them yet because I don't want to hurt them. I'm worried about what they'll think and how it will affect them. Having come from such a lousy childhood, I wanted to be to my kids everything that my mother was not to me. There will be a need to tell them because when I leave home they will want to know why I'm leaving. I've been in the closet so long I need to do this. It will be such a relief. I don't find it so difficult to maintain secrecy, except with the kids; that's difficult. I want to get over that hurdle.

I don't think I have a lot of fun in my life at the moment. I am very busy. I'm just learning to live again. About a year ago, I became incredibly depressed. I couldn't sleep. I'd wake up at 2:00 every morning, no matter what. I couldn't eat; I had no appetite. I lost about 50 pounds. It was a really bad time, culminating in coming out to my husband.

During that time, I couldn't do anything fun. I'm feeling well again and I'm just starting to do things for myself. My husband is so depressed that he doesn't want to do anything, ever. So, for so many years we haven't done anything. He just reads. I felt I was being dragged down into his depression. So now I've decided that I really have to look out for myself and I have to make my own happiness outside of the marriage—outside of the home. I'm starting to get to know people and making plans to do things.

At the age of 50, clearly, I have to think about the future. I don't earn very much myself financially, and it is going to be very, very hard. It's really scary. I have lived in the U.S. for 26 years. My degree in nursing is from London University and was so many years ago that it isn't of any worth now. I work as a medical assistant in a doctor's office. I am not licensed as a nurse in this country, since it would have been like starting all over again to try to get licensed. There is no market for my other degrees. I don't look forward to retirement.

I am not currently seeing anyone. I don't have any special person I can go to or spend the rest of my life with. I just don't know about the future.

If I had it to do over again, I wouldn't make the decision I made; I wouldn't let my lover leave while I stayed home with my husband and children. I regret it very much. I've seen her just three times since she left and we talk once or twice a year on the phone. In the past couple of years, she has been in a relationship.

I have a lesbian therapist, which has been a godsend for me. It was real important to me that she be a lesbian. The last thing I wanted was to go to someone who would want to cure me. The organized lesbian groups have been very supportive. I've done a lot of reading on lesbian subjects and now I don't have to hide these books.

I regret so much getting married so young; I was 21. I knew I didn't love my husband, but it was back in the time when you looked at getting married as incredibly important. It was your meal ticket, and women needed to think about those things. I didn't think of it so consciously then, but I had very few options at the time. I thought nobody else would come along and I had to find myself a man! I regret that hugely.

I told my kids to use their twenties to grow up and enjoy life. They are both doing that. Neither of them is interested in settling down yet. I'm really pleased. I've done that right.

I'm scared about the future. I wish I'd done this younger. Right now I'm thinking of getting out and being on my own, and being self-sufficient. I've never lived on my own. That's a big step for me.

Ginny

*I think things would have been different if
I had come out a generation later.*

When I was twelve or so, I had a special friend named Candy. We were very close. We were best friends and it turned into something a wee bit more. We never became lovers and it was nonsexual, but it was more than friends. It was kissing, holding hands, saying we loved each other. So, it was physical, but not sexual. I think the two of us were too afraid. Then, her parents found our love letters. There was a big emotional upheaval in both our families. Our families had become very close because of our friendship and, at one point, my dad worked part time for her dad who was an upholsterer. They played cards together every weekend and our families spent a lot of time together. When all this came out, there were accusations back and forth. They were so upset they didn't know what to do. This was back in the late sixties. There was no such thing as gay rights or awareness. Her family was religious; mine wasn't. I think there was a lot more pressure on her than there was on me. My parents said, "We'll take you to a psychologist." Her parents were more into exorcising demons. The upshot of it was that we weren't allowed to see each other for awhile. At that point, it was almost a relief because the whole thing was so emotional. We felt that we had done something bad and were wrong. We felt so much shame. We thought we were bad people and shouldn't have had this thing going on between us. It also broke up the friendship between the two families.

I didn't get taken to a psychologist because my dad was in the service and something like that would have been put on his record and he couldn't have that. I think my dad asked for a transfer because about six months after that he got transferred out of Duluth. So, I just put the whole thing away. I just put it in a locked closet—it was a part of me that I would never acknowledge. Being the good Catholic girl that I was, it was always important to me to please my parents. I was a good student, never got into trouble and never did drugs. The whole good-girl image was very much internalized.

I have a younger brother and sister. I asked my sister much later if she remembered any of this. She said that she was aware that something had happened, but she did not know what it was.

The first year of college I met the man who later became my husband. We were being honest with each other and I told him about the girl in my past. Right after I had my first baby, Candy tracked me down and called me. She had married while she was still in her teens, shortly after our experiences, and started having babies right away. She had two kids. This was really a monologue on her part, because I really didn't want to have anything to do with her. I was over that. So, I was not giving out very much of myself. What I found out was that she slept with my picture under her pillow every night. Her husband knew this. She was quite obsessed, and she was very open about her obsession. She had a very bad marriage. Her second child was due to him raping her when he was drunk.

I am not sure why she called except she said she wanted to see how I was doing. I told her that I was married and had just had a baby. She said she was happy for me and that was pretty much it. I think I corresponded with her once and then just dropped it.

When I was freshman in college, I had a roommate who felt as displaced as I was. I had come to Seattle and knew no one. I was living with my grandmother, which was not a good thing. This other woman was in the same sort of position. We bonded right away and became good friends. Then, she got a roommate and they became lovers. I totally rejected them. I didn't tell them why. I just said that I couldn't have anything to do with them. They took it as being real basic homophobia, which it was. I told my old high school friends in Denver about this and how I was freaking out about it.

Then, when my son was about a year old, my good high school friend, Debbie, called me up and told me she had divorced her husband. I was thinking to myself that I was so lucky—I have a young son, a perfect husband, the perfect marriage. I felt sorry for all those other people because they weren't as lucky as I was.

A little later, Debbie called again and said that she had some news that she was afraid to tell me. Then, she came out to me. Well, about that time, I was starting to have some questions about myself. I had joined a softball team and half of the women on the team were lesbians. All the ones I got really close to were lesbians. So, I just started to think about myself. I told Debbie that her news was fine with me; it was no problem. Later, I took a trip with my son to visit her. She had just come out and she wanted all her friends to support her, so she invited us to her coming out group. I thought it was cool. All these women were telling their stories and they knew that we were Debbie's straight friends and there to support her. I brought my son with me and he played with everybody and they just loved him. All these women were telling their stories and that was it for me. Yeah! I felt that this was who I was and what I was about. This was the truth of it. I felt this was true but that I wasn't going to do anything about it. I had a life to live. I didn't tell anybody.

I went back home and had another baby—a daughter, Carleen. I call her my miracle baby because it was the one time we had sex that year. I wanted another baby, period! At the time, we did not have a lot of money. So, I was trying to supplement our income by having several part-time jobs. I was also escaping from the marriage. Not only was I working a couple of jobs, but I was on two softball teams and a bowling league so I wouldn't have to be home. I was too busy to deal with anything on an emotional level. I was busy with the kids; I was busy with school. I was a busy girl and it worked for me. What I didn't know at the time, but found out later, was that my husband was just about as unhappy with things as I was. But, he had the perfect wife, the perfect children. Everything was perfect.

During the course of one of my part-time jobs, I met Lisa, who had graduated from school and couldn't find anything but part-time work. I was immediately attracted to Lisa and I would try to plan for her to be on my crew. The attraction was mutual. One day, we were just sitting around talking and she asked me if I wanted to go see a movie. It was a date. We never said so, but it was definitely a date. God, she was crazy—she was nuts. I'm straight and have two children and yet she was pursuing me! I didn't give her anything back, saying that I didn't want this at all. But, we went to this movie, and it felt like an honest-to-God date with all of the tension that was going on. As we were getting into the car, she told me that she was really attracted to me. I was dumbfounded because it was out in the open. I'm not used to having things that are uncomfortable out in the open. I don't remember if I said anything back.

That weekend I went nuts because everything just sort of opened up. I made a decision that I was gay—whatever that meant. I knew that I needed to find out what that meant and I also knew that I couldn't take my kids with me. I called her saying that I had something I needed to talk to her about and we arranged to meet at a park. She was very nervous because she thought I was going to say that she had been very inappropriate and that I didn't want to have anything to do with her. I said, "Look I feel the same way about you." I told her my story and that I had known this all along but had denied it. I knew this was a fact when I was at Debbie's coming out group. Actually, I had decided that when I was forty, the kids would be old enough and it would be okay. We kissed and that was it.

Unfortunately, the timing was really bad because we were celebrating Easter and my son's and husband's birthdays all at the same time. I wrote a letter to my husband, Chris, and actually showed the letter to my best friend, who was in a mothers group with me. She was very accepting of it and I was very surprised. I needed to talk to somebody. This was another friend named Debbie. We had kids about the same age and baby-sat for each other. We just had a very good connection. Somehow, I knew that she'd be okay with it. She told me that I was so brave. It wasn't that at all; it was just something I had to do.

To make a long story short, I gave the letter to Chris. He said he was sorry that we couldn't have talked through this before. He said he was sorry that I'd gone through all this. He said, "You also need to know that I won't give up the kids." I told him that I knew that and that he was the perfect father for them. I told him that they were better off with him and that we'd work something out. I knew that I would not take my kids into something that I didn't even know about myself. So, that was it. I packed up some clothes and left. It was tough. My son was four and my daughter was not yet two.

Anyway, my relationship with Lisa lasted three and a half years and went two and a half years longer than it should have. It was a very dysfunctional relationship. I was going to make things work just like I'd always made things work. Finally, my health was suffering and everything else was going to pot. I was in so much pain that I broke it off.

Four months after I left, I was working part-time. I could not get a job. I had been out of work for five years. I had a degree in psychology, but what was I going to do with that? So, I was working part-time and trying to figure out what I was going to do. I was working as a Kelly Girl for an occupational therapy business. And, there I met Susan with whom I had a immediate bond. It was great. I talked to her about all the problems I was having with Lisa. She was very open. She had her own turbulent life. She'd been married once and had a son from that marriage. She'd divorced her husband about the time her baby was born. She was a bit older than I. So, we'd walk around Green Lake and I'd tell her my tribulations and she'd tell me hers. Finally, she told me that she just had this real problem meeting good men. I said, "Well, I got one for you!" I told her I thought he was the best man in the universe. So my ex and she got together and were married about a year later. That's been 14 years now—the perfect marriage. They are the same age, like the same things, and are very companionable and compatible. So, that took care of him! She proved to be a good mother, too.

I've seen too many broken homes with the kids all screwed up and I was not going to be the cause of any of that. The kids know that I'm their birth mother and they still call me Mom, but Susan and Chris are their parents. I didn't want this push-pull stuff with the kids. I probably pulled away too much, but I see them five times a year. It's gotten a little worse because the kids are busy now. My son just turned seventeen and my daughter is fifteen. My relationship with both of my kids is very good. Neither one of them has gone through a rebellion stage. They are great kids!

It was a good decision I made for them. I feel guilty sometimes but it was still the best decision I could have made for them. My dad sees the kids more often than I do. Back when I was leaving, Chris asked me if I wanted him to talk to my dad. That's Chris. But, I came out to my folks. My dad, the military guy, came over to me and said that he loved me no matter what! I've been really lucky. My mom just cried and cried and cried. My dad was afraid that he wouldn't be able to see the kids. I told him that Chris would never do that to him or the kids. My mother never did say why she cried so much. I just let her cry. The big thing for them was the divorce and being able to see the kids, not my lesbianism.

After my break-up with Lisa, I went kind of crazy. I was thirty-three years old and I thought I was pretty hot stuff. I was on a lesbian softball team. Right away I had a sort of fling with a gal on the team. My friends were introducing me to other women. Then I was dating--nothing really serious or anything. It was fun. Shortly after that I met Claudia. That was in April and we got together in May. I always consider a relationship like a marriage. I met Claudia in a women's study class at the University of Washington. We called the class Lesbianism 101. She knew that I had all these things going on as we were getting more and more serious. She told me that I had to tell these other women that I was no longer available. So I did that. It was okay with me, but it was difficult.

That was almost ten years ago. For the most part it's been great. To me, it's a forever thing. I am forty-two. I do computer networking for a company.

I think things would have been different if I had come out a generation later. There would have been more options. I would have had more information. Kids, nowadays, come out in high school. My parents don't talk much about my situation. Chris has been very supportive. He was the first person I talked to when I broke up with Lisa. I thought it was necessary information for them to have because it was a big change in my life.

With Claudia, it is her choice about how much she wants to do with my family. We go back and forth on this. She knows my guilt trip about my kids. I want the small amount of time I have with them to be special. I want them to like me. Claudia knows I overcompensate and she's there when it is convenient for her. So, I try to make it convenient for her to be included. The kids don't have a problem with her. If she's not around they will ask about her. With my parents, I didn't give them an option regarding Claudia. I said that this is who I'm with. You don't have a choice. They've actually been very good about that. When they were married, it was considered an interracial marriage because my mother is Hawaiian. Back in the fifties she was considered colored. My dad was told that he couldn't be stationed in Mississippi, for example, because of his interracial marriage. My dad's family didn't want to have anything to do with her. He just went to them and said, "This is my wife and my family and if you don't like it, tough! " He gave them no choice. I did the same thing. It actually worked.

Regarding my siblings, my brother and sister and I have always been close because we are so close in age. My brother is fourteen months younger than I and my sister is three years younger. So, when I came out, my brother said that if there was anything he could do for me or the kids to let him know. He's a different sort of a guy. I think he was really uncomfortable and didn't want to say anything. Our family was raised to take pride in the family and not talk about uncomfortable things. I remember his words because I didn't expect them. My sister was very supportive.

I don't know how unusual my story is except that I've heard some really wretched things when other people tell their stories. I have had lots of family support.

For me, Claudia is my perfect mate. Lisa had brought out all my co-dependent leanings in a very negative way. I was always taking care of her and making excuses for this and that. I was always needing to fix things all the time. I did some reading and some counseling on our relationship and realized this was not a good thing. I realized that I was never going to fix her and, while she was with me, she would never get fixed. I knew I couldn't be healthy in that relationship.

I think the quality about Claudia that I treasure the most is that I don't feel like I have to fix her. We talk about all the problems that we have, but I don't feel the need to fix them. I give her support and sympathy, but her problems are hers and whether she chooses to deal with them is up to her. It's only when it affects us that it becomes a problem. That's when we have to talk. In terms of the healthiness of the relationship, I think other people think it's kind of odd because we don't have very many of the same activities.

She has all her hiking and biking which I have nothing to do with. I like to play golf, sit in my chair and watch *Star Trek*. She wants nothing to do with these things either. We do have many of the same values. We have a very good companionship and are still building our relationship. I'm going back to school and both of us have our work. We have our together friends and our separate friends. Claudia is just very important to me.

J . C .

It was like trying to fill this spot that never got filled.

I understand a lot of women know that they are lesbians early on. But I grew up in a capsule. My father was a professor and a part of a medical community, so we had a very protected environment.

I did very little dating while I was in high school, as I was very involved in art and music and performing. Then, when I got into college, I started dating a lot. I was always attracted to people who were very bright and, in my sophomore year, I started living with a fellow who was a physicist. Our relationship was fine as long as it was intellectual in content, but when it got down to the day-to-day living, problems came up. He said the way I responded to him after sexual activity was like I had been soiled. At that point in my life I had no idea that there was an alternative. I didn't know anybody gay, you know?

So, I lived with him for four years. My relationships always started out with a lot of heavy sexual activity and then, after a period of time, it came down to nothing. That was true in this one, too, and it created a lot of conflict. Then I finally moved out of there.

After college, I was living in Seattle and I met a fellow who lived in New York. He did all those wonderful things that are taught to us in little fairy tale books. He sent flowers every three or four days. I was real impressed by that. All the women I worked with thought he was wonderful, and I ended up marrying the guy and moving to New York. That didn't last too long because he drank a lot. I thought he was a social drinker, but actually he was an alcoholic. I was fairly isolated, too, because I didn't really know anybody there. It's interesting that he still calls on anniversaries and stuff. We didn't bury the hatchet in each other. I divorced him in the early seventies.

Then, I got into banking and banking management. That's a real neurotic occupation. I did well at it. I met a fellow there who was a lobby guard. I was engaged to him for a while and then started dating a friend of his.

Most of my relationships had a three-month span. I dated a lot of different people because nothing very satisfactory seemed to be happening. I was pretty sexually active, but as I look back on it now, I know that I had an underlying attitude of disrespect of men. I think sex was their primary focus. Relationships were very disappointing to me, they were lacking in depth. I thought, "What is it that I'm supposed to be experiencing?" I wondered what everybody seemed to get so excited about. I dated men with a lot of different ethnic backgrounds and occupations.

Finally at 29, I thought it was time to be married and have a family. All that family pressure stuff. I was introduced to a fellow who was a widower and he had a three-and-a-half-year old daughter. I married him within six months. Then I became pregnant and, within the next year, I had another daughter. I was used to changing relationships, but now I had a real commitment to being a parent and I felt I should honor what I had started. I was married for seven years. He was a very controlling, abusive person and a police officer. Who better to take care of me than somebody strong and in uniform? Big lie!

Then in 1985, my mother was dying of cancer. For the last three months of her life, she was totally bedridden. So, I took the girls with me back home and cared for my mother until she died. As her life was ending, it really made me think about the direction my life was taking. I decided that I did not want to go back to this marriage. I could see how little caring he really was capable of. I had a big awakening. I knew that I needed to do something else with my life. So I came back and divorced him.

That was a traumatic process. He has still not made it easy after all this time. I realized that I had to make a living and support myself. I had stopped working when my daughter was born. To move away from the work force is very disabling, no matter how strong you are. I decided to make a living doing something that was more suited to who I was. It was scary, but I believed in myself.

My daughters were in a private school at the time. I started putting together my music and my art, and I was able to create the music program at that school. I did that for three years. I had free rein to just create it, and it was very successful.

There was another private school in the area that had heard about the program; soon I was doing two private schools. During that time I started doing music education classes with little people —two-year-olds and a little older. I took those kids as they grew and they became my piano students. I did some advertising and sent out fliers. At the present time, I don't have to do anything to create a full load. I have more people than I can fit into my schedule. So making an income finally took care of itself.

I was working at this private school and I had this free hour-and-a-half on the days that I taught, because I had to wait to give my daughter a ride home. I always went to this one particular place for lunch during that time. There was a woman working there whom I started having little short conversations with and it was really nice. All of a sudden, one day, I realized that I really looked forward to going in there and talking with her. Then it dawned on me that the reaction I was having wasn't like a lot of other friends that I've had. It was a real attraction and I thought, "Oh, dear!"

When I was in college, there was a woman who lived across the hall who was lesbian, but I didn't know it then. She used to arrange dates for me with her gay male friends because I preferred men who were polite and knew how to behave appropriately. They were always a terrific date. When I moved here, I sent her a card and she came over with her roommate at the time, and it was like, "Oh— your roommate." It never occurred to me then. That was my only contact with lesbians. When I was working at the bank, I also managed an apartment building. In the building, I had a number of tenants who were gay men and I got along with them really well. These were my only contacts with the gay world.

So, here I am at the restaurant saying, "Hm . . . this is really different." As I continued to go in there, I began to consider myself in the middle of something like a teenage infatuation. It was terrible!

Then I had a woman who brought her daughter to me for piano lessons, and she was noticing some of these changes I was going through. I was noticing her a little bit, too! One day she brought me some music tapes and told me that she had brought me some women's music to listen to. I thought that was fine because I was a feminist. She said, "You may want to listen to this when you're alone." It was a tape of one of Olivia's anniversary concerts. She told me there was a concert coming up and asked if I would be interested in going with her and another friend of hers. She had brought her roommate here a couple of times with the kids, and I kind of wondered about it.

Finally, I started to talk with her about these feelings I was having. All of a sudden, she up and moves to New York! Always before in relationships, it was no big deal when they were over. But in this case, I thought somebody had ripped my insides out when she left. I was just devastated.

In the meantime, I was looking for a counselor as I felt very edgy and confused. It was important to me to have a counselor who was a lesbian and who had a stable relationship because I knew nothing about stable relationships. I wasn't sure that stable relationships were ever possible. A friend of mine recommended a counselor, and it has been a very positive experience for me.

Anyway, this friend who recommended the counselor shared similar experiences with me. She said, "There is something I want to share with you." And then I said, "There is something I want to tell you about, too." As it turned out she had a crush on somebody she worked with and I had this big hot crush on this waitress. We thought that was pretty entertaining! So, I was able to start moving through my confusion to some clarification. My friend and I ended up coming out about the same time.

I absolutely consider myself a lesbian now. In retrospect, I can see that there were a lot of things I didn't cue into growing up— a lot of things I didn't see.

I had a good time telling some of my friends. I really enjoyed it. It was like this great discovery that I had made. I told some very old friends of mine and I've had no backlash. They were just fine. It speaks of the quality of friendship I had established. My feeling was that if it was something they couldn't handle, then I had made an error in evaluating the things that our friendships were based on. Acceptance of differences is important to me. This one woman that I told had always kind of looked to me as the person she always wanted to be because I did a lot of dating. It took her about a week before she could talk to me again. But, she called back and said that she had had a real hard time with it. Then, she introduced me to the first woman I was physically involved with.

My friend had said that she knew this gay fellow who had a lesbian roommate who was about my age, and that maybe we could talk together. She knew that I had lots of questions.

I got involved in that relationship, and the woman needed a place to live because the fellow she was with was moving. We were dating at the time and she asked if she could move in for thirty days. I didn't know how to say no to her. I didn't want to tell her that I wasn't ready to have anyone move in with me. I had two children that I was not out to. I had all this stuff to consider and I really didn't want to make that as a choice yet. But, at the same time, I wanted to be a nice person. So, she moved in. That was two-

and-half-years ago, and she is still here. During the time she's been here I have always said, right up front, that everything is a day at a time.

There was one time in particular that I was just a touch involved with another woman who came along during this time, and who is still a friend of mine. I felt that I needed some more experience. I needed to know whether I was committed to this change or whether I was just fed up with the male population. Men just make me crazy.

I find the energy with women is entirely different. I do have a real preference. There is a kind of being present in an emotional way with women. I had a lot of opportunity to experience this with men, and they just weren't there emotionally. It was more like something was done to you. You might both be participating, but there was nothing mutual about it. There were a lot of things lacking that I think are more prevalent in the nature of women. I think there are biological differences that show up in those areas.

People say, "Well, what can women do?" I had that question, too. I found out it is more than satisfactory for me. I would like to think that somewhere down the road there would be a relationship that is really fulfilling to me in a lot of areas. The person I've been with is very, very nice. We've had very little conflict. The problem is me, not her. I think that I need to find a relationship that works in more areas for me.

When I was in high school, there was a young woman who was involved in music with me who discovered her sexuality at that time. I knew she was a very warm, tactile person, and I really liked her a lot. I realized later that I was very jealous of the fact that she was very attached to one of the women in our vocal ensemble. We were really good friends, and I really didn't like that she was so attached to her. I was her friend and I was jealous, but, at the time, I didn't identify what was going on. Now she and I are corresponding, and we see each other from time to time. Incidentally, she never married.

I have this really scary feeling inside that at some point down the road there is a relationship that could really work out to be something of long-term value. I'm glad that it isn't right now because I have a lot of other issues that I'm working through—parenting stuff.

One of my children is going to be 19 in February and has been living at home until just this last month. She has gone through a lot of rebellion, and her father has just been a phenomenal jerk during this whole period of time. I cannot be out with my children because of him. He is a raving fundamentalist—and a cop. He is a rigid, vengeful person. It would be a big court battle and all that —not because he wants the children. The oldest child, whom I adopted, is his child from his first marriage.

My younger daughter is 12. They are completely different. The younger one is very musical and is extremely intellectual. She is talking about the full scholarship to Stanford that she plans to have. She is a scholar, and she could pull it off. I have some feelings about watching her. I don't know what the inherited genetic programming may be. There is the potential that this child may one day come home and say, "Mom, there is something I want to tell you." She has said that she knows she could date someone who is Jewish or black—or could even bring home a girlfriend, and not a boyfriend. She knows it would be okay with me if they were good persons.

While I am not out to my children, I think at some level they know. I would eventually like to be out to them. I'd like to reach a point where I can just be out, period. It's not part of my nature to be secretive, and it is extremely difficult for me. I deal with a lot of small children who belong to parents who have different attitudes than I do. It could be very impacting on my business. If I can create some income that is not from the teaching, I could do more things, one of which is to be more out.

It could be difficult for my kids, with all the emotional things they have had to handle. I have told them that we have friends whom we have known for a long time and whom we love and respect, and they are gay.

148

I am a terrible flirt; I have no problem with that at all. I don't mind being somewhat demonstrative in public within the limits of what is appropriate for anyone. If you hang and clutch at someone, I think that makes other people uncomfortable. The thing I resent is going to a restaurant and seeing this fellow and his girlfriend holding hands. I feel cheated when I can't do the same; that hurts me inside. What ends up happening is that I choose to go to places where there are a lot of gay people. I resent the fact that I can't go just anywhere.

I am not out to my relatives. I think they have a question about me because I've had this woman living with me for a couple of years now. She just sort of goes everywhere, like family. My ex-husband made some comments about it. He thought it didn't look good for me to have another adult woman living in the same house. He said to my children that maybe I was a lesbian. They came home and they were all upset about that. I told them that I was sorry that he was concerned with that, and that they know who I am and the kind of person that I am. I said that it wasn't his job to mind my business. It is hard for me. I don't want to lie to them, but I don't want to put them in a strange position.

I would like to be living in a more isolated place. If it were overlooking the ocean that would make me happy. I would like to have a studio there. Besides my art and musical composition, I write. Eventually, I'd like to think of residuals and walking to the mailbox and finding checks.

If I could have the kind of relationship that I really want, that would be great. I know there are going to be very few people who are going to be in that accepting, wise, intellectual, spiritual place with me. I need those things to match up.

I have a very wide range of friends who are lesbians. I decided I needed a social circle, and I just went about collecting friends. I know a lot of really fine people, and the percentage of gays and lesbians in our population is not ten percent—it's closer to thirty!

I'll bet you money on that. I've got excellent radar.

I wish I had known back in high school what I know now. It would have saved me a whole lot of pain. I had a certain amount of integrity in relationships, but there was borderline promiscuity. It was like trying to fill up this spot that never quite got filled.

Kristen

*While I was married, I was totally unaware. I thought all
lesbians lived in San Francisco!*

I was married in 1970, and it lasted for 12 years. I dated an
older man when I was in high school and I married him the day
I graduated. I moved right out of my mother's house into his.

It was a very chaotic marriage. I had a lot of emotional problems
and a lot of depression. He had problems, too, but I don't think he
dealt with them. There were a lot of times when we really enjoyed
each other's company, but overall, it was very hard. We had a lot
of arguing and a lot of instability. It seems we took turns trying to
leave each other and the other one would be threatening suicide
and be really devastated.

His goals were a lot different from mine. I enjoyed the
relationship, home, and a lot of continuity. He wanted to be a go-
getter professionally and to make a lot of money. He was a very
hard worker; he worked over 80 hours a week, and I felt abandoned. We fought about that a lot. He worked as a financial
analyst and on the side we owned a tavern. He was either at one
job or the other, and I got fed up with that. He finally moved out
of the home to do more things he wanted to do. I finally just
wanted the marriage over. We had one child. She's 19 years old
now.

While I was married, I was totally unaware. I thought all
lesbians lived in San Francisco. Every so often, my husband would
rent pornographic movies and I would often watch them with him.

There often were scenes with two women, and I would be aroused by that. I think I had had attractions toward some women friends, but I just dismissed them. I told my husband that if I weren't married to him, I'd probably investigate those feelings, but it wasn't an option to me when I was married.

I consider myself a lesbian now, but I wonder if I'm truly bisexual. I choose to be in a lesbian lifestyle, and I really enjoy it a lot. I am currently in a relationship which has continued for a little over five years.

I guess what led me to explore my lesbianism was that there was a woman who was an obvious dyke at the place where I worked. She used to flirt with me; I started flirting back and we had a little fling. That kind of propelled me into investigating the gay lifestyle. I visited bookstores and did a lot of reading and talking to other people. I went to the Seattle Counseling Service and talked to a counselor there. I did a lot of thinking about it.

After my exploration, I immediately got into a relationship! I've been a recovering alcoholic for seven years. While doing my exploration, I was becoming disillusioned because the people I met were also other alcoholics. I started feeling that that's just what we all were. Anyway, I met this woman at a bar, and we were very attracted to one another and we stayed together for three years. My getting clean and sober ended that. After that, I fell in love with another woman and we were together for about a year.

I met my current partner in 1985 at an AA meeting. This relationship is going great. A little over three years ago we had a commitment ceremony. We feel very married. We've bought a home together, and we are doing a lot of work on it and it's very rewarding. We go to couple's counseling to learn to live together better. It's been really helpful.

My child lived with her dad after I left until her last year of high school, and then she came to live with us. She's out on her own now. Once I made the decision that I was indeed a lesbian, I talked to her about it. She was about nine years old. I talked to her in terms of relationships. She was one of the first people I talked to about it. I felt it was important for her not to be confused about what she saw and heard. I wanted her to feel that she knew what was going on.

I think she was worried that she wouldn't have as much attention from me. I think it would have been the same if I had been dating men. Now she is very accepting. She went through a stage where, while accepting, she wanted to keep it very separate in her life. She didn't want other people to know. She was fearful of reactions from her friends. She is now very loving toward both my partner and myself and she is very supportive of our relationship. It feels great.

I'm out to everybody. My mother, who has died, knew I was gay. She was worried about me being shunned by society. She didn't want me to tell my grandmother or my father because she was worried about their reactions. After my mother died, I told my grandmother and she has been my biggest supporter. She has been right there. We don't see much of my father, but he also is supportive. It feels good because he's made quite an effort to understand.

I work at a facility now where the clients are gay and most of the people who work there are gay. I have worked in more traditional institutions where I've been out, and for the most part I haven't had any overtly bad reactions.

Gayla

I love men, and just, also, happen to love women.
I found my soul mate in a woman.

I did all the right things. I got the degree and got married and went to work. I was married in June of 1967, six days after I graduated from college. My first son was born three years later and my second son was born two years after that. We also took in a foster daughter when my eldest was eight. We had her living with us until she finished high school and we had to move away.

I married, yet I was aware of having difficulties with men. I had been raped four different ways by four different men before I was married. I had told my husband when we were courting that I was aware that I might not be able to be in a relationship with a man after those experiences. He felt that it was going to be okay. He had a lot of faith in me and in what we were doing. I had a lot of respect for him, and so we got married. While I had feelings of warmth and respect for him, I don't know whether I was in love or not. It is still hard to say.

I had had this wild Latin fellow interested in me at the same time, and he thought he was going to get me over all my hang-ups—but I wasn't sure I wanted to get over all my hang-ups. In contrast to him, Bob was kind, steady, and had a pretty clear picture of what he wanted to do in life. His values coincided with mine.

Bob had come from a very strange family situation and wanted a family and loved mine. He was very much attracted to the way my family operated. I think he married my family as much as me. It was the image—we were a big, noisy, very tightly-connected family. It was nice, and it still is. I admire and respect a lot of my brothers and sisters. I had a great deal of respect for my father and, while I had a difficult relationship with my mother, I also respected her intelligence.

The marriage, however, was one of those difficult situations. Bob was from a Scandinavian background, and his step-father had abused him. As a result, he had some difficulties with relationships. If I got too affectionate, he would do something silly to distance himself. I'm a very physical person and I like contact and touch. He was very patient and undemanding and gentle and very sexy. The combination was very attractive and the relationship was very satisfying sexually. We seemed to have an equal sexual drive. He had a wonderful body and still does. In our relationship, our physical relationship just got better and better but our emotional relationship did not. He was a very private man and he preferred to do things alone.

After two years we moved to Detroit . We raised our sons and took on a foster daughter. That was very challenging because she was sexually ambivalent. She really pushed all my buttons and challenged all my issues. She was extremely intuitive so she read a lot in me that was accurate and hard to come to terms with. I had been very relieved that my second child was a son. I didn't want to bring a girl into the world. I didn't think the world was very responsive to females. We had the girl for three years when I decided to go into the ministry; my husband changed jobs, and we moved out of state.

With this move, Bob reconnected with his father and sisters and he got a little warmer emotionally. Then it wasn't too much later that he asked me for a divorce. I knew he was involved with another woman. He said, "Maybe I can stop hurting you." So, at some level, he was aware of some of my pain. I don't think he had the capacity to be emotionally supportive, given his own emotional background. That was an arid part of my life, and I sought intense female companionship because of it.

Relatively early in our marriage, I became aware that he was looking around at other women, but he had always said that he was committed to family and he behaved that way for a time. Then it became really obvious that he was looking for something else, and things started to go down hill. It was my first ministry and he was not accustomed to my being the center of attention. We went through mediation divorce because we didn't want the children pulled every which way by the break-up. He wanted to be fair financially, and I think he was in so far as he was able. As much as I was in pain, I had an awareness that fighting in the courts wasn't going to change the pain. It was hard! Both of us were very clear about our obligations to our children. He still is; he is helping support them through college. He maintains close contact with those boys. We were married just short of 20 years.

Even before I got married, I was aware that I found both men and women physically attractive. I have a sense now that both my parents were bisexual, and they had gay and lesbian people come to our house. We knew it; it wasn't a secret. I grew up in the New York metropolitan area where there were openly gay people.

When I was about seven, I was a tomboy. I was always with the guys and many times it was older guys. Because of that I was sexually active at a very young age, and I came as close to intercourse as you can get with immature males. I enjoyed it immensely. I thought it was wonderful. I liked the physical contact. I was aware of being sexually compatible with men from seven or eight. In pre-puberty, I was aware that I was attracted to women.

In high school I had very intimate friendships with girls. I don't recall making love but I was obviously in love. I was in love with one of my counselors at Girl Scout camp. There was a woman who was a year older than I was in school. I was so impressed with her. I thought she was spectacular!

In college, my freshman year, there was a senior who was also a French horn major who mentored me in some wonderful ways. She enjoyed my mind and there was no question that I was in love with her. We used to kid around about it because we were both aware of the implications of the time we spent together. We were not intimate. I fell in love with all kinds of women. It was all sort of progressive. It's hard to say where it starts.

I also fell in love with several men and women during my marriage. However, I had a very strong code of honor about behavior in marriage and I was not prepared to have an affair. But I was aware I had feelings, even though I did not act on them.

There were two major lesbian relationships in my life prior to the one I have now. One was a much younger woman who seemed to bring out my nurturing instincts. It was very confusing, and we were not sexual. Then there was a woman more than 10 years older than I with whom I was intimate. That was at a time when I realized that my husband was really looking elsewhere and I was trying to determine who I was. It was an experiment as much as anything. We had some common spiritual beliefs, which was a very strong drawing point for me. So there were these two women who came at a very confusing time in my life. I felt neither would last, and therefore, didn't give my full commitment. However, they were steps along the way for me.

I met my present partner, Karen, when I was seeking my first settlement as a minister. Her husband was on the search committee. The committee called me to the church for an interview and she was working in the church as the administrator. The first time I looked into her eyes I thought, "This is a person who is going to be very important in my life." It has nothing to do with gender. It has to do with the individual and his or her spirituality. When Karen and her husband drove my husband and me back to the airport at the end of that week, I was aware of those vibrations and was very concerned about what I was getting into.

Karen and I worked together as colleagues. One of the first things she did when I got into this ministry was to make it very clear that if it didn't work out for us to work in adjacent offices, she could be gone. She knew the congregation and was very supportive and helpful. As time went on, I was still having feelings for her, but I was also aware that we were both married. At this point, I put myself into therapy. I began to deal with family issues and my sexuality.

Karen was supervised by the board, not by me. We were sort of co-equals in the office. The set-up was very unusual. She told me that she hoped I felt safe and comfortable with her. Something in me snapped because I realized during therapy that feeling safe and comfortable was not something I had experienced in my life very often. While my household was in many ways very loving, it did not feel safe for me as the eldest and the responsible one. I was always in a performance mode. Eventually, I told Karen that I had feelings for her. She had been talking to a friend about how well we got along and he said to her, "Look, if this were a man, you would know this was courting behavior." He tried to get her to be more aware. She did not respond to my statement, except to say that she didn't know what she was going to do. That remained unchanged for years as I continued counseling and she was doing her own work. I finally asked her if she would be interested in pursuing some spiritual work together. We worked together as spiritual peers for several years, doing co-counseling work.

My counselor said that I was doing all my work with Karen, and I just debriefed with her. That was true—because I felt I needed a neutral third party that I trusted to monitor my process. The potential for self-delusion in love relationships is so powerful. So we worked very hard as spiritual co-counselors, even going to retreats together.

Somewhere in this process, my ex-husband found another woman. Actually she may be the perfect person for him; she is as disinterested in public life as he is. The problem was that she was the mother of my son's girlfriend, and also in the church, and when they got together it caused a scandal in the congregation. Actually, my son stayed with his girlfriend until his father and her mother married. Then she couldn't deal with it, dating her "brother." They have both since married other people. My younger son calls the whole thing a soap opera. It was just awful. It's a miracle that I managed to stay in the ministry. I was so devastated by the way it went. It was terrible for me and the congregation. Karen was a rock through the whole thing.

Anyway, during our spiritual mentoring she mentioned that I had been wandering around in her meditations five years before I showed up in the flesh. That's why our first meeting was powerful for both of us. Since she processes privately she didn't say anything about it for a long time.

Sometime before my divorce, she told me that her marriage had been over for 10 years. Her husband had been engaged in a three-year affair and wanted a divorce. So, one month after their youngest graduated from high school, they filed for divorce. It was a very civilized, quiet divorce; they just did it. We had been through all this garbage. She saw me through my divorce and I saw her through hers. Suddenly we were able to be together and we just got closer and closer. We are now living together after some seven years of knowing each other. She moved near me and we finally bought a house together and finally we had our commitment service.

Right now, my professional life is falling apart and the relationship is keeping me together. It's very supportive. We both have very busy lives. She works in Seattle and commutes. She has a 12-hour day. I work in the town where we live. I'm a public person—very active in the community. I have meetings almost every evening. We make time to be together.

I think the most heavenly time of the day is when we can just spend a few hours snuggling up to each other in the evening. That time is just really special.

Here in Seattle, I'm totally out. In the community where we live, I'm out only to the congregation. They were invited to our service. I'm in the process of a negotiated termination from my ministry, not just because of my lesbian lifestyle, although that is a part, but because of the intensity of my personal style—my East Coast style, in some ways. I think the congregation was just asked to go through too many changes with me. It is a very conservative group, and I think they reflect the community as a whole. The majority of them want me to stay, but it has become an untenable situation.

I suspect that I'll have at least one more ministry, but I'm also hoping to be a published writer. I have four books of poetry that I'd like to send in. I would eventually like to be lecturing and traveling. It would be a ministry—but different than I have now.

I am out to my children. I was out long before I was in a relationship with Karen. My elder son is delightful about it. He had had a dear friend from childhood, who goes to his school, tell him that he was bi-sexual. He tried so hard to empathize with his friend. It was very touching when he came to me with his struggles with it.

I came out to my husband in the process of the divorce, before I was in a relationship. He wasn't surprised. He tried very hard to tell me that it didn't change the way he felt about me. His feelings about me had more to do with my intensity and his difficulty dealing with that. He wanted someone who was more easy with life. He and his wife attended our service. All our kids were there for the service.

I want to be very clear that I have very positive feelings about men. I have had male mentors professionally who were wonderful to me. I feel very warm toward my sons. That's one of my reasons for coming out to them. I feel that our society forces men into boxes that are just as constricting as women's boxes.

Both sons are very sensitive to these issues. My younger son just wrote a paper on how difficult it is for a person of conscience to be a white male. I have a friendship with my sons as well as a parent relationship, and they are just precious to me. I see them facing a very hard time in the world. I love men and just also happen to love women. I found my soul mate in a woman. Karen is my life companion.

Denise

I was going to show the world that you can get over your homo-sexuality. I was going to prove I could do it.

In 1971, when I was a sophomore in high school, I got on the basketball team. I was the only sophomore; the rest were seniors. The senior girls adopted me. It was so wonderful to have these 18-year-old women hang around with me. It was the first time I ever felt loved in my life. I couldn't believe they accepted me. I didn't have that at home. My parents provided us with a good Catholic education and food on the table. My mother was the dominant one and my father was quiet. She laid down the rules. As far as the emotional stuff, there was no tenderness between any of us. There was no affection. I may have seen my mom and dad kiss once as I was growing up but there was a real lack of emotion. So I didn't know what liking girls was. I had never heard of the term "lesbian" or "homosexual".

I was raised in a very strict Catholic family, and after high school I went to a small Catholic college. I was really good at basketball and played my freshman year. There was a gal, Gail, who was a junior and she started showing me a lot of attention. She would say, "Hi." to me a lot and we played basketball together. She eventually brought me out. It was so exciting to me. This was what I wanted! I was eighteen. She had a boyfriend at that time, too. As the relationship went on, I got jealous because she had had this boyfriend for three years but they never had sex. I think this boyfriend was sort of a cover-up because all her roommates were straight and they all had boyfriends. Our relationship was great because up until I met her I'd never been anywhere. That Christmas we went to San Francisco. It was wonderful. She showed me everything. I just loved it. During the three years at St. Martin's College, there were always rumors about us.

Then, I moved to Bellingham where they had a good basketball team. I felt I had a very strong religious belief and I didn't know how the Bible was with this thing with women. I used to work in the gym as a part of my work study and the secretary was a Jehovah's Witness. I don't know how we started talking about it but she told me that the Bible said it's an abomination. I went and looked in the Bible myself and I found it and thought, "Oh, my God, I'm going to go to hell!" It scared the shit out of me. It always stayed in the back of my mind that I was going to hell for being with a woman that I really liked. Gail had stayed in Olympia to take an extra course and I was up in Bellingham but the relationship continued. Then I made the team. She graduated the winter of '74 and things didn't work out job-wise for her, so she came up to Bellingham. She wanted to be a teacher but she also got involved with the basketball team. Finally, she became emotionally involved with one of the other players. I got very upset and jealous about it and we broke up in '75. She moved back to California. Oh God, was I hurt! Eventually, I did get over it.

After my junior year in Bellingham, I went to Campfire camp as one of the administrative people. I met a woman there, Linda, who was one of the counselors. One Friday night we were all in the counselors' lounge area. I remember just looking at her and thinking how cute she was. I walked her back to her cabin and had my arm around her and I thought I was going to die! Finally, about three weeks into the camp, I told her that I liked her. We spent some time together. She hadn't ever been with a woman but she remembered having feelings when she was twelve or thirteen.

She and I would stay up late and talk and eventually had a relationship. Later, we went down to California to see her dad and we stopped off to see Gail and her new girlfriend. Gail was so jealous. She couldn't believe I was with somebody else.

When Linda and I came back, we both had jobs in a group home as counselors. We lived in this group home with twelve girls. The girls had had trouble with the law and some of them were pretty hip. Linda and I had the downstairs basement. We were together a year. I graduated from college in 1977 and she went to visit her brother in Oklahoma and then came back and told me it was over. I was devastated.

This thing about the Bible was still swirling around in my head. So, I decided I would give up being a lesbian. I decided I was going to give my problem to God. I went to the priest at the Catholic church. I told him I wanted to have the love of someone like Christ had for the church. It's unconditional; it's lasting and forever. I was going to show the world that you can get over your homosexuality. I was going to prove I could do it. I started a journal. Every day I would write how I was doing and feeling.

I got involved in the Church. I was teaching religion classes to little kids. When I got out of school, I really didn't know what I wanted to do so I went to the church's education director. I wanted to get in some sort of program. He told me about a program in Seattle called Channel. It's a ministerial development program. It trains kids out of college to be youth ministers—lay persons working in the Catholic Church. Since I had a lot of experience working with youth, I came to Seattle to interview to be a youth minister, and got the job. This was the fall of '78. I went through training and I was the born-again Christian in this program. They were really taken back by how strong my belief was. I was very serious about this. I finished my training and was to be the youth minister at St. John's in North Seattle. There was also another woman there who did all the work with adults. She was a former nun who happened to be a lesbian and she had a crush on me. I'll never forget it. I was playing basketball with the kids and I hurt my back and she wanted to put this cream on it. Of course, I let her. She knew I was a born-again Christian and the whole bit. She didn't believe me. But I told her about my beliefs and that I was going to get married some day. She put this cream on my back and I'm sure it did something for her.

The following year, as I was working with the kids there was this big Christmas ball. I prayed to God for a guy to go with. For two weeks I prayed for a date to this ball. And, sure enough, this guy came into my life. He had just become a Catholic. He decided he wanted to work with the kids. Anyway, he asked me if I wanted to go to this ball and I said, "Sure." We went to the ball and had a great time. He started asking me out to do more stuff. I wondered if God wanted me to marry this guy. I never had any feelings for him except in my head. I told him once that I loved him as a friend and he said that he thought I loved him more than that. So, he ended up asking me to marry him and I said I would. After all, he was the one that God had brought into my life. I was also a member of this charismatic prayer group that met with some older adults. They were praying for me.

He and I went to a marriage encounter. We had such strong faith. At that time, I was considering going to graduate school at Seattle University to become a pastoral minister. Anyway, we decided to get married in September of 1980. I was very nervous about it that whole summer. I started moving my things over to his place. We never had sex; we didn't have anything. I told him that I had been a lesbian and that God healed it all. I convinced everybody this had happened.

I got married at the church where I had been the youth minister. The kids were involved and two of my former lovers were bride's maids. I had acquired this powerful nun to be my spiritual guide who had guided me in my spiritual turn-around. I would see her sometimes twice a week. I could call her on the phone. She really was a dynamo of a woman. She told me that Jesus was with me. She did the sermon and the homily at the wedding. There were a lot of people there. This was a big thing.

My family was involved and we each wrote our own vows. Somebody commented that when I was reading the vows it sounded like the pope. I said all the right stuff even about having kids—even though I knew deep down that I didn't want kids.

We were on our honeymoon and I don't think we had sex that first night. I had never been with a guy before. We only had sex five times in the year and a half we were married because I just could not do it unless I was drunk. Sleeping in his bed with him —I cringed. I still believed that God had changed me and that I could be sexual for my husband. Every day I would write affirmations of "I love Craig; I love sex" in my journal. I even went into therapy. I said to myself that I had made this big change and asked when God was going to do the rest. I worked very hard because I wanted to make this happen. I believed that this is what God wanted me to do. To me, it was hell trying to be something I was not. I didn't know that was what I was trying to do at the time, but to deny myself like I did was extremely painful. I believed that I was doing the right thing. You know in the Catholic Church you have to suffer and this was my cross to bear. It was my own hell. I know what hell is—it's trying to be something you are not.

Near the end, I found myself going to the Safeway store; there was a checker there and my feelings were all coming back. I thought that she was cute. I went to a movie written by Lillian Hellman and all this stuff started to come up and it scared the shit out of me. I thought God had changed all this. I gave it up; why was it coming back? I was so scared. Craig and I were seeing a marriage counselor to figure out why I wouldn't have sex withhim. I was seeing a therapist on my own and I nearly had her convinced that this born-again Christian stuff really had hap- pened to me. I was doing it all for him. That's what a good Christian Catholic woman was supposed to do. Finally she said to me "When are you going to accept that you're gay and Catholic?" I said, "Never." I stomped out of her office. I was close to suicide.

I started talking to Craig and saying that I didn't know who I was anymore. It was horrible because he was saying that we had made a commitment. He brought back all the marriage vows—everything. I kept saying that I was so sorry. I felt so betrayed by God, I was having nightmares.

I went to a garage sale and found a book by Thomas Merton. I found a section called *Your False Self*. It was about this self I was projecting to the world who wasn't who I was. It was the hardest thing to finally admit that I was a lesbian. I was so angry, I ripped up my Bible. I was so pissed off, I had a picture of Jesus and I threw darts at it. Near the end, I thought I was pregnant and it scared the shit out of me. Luckily, I wasn't.

My therapist suggested that I contact a group of Carmelite nuns that lived close by. I got to know the head of the group and we have corresponded for fourteen years. She became a mother to me. What is so neat about it is that I came out to her in the letters. Someday I want to put our letters in a book of my own. The love and the care she gave me showed me that it was okay to be who I am. There were a couple of letters in which I was very angry because the church says this and the church says that. She accepted my anger and gave me the love I never had when I was a kid. It helped me come a long way in accepting myself. I think it is so wonderful that we had this relationship and that she has mothered me through it all and that I have all her letters.

After I was no longer married, I moved back into the house where I used to live when I was doing the youth ministry, and went back to counseling in a group home. In the fall of 1982, I fell in love with one of the girls. She had just turned eighteen. She had fallen in love with me. I was twenty-eight or twenty-nine. I just thought, "Oh my goodness!" When you turn eighteen, you have to leave the home, so after she left, we got involved. I was just starved for a loving relationship. Anyway, after she left, I lost my job in the group home because they found out. It was very humiliating and I felt very ashamed.

Then I got involved with Dignity which is a Catholic group of gays and lesbians. I liked their community. I met this nice gay couple and they took me under their wing. They are about ten years older than I. I was floundering around. In 1986, I went to a rap sessions at The Lesbian Resource Center. There was a woman there; it was the first time I had seen her there. I thought she was kind of cute and just left it at that. Oh yes, I gave her my phone number. She ended up calling me and she wanted to go out. We went for a long walk. She knew she was a lesbian but had never had a relationship before. She was just coming out. I thought, "Oh God, here we go again." She told me her story, and I started feeling sorry for her. But here again, I was so much trying to find love. We ended up getting involved and moving in together. We were together for five years. I wanted to save her and all the time I was angry and bitter inside because there was no feeling there. I thought I was doing the right thing. I found myself getting more depressed. We finally broke up in '92. Before we broke up, we were in therapy together. I really liked the therapist we had, so I began seeing her by myself. I finally started looking at my issues. I was looking at all my lesbian and my family relationships. It took four years to go through that stuff, but I thought I was feeling great.

I decided to put ads in *The Weekly*. I was ready for a relationship. I got involved in a different church and I had the group praying for me that something would happen. I met this gal and we walked around Green Lake and we really hit it off. We had a lot in common and I decided that this must be it. Here, again, I was thinking that God had brought us together. What happened was that her personality started to change. She started getting into car accidents and she began to be really sad all the time. I didn't understand what was happening. She was drinking a lot more alcohol and having a hard time talking to me. Later I found out she had been on medication, but was off it because she couldn't afford it any more and had gone into a very deep depression. I was surprised but I understood it because I had been in one. The drinking got worse and I didn't know at the time that she was also into drugs. That's why she was getting into all the car accidents. She probably didn't know what she was doing. I was going to tough this out with her, but she decided that she wanted to leave to work this stuff out on her own. So she left. I found out from her new roommate that she was an alcoholic and addicted to drugs. She was also addicted to sex and was having relationships all over the place. I couldn't believe it. I wondered how I had gotten into this. How did I attract this into my life? I realize now, a couple of years later, that that relationship really brought me to my knees. All these times I was trying to be something for somebody. I didn't know what the hell love was or what it meant. I was going to wait for her while she was off getting well. When I found all this out, my therapist said, "You better give this up."

I was really faced with myself. It was the most wonderful thing because I finally got to the core of my own poor self-esteem and my own lack of love for myself. I had to dig out more memories of my childhood and some shameful ways I took care of myself. I went back and did the work.

After all those experiences, I now know what love is. It's inside of me and no one can take away the feeling of self-satisfaction. I'm not even thinking of a relationship any more. I feel good. I feel whole and complete. One of the neat things about this is that I'm back to being creative. I know what born-again means now because I'm such a totally different person. The energy is no longer blocked. I'm writing now and I'm on my fourth rewrite of a story about the earth—how she came to be; how she is now. It's basically a spiritual fantasy. It's so exciting for me

I am so grateful that all this happened. I don't belong to the church anymore. I've had a ton of therapy and I've learned so much about myself. I was searching for love. My parents were not good role models because they only functioned out of their heads. When I came out, I became the mutant of the family. The beliefs that my parents gave me were hand-me-downs and I couldn't wear them. I really, really tried. I love myself now. I feel confident and my self-esteem is good. I know what it is like to try to force yourself to be something you're not. There are so many people who do that. The gift that God has given me is to let me grow into the person that I am.

I look back on my past and say. "This is good." I'm now doing creative work in my life. That's why we're here in the first place. I want to make this place more loving and the world more compassionate. I'm am so grateful to have been through all that I have. I'm happy!

Jocelyn

*I'm very blessed . . . and I feel very sad for that
young girl that I was.*

I was 19 when I first married in 1948. I was married for 25
years and had six children. The marriage ended because he was a
gambler; at least, I want to blame it on that. We got married
because it seemed to be the thing to do. I was running away from
home and my alcoholic father. In hindsight, I think I was also
running away from my own sexual stuff.

When I was in college I was seduced by a woman, and I found
it very confusing. I thought, "Well, at least I won't get pregnant."
Pregnancy was a big issue in those days. I was very high Episcopalian. One time, when I went to confession the priest told me I
wouldn't get in any trouble no matter what I told him and I lied.
Thank goodness I had enough sense to do that!

I was in pre-med but couldn't afford medical school, so I went
into nursing. Then John and I started dating. He was very clever
and a lot of fun. I was an only child and had been lonely, and I
remember always wanting lots of children, and I could see that he
liked kids. I wanted to show my parents how families should be
done. So, I married John.

We had only dated six weeks, but he was very assertive and I
wanted to have someone sweep me off my feet. I went to work and
he finished school. He got his degree in engineering and I helped
him get his company started. I was twenty-one when I had my first
child. I had six children in nine years. We got to be a good little

family—went to church and the whole bit.

John was a gambler, and it got progressively worse. I started seeing a therapist to straighten my husband out. And it turned out that the therapist was a sex addict. He was inappropriately sexual with me and I went right along with it. Now I know it was because I had been sexually abused as a child. He had a group and he encouraged the members to hug each other. Then we had parties and we would go swimming in the nude. The group would always go out drinking.

My own drinking was increasing at this time. I was a binge drinker. I would go to Las Vegas with my husband and I would drink. At a holiday party, I would just get awfully drunk and become very sexual and flirt with all the guys. One time we had a suite at one of the hotels downtown and I got drunk. The hotel suite had a grand piano in it, and I went knocking on doors trying to find someone to play the piano. I finally came to this place where these two couples were, and one of the guys said, "Yes, I can play the piano." He went on down to the room and his girl was there on the bed and I propositioned her. Thank God she didn't take me up on it! When I was drunk these things would come out.

My marriage was deteriorating. John's gambling was getting worse and I was in this group doing very inappropriate things. John's game had been that when he won big, I would get half of it for whatever I wanted. I would fix up the house or things that ordinarily would get done anyway. I was beginning to be a little more independent.

One year when I was about 44, he won a lot of money. I got all the kids taken care of and I went off on an adventure to a dig in Africa. It was wonderful and it was the first time in my life I hadn't been someone's daughter, or mother, or wife, or teacher. It was a wonderful trip. There were 17 people and I learned that I could like myself and enjoy being by myself. It was a real marker in my life.

172

Right after that, my marriage really deteriorated, and I got a divorce. Then I started having an affair with this man who was from the therapy group. He was about 20 years older than I. My alcoholism really got going, and I did a lot of acting out. I was still with this group and we had group sex and everything. For me, it was just an excuse to be with another woman. I lived such a double life.

Then in 1979, I met Bob, who was a fine upstanding man. He represented decency, and he was so different from how my life was. Eventually, after five years, we got married. I finally broke away from the therapist. Bob was also an alcoholic. In marrying him I knew I could drink as much as I wanted to. His drinking got worse. Bob had had a very tragic life. One of his sons killed himself while on drugs six months after his mother, Bob's wife, had died. This son was gay and had just found out he was HIV positive. Bob was homophobic.

When Bob and I got married, we both got into recovery. About two years later, Bob got lung cancer. He died about six or seven years ago, and then, six months after Bob died, his other son killed himself. That whole thing was a Shakespearean tragedy. I had a lot to work through, but I stayed in recovery.

The first time I ever felt sexual toward a woman was back when I was 10 or 12, which seemed normal at that time. Being a lesbian is complicated. Once in the recovery group with Bob I said that I was bisexual. I know lesbians don't think you can be bisexual, but I think you can!

A few years ago, I opened a retreat center. A good friend of mine came out and lived with me. She was such a help in opening that center. We lived together for a long time, and we finally became sexual with each other. I was really thrilled and it was very good. She was a wonderful person and I am still friends with her. We have a lot of work to do, but we are thinking about getting back together some day.

I was very ready to be pretty open about being a lesbian, but she wasn't sure she was a lesbian. (I found out later that she had had an affair with a younger woman in college). She was really depressed and confused at the time. She went into treatment and started working on her own problems. Then she came back and we were very miserable. About six months later she left and got a good job. The separation was very painful for both of us. She nearly killed herself, but she also got to work on her own stuff. She is now in a pretty damned good place. We see each other and we go out. In the last year, I have told four of my kids about my sexuality. It was hard for me. I also think all the secrecy was hard on my relationship. I thought, "Here I am in a 12-step program, and I'm a counselor." I finally went to the Cottonwood Center for a month to work on my sexual abuse. The whole thing is that you are as sick as your secret. After that I thought I needed to tell my kids.

The oldest one had a friend who was a lesbian. I told her that I might have a relationship with a woman. She said that she suspected that, and she was easy about it. Next, I told another daughter, and she is praying for me. She thinks it's evil and not natural and so forth. However, it hasn't ruined our relationship.

Then I told my oldest son. His wife had known for a while. I told him that I was working on my sexuality now and that I thought I was gay. He said "Mom, I want to tell you that there was a time when I wondered about myself." He told me that it was okay and that he understood. He was more worried about his career and family than what I was doing sexually. He said it was nobody's business.

Then I told my hippie son and his wife together. He said, "I wondered what you were doing for sex." Then his wife said that she'd had an affair with a woman once. They were wonderful.

I still have two children I haven't told. One is far away and the other is a fundamentalist Christian, and I'm not sure I'd have such a nice reception there.

I know I'm more attracted to women than men. In some ways

it makes it easier to deal with men because I'm not looking at them as sex objects or take-care objects.

I'm not out and I'm not closeted. If it is appropriate, I tell people. I don't think God is going to get me. I think, too, at my age, how many men are left? It's almost a practical thing if you are sexual. I have read books which discuss older women deciding to be sexual with women. Women are more open. Most of the men I know in this part of the world are pretty rednecked.

I'm 62 and just now am beginning to give myself permission to have fun. I have come out a lot in the past year and everyone has been very nice. Of course I am still very selective about who I tell! I'm very blessed and I feel very sad for that young girl that I was. I'm also very glad I had my kids.

Claire

At first I thought I wasn't a lesbian—I was just very
attracted to this woman!

I was married only once, and once was enough! I have no children.

My marriage was kind of a curious situation because I married my psychiatrist. We actually got married after I had been his mistress for years. The reason I got into therapy to begin with, as a 19-year old, was because I felt strange. I felt like I didn't fit in. I felt that something was wrong but I didn't know what it was. I went to college, but I didn't feel drawn to date boys.

I felt that I didn't know the emotions that other people were talking about. I felt odd and I didn't know why. I couldn't seem to cope with the world. I went to college and I would make A's and would get terribly afraid and drop out. I told my parents that I just felt desperate. So I went into therapy. As it ended up, we never really addressed the issues. We got involved sexually shortly after my 21st birthday.

I felt it was a fairly good and interesting relationship. He was 28 years older than I. I thought maybe the problem had been that I just didn't get along with young men. I thought I had a problem relating to men my age. After I got divorced and came out and got into therapy again, I started discovering that our relationship should never have happened.

When I look back on it, it was not a good relationship for a number of reasons. I was 28 when we got married in 1978. He was very domineering—and an alcoholic. When I was married, I have to say, I was an alcoholic and I smoked a lot of marijuana. After I got divorced, I thought my problem with it would stop, but it didn't. I realized I had a big problem with getting numb—with having to stay numb. So I got into therapy, and I'm good now. I got over it and I'm amazed at what it feels like not to be numb.

Now I drink very little. I made a contract as to how much I would drink. I have only two glasses of wine and only when I'm out with people. I haven't even maxed out on that. No marijuana now.

It was an abusive relationship, both mentally and sexually. He had the advantage and he didn't mind using it. He would have too much to drink and start out on a tirade about women. He had a lot of issues about his mother sending him off to a very strict private school in England. He never said anything nice about his mother. He would get on these tirades and he would talk for hours, just saying all the terrible things he could think of about women. I thought that no one had ever shown him what love was and I tried and tried and then I thought , "Whoa! This is getting nowhere; this is a lost cause."

During the last year of our marriage, something made me realize that I had been noticing women all my life. I realized that I paid them more attention than I had paid to men. It wasn't anything in particular that made me start thinking about that. Part of it was that Frank was more and more sexually abusive, and I got to thinking where my interest had been all along. Because he was a psychiatrist, I talked to him about the fact that I might be sexually interested in women. I thought I was bisexual. He was more interested in saying that he and I should have an open relationship sexually, which meant to him that he should be free to do what he wanted with other women.

Frank was making plans to retire to a town in Florida, and I moved there a year ahead of him. I realized that I had looked forward to being away from him and living by myself for awhile.

In that year, I started to really think about myself and what was going on. At that point, he wrote to me that he had gotten sexually involved with a patient. That's when I began to know that something was really wrong.

In the meantime, I was very much attracted to a particular woman. But when I talked to Frank about it, he wanted the three of us to get involved. I got very mad because I felt that he wanted to take everything away from me. I said, "No, I'm not going to get involved with you and another woman." Then I began to focus on women rather than denying that I had been more interested and more emotionally drawn to women all my life.

These new feelings seemed perfectly natural to me. I did not know any lesbians; yet, I knew I could love women in a heartbeat. I didn't know I was a lesbian. From the pictures that the culture painted of lesbians, I thought that they were a very hard, rough bunch of tough women with tattoos and leather and butch haircuts driving trucks. I thought, from that, that I wasn't a lesbian. I just happened to be very attracted to this woman; but I'm not a lesbian. I'm not one of them!

This woman that I was so attracted to was a woman working at the same place as I. Her husband also worked there and was putting the moves on me. I kept telling him, "No.'"and, "Get away from me." His wife was someone I really liked. I wanted her to be a good friend of mine . . . and, yes, I found her terribly attractive. I wasn't attracted to him at all, but he was very sharp. He figured it out—that I was hot for his wife, which I was. He lied to me and said, "She really likes you. You ought to come to our house and spend some time with us." Actually, he wanted to get in bed with me. He wanted to get in bed with anything that moved.

My first sexual encounter with a woman was with the two of them, and I realized during that episode that I was crazy about her and had no feelings about him. The terrible truth of that was that he had lied about his wife. She really was not interested and really wanted nothing to do with it. I left that experience feeling very

178

used and stupid. But it did confirm for me that my emotional pull was toward women.

Later, that woman went out to lunch with me one day because she wanted to talk to me. She said, "I don't know what is going on but I find you so incredibly attractive." I said, "Fine. I'm delighted that you are and I don't find that odd at all." Nothing ever came of it, though I would have welcomed it. She was not able to think about anything other then being close friends. We have stayed good friends, and recently we got together and talked about what happened between us in 1986. She now says that she isn't interested in sex with anyone.

I've had two lesbian relationships. The first woman had been a friend of mine when I was married and had been a very closeted lesbian. I was still, at that time, a lesbian virgin. I had decided that I had better look into this situation. I went to a women's music festival outside of Atlanta in 1987 with this closeted friend and another woman. Eventually, my friend and I were involved for a couple of years.

Then I moved to another town in Florida where there was a women's community. I went to some of their social events and was learning how to make contacts. I met my second partner there. We had what I thought was going to be a long-term relationship, but it only lasted three years, ending a year ago. We had thought that it was going to be a pretty committed relationship, but it was a very painful breakup. We weren't getting along very well the last year, and I finally realized that I had quit loving her. Then, I decided to move out here. I am not currently in a relationship.

I am not exactly closeted. I decided that when it would occur naturally, I would let people know. I would be honest. As I make new friends, and the discussion comes up, I tell people where I stand. I share a house right now with two straight people I work with, and it hasn't come up that I should have to explain my lifestyle to them.

I had made this agreement with myself that I wanted to be closer to my family. All the time that I was married, my husband had had this successful campaign to drive a wedge between me and my family. Since the divorce, I've gradually tried to make better ties with my family . At Christmas time, I was taking a walk with my mother and the subject of homosexuality came up. I came out to her then, and she was the most wonderful person in the world. My mother was 70, and she was wonderful about it.

I didn't talk to my father, as he's always been the difficult one for me to talk to. At any family discussions, all during my life, my father and I have been at odds. He is not the open-minded kind of person that my mother is.

I have an older brother who lives in California. I called him up one time when I was pretty lonesome. He had met one of my partners earlier when we went on a trip to California. At the time of the call he said, "Well, isn't she with you?" I said, "No, Frank, I better explain that to you." So I explained to him that she and I had been more than just friends and that I had broken up with her and had moved here by myself. He said, "Hey, okay. Whatever you do is your business. It just seems like you've picked a really difficult lifestyle." I told him that it wasn't more difficult than trying to be something I'm not.

I've since been to see my brother and we had a wonderful visit, the closest visit that we've ever had. I have a younger brother who doesn't know a lot about me. He is a fundamentalist-born-again-kind-of-guy. My younger sister and I get along fine, and it just hasn't come up. If it does I'll tell her.

Sometimes, I find that it's a pressure to not come out. It's enough of a pressure to create a lot of stomach acid. Sometimes, I think, in maintaining secrecy, I feel that I'm about to burst. Sometimes, I think it's not worth it. I just haven't found the ideal way to do it.

I had a friend back in Florida where I was working and she figured out about me on her own. She just said something to me one day—without using the L-word—that let me know that she knew I was in a significant relationship with a woman. In my working relationships, it creates some distance between me and the straight people I work with.

To be a lesbian feels like a natural thing for me. I have a little problem wondering if I'm fitting into the lesbian community. Sometimes I feel a little intimidated by people who have always known they were lesbians. For me, it's just been since 1987. That is one reason I picked this area to move to because it's supposed to have a large women's community. I live with a straight couple, so my next move is going to be either to share housing with people in the gay community or to just move on my own and associate more with lesbians. I've been here nine months and I've met a few people who now feel like old friends.

I work in an operating room and wouldn't it be wonderful if I could find a lesbian surgeon to work with in a collaborative way? However, I'm not going to be worried about chasing down the perfect relationship. I'm going to let that happen when it happens. I would like to be in a committed relationship.

LULU

It was a real sense of homecoming for me.

I got married in 1966 and was married for 16 years until my husband was killed in an accident in 1982. When we married, I was 18 and my husband was 20 and we were very young for our ages. It wasn't the best marriage in the world, judging from others that I've seen. Yet, it wasn't the worst, either.

The happiest part of the marriage was the first three or four years. There wasn't any kind of abuse or drinking or anything like that, but certainly a lot of ups and downs. I had two children, who both passed away. He was in the service, so there were periods of time that we were separated.

After he left the service, and for the better part of our marriage, he worked two jobs. I also worked, so we didn't have a lot of time to spend together. After we had been married 11 years, we adopted two children—first a daughter, then a son. They are now 15 and 13, and they live with me.

To decide that I was going to be a lesbian took years. When I was still married, I had fantasies involving women. I never acted on them because it just didn't seem right.

After my husband passed away, I tried to start dating men again. I really didn't want to because my good comfort levels were with women; getting together and talking and having a good time was always with women. I tried to date, and it was just awful. I was miserable and I made the man miserable. I was just not a nice person on these dates. I didn't think they were very nice either, but that might have had to do with where I was coming from.

I gave up dating but still hadn't come to terms with my relationship with women. Then, slowly, I came to realize that it was possible to pursue this dream that seemed so outrageous to me. I had a phone number to call, and I must have called that number 50 times and hung up. Finally, I did call, and the gentleman gave me the number of a couple of women who were in a partnership. I called them and I got to know them better than a lot of my friends. They were very helpful and they invited me to go to the Metropolitan Community Church.

I was terrified to do this, but I did it. It was a real sense of homecoming for me; it was wonderful! There were moments when I would have second thoughts, like the first time I went into a gay bar. It wasn't that it seemed wrong—it was just that it was something I had never seen before. These women I had talked with didn't paint a pretty picture. They said it was a very hard and difficult life, and that acceptance was hard to come by. They were very frank and honest; they talked about the good as well as the bad. This was in about 1984. My mind-set has changed in an extraordinary fashion over these years.

The first woman I started seeing was a couple of years younger than I. I don't know whether you'd even call it a relationship because I just started having coffee with her and we went to a bar. It was very comfortable being with her. Then we moved on and started having romantic things. I didn't have any problem with it, but she had a problem with it because she didn't want to do anything unless there was a commitment, and I wasn't prepared to do that.

I didn't storm the bars and start picking up women right and left. I don't do that; I never did. I've only been with four women. The second one was someone I was very attracted to; she was from California, and that was just a weekend thing. We still communicate. She is a lovely person and I enjoy her. I was with the third woman for four years. We are not together anymore; we just found the differences were too great.

I am currently in a year-old relationship and it is wonderful. It has its problems, but I think there is enough maturity and caring and sameness in our outlook that this one will work. I really hope it does because I really enjoy this woman's company.

I consider myself a lesbian now. My children don't like that at all. My son's pretty okay with it, except when his friends come over for the night. He requests that we sleep in separate bedrooms. He is also uncomfortable with that—because it is a lie. He would rather have the lie, though, than us sleeping together. My daughter thinks it's just awful. Her dearest wish is that I find some rich, handsome man. When I first told her that I was a lesbian she said, "No, you're not!" That's been about four years ago, and she still hasn't really accepted it.

My partner has been in other relationships before, and the other women have always lived with her. This time, she is living with me; she's never done that before. That's one of the things that's causing an adjustment problem. In addition, two acting-out teenagers don't make life very easy, either. My children like her, but I have the impression that it wouldn't make any difference who it was or of what gender; there would always be some resentment. They want more of my attention.

My kids are involved with a lot of sports activities. My previous partner went everywhere with me. We would go to my son's games, and everyone was really aloof and no one would talk to me. Then we would go to my daughter's sporting events and everyone was just wonderful. We came to be very good friends with several of those people. They were couples. We would go to parties and have them over for dinner. Nobody in that group has ever said anything, and it had to be obvious to them. That's kind of pleasant, and it doesn't bring you to the point where you have to blurt things out.

I told my younger brother and sister quite some time ago, and as I told them, they just kind of sat there. Now they seem to feel okay with it. With the exception of me, my family doesn't talk much.

My parents are living and my stepmother knows I'm a lesbian. I just told her last summer. When I talked with her, she said, "Oh, I'm not surprised with all you've been through." She didn't want me to tell my father, as she thinks it would kill him. I was prepared to tell him. We were sitting down at the dinner table and he jumped up and watched T.V. I just couldn't after that. So I just told her, and she was pretty horrified. They now live in Arizona, and I see very little of them. It is not something that I'm faced with frequently. Maintaining my secret isn't much of an issue for me.

When I realized that being straight wasn't an option for me, I found that the hard part was being honest with the people I had been around for all those early years—husbands and wives and their kids whom I knew when I was married. That's still really uncomfortable for me. Some of these people are not very open-minded. In fact, they are bigots. It was hard and it is one of the reasons I decided to move.

If a woman were contemplating changing her sexual orientation, the very first thing I would advise her to do would be to talk to somebody who is in the lifestyle. I'd suggest going to places where there are lesbians and gay men and find out what your comfort level is. I would also suggest going to the bookstores and reading.

Gail

Once I became involved with a woman, I realized that
that was what I wanted for the rest of my life.

When I first realized I was gay I didn't do a whole lot about it. I was both guilty and confused.

It happened at a time in life when my job allowed me to just sit and think. After a while it occurred to me that I was no less a person of integrity. I was no less nice. I was polite. I was no less of a friend than I had been before. It was not very hard to accept it.

That process took a few months; then it was done. I was in a marriage and I was not financially in a position to leave. There was no strong reason to leave. I was being treated so well.

I was married 19 years because it was the thing to do. It was the only thing to do—I did not feel like there was any other alternative. I felt that I was in love for a while. My husband was going to graduate school and felt so guilty about me supporting him that he took over all the household tasks. That never changed once he got his Ph.D.; I was not ever a housekeeper. We were very tolerant of each other and just kind of co-existed. It was boring. We did very little together. The only thing that made the marriage work was that he never forced me to stay home and I never tried to force him to go out and be sociable with me. We did that for a long, long time.

Once I became involved with a woman, I realized that that was what I wanted for the rest of my life. Then I was impatient to get out of the marriage. With this marriage, I probably could have stayed married and led two lives; but, I didn't want to live my life that way either. So I finally left and filed for divorce. I was involved with a women for a year and a half while I was still married and then she left me for another woman. After that, I stayed married for another year. It took a while to make the transition and find a community.

My ex-husband and I have never discussed this, but I'm sure he knows. When I was having my first affair with a woman, he was very tolerant. He never asked where I had been when I came in at 2:30 in the morning having been to the bar and smelling like smoke. He didn't want to know.

My parents are still living and are in their seventies. I came out to my mom and she took it very hard. When I got divorced, she thought I would find another man and give her a grandchild. She took it very hard, but she is adjusting. She wants what is best for me. When I told her this would make me happy, she wasn't real pleased but she said,"Okay." Then Mom said, "Don't tell your father, it would kill him. Don't tell your brothers because they might let it slip to your father and it would kill him." But my dad has been guessing for a while. I was telling him about my new job and that it was a woman-owned company and he said, "Is she a member of your crowd?" He knew without a doubt. They are not the type of parents who would disown me—never.

I'm out in the community. I had a party a few weeks ago and got to invite 55 people. I'm not out in my work because I'm in a new job. In my previous job it was not an issue. Some people knew and some people didn't and I really didn't care who knew. I didn't expect any problems. There were other gay people there, and it was a very comfortable environment. I've been on TV—I've been on the news. I went marching in Austin and my face showed up on the Houston news. I belong to Heartsong, a lesbian chorus.

I am not currently in a relationship, and I have mixed feelings about that. Sometimes I think it is wonderful because I have all my time to myself. Then, there are times I just get so lonely; I wish that I had somebody in my bed. There is a real duality about that. I attend lesbian groups to meet friends. Relationships for me either happen or they don't; I don't seek them out. Recently, there was one that just almost happened, then didn't. I don't worry a whole lot about whether I'm involved with somebody.

Ten years from now, I want to be running a retirement home for women. I'm not in a position to act on it yet. I think it is needed in the community, but it is a big project. I feel that to do this I'm going to have to go get a master's degree in healthcare administration. I want to know how to do it, and I want to do it well because I know people in the community will be investing in my project.

My advice to young lesbians is to take care of your career. If you have financial freedom, you can buy other kinds of freedom. For women who are contemplating leaving their husbands, I have the same advice. Have your career in order first. I thought mine was; but it wasn't. I have been suffering financially; although, I did do some things right. I had checking accounts and credit cards all in my own name for years. I'm proud of myself.

Anna

There was no word for lesbian at the time, and no one told me
I was doing anything strange.

I was married in 1969. My marriage was really boring. I think
I was married to the idea of being married. I think it lasted as long
as it did because my ex was in the military, and he was gone a lot.
We started having a lot of problems when he got out of the
Marine Corps and we had to spend more time together.

We had two children. I was four months pregnant when we
married. My oldest son is now 22, and the youngest is 20. My
marriage was boring, but at the time, I didn't know it was boring;
I thought everybody was like that.

I didn't know what an orgasm was. I was married three and a
half years before I actually had one.

I think the most satisfying thing about the marriage was the
time I spent alone. Even when my kids were there, it was still a
quiet kind of time. I had access to all the reading material I could
possibly want. My husband thought I was reading too much of
that "awful feminist literature" and blamed it for the decline of the
marriage.

During the first five years of my marriage, 80 percent of my
time was spent alone. When I look back on my marriage, I find
that time kind of strange. I was legally married for 11 years, but
we were separated for the last three.

I do consider myself a lesbian now. I have ever since my first
adult physical and emotional encounter with a woman. I had

had encounters when I was a child—hugging and kissing with a girl friend who lived next door to me. I thought this was the most common, normal thing to do. My brother was there and it didn't seem to bother him. It just went on and I had experiences after that, too. In fact, everywhere I lived there seemed to be some female child in the neighborhood that I was cuddling with. That went on until junior high school. There was no word for "lesbian" at the time and no one told me I was doing anything strange.

My first relationship with a woman came when I was 27. I was separated from my husband, but we hadn't divorced yet. I was living with a woman and a man who worked at the same place I did. They had been living together for about eight years and were just about to get married. We had rented a large house together. I'm black, and they had a group of racially mixed friends that I became involved with.

Anyway, there was this woman who people in our group seemed to keep a little bit of a distance from. I didn't think much about it one way or the other. She just seemed to be this man's lover and he had several different lovers at different times. But anyway, I noticed a connection between this woman, Laurie, and me; but I didn't know just what it was.

Then, later, a kind of weird thing happened. I was bowling on a league, and there were four of us women who were going to go out after bowling that night. I had had an accident that day when playing softball and had a head injury. When we started to go pick up this other woman, I got sick. I felt nauseous and had a throbbing headache, so I told them to go ahead and I would just stay there and sleep. I happened to be at this couple's house. Anyway, I stayed there, and they went out.

When I woke up at about 3 a.m., there was Laurie—in bed with me. We started to talk, and the next thing I knew we were making love. I knew that her boyfriend, George, was in the living room but I didn't really care at that point. That's how it started.

It was extremely intense for me. I didn't realize what was happening at that time. I became a real pest where she was concerned; I would not let go. I was later told that she had had encounters with other women in that group of friends. She just enjoyed having those encounters.

I really liked it, and didn't want to let go. I tracked her down to wherever she moved; I sent flowers and balloons to her at her job. She didn't return my phone calls or anything. It took me about six months to come to my senses and start to get over that. I had just about done it when I got a phone call from her at work and it started all over again. Anyway, she finally married and moved to California, and that was the last I saw of her. I actually went to the reception.

That was the beginning for me because I had no interest in men after that. I was seeing one man in particular once before that. I wasn't in love with him but I enjoyed the time we spent together and I enjoyed sex with him. I enjoyed how sensitive he was. We could talk and I'd never had that with a man before. I had a couple of one-nights with guys that were just awful. That was all before Laurie.

After Laurie, I was running from therapist to therapist trying to figure out what the hell was going on. I didn't really have a name for it. I guess at the time I didn't think I was a lesbian. Of the first three counselors I saw, I seemed to be talking about only half of myself. That was the part that had been married and the childhood part. There was a whole other part that dealt with the experiences with girls when I was young. I didn't deal with the complete me.

One friend finally suggested that I call the Lesbian Hot-Line to find a counselor to deal with that. At the time, I was still in the throes of Laurie. I wanted to find a way of being over that, so I called the Hot-Line and they gave me the name of three therapists. I settled on one and I saw her for about five years. It was through her that I got involved with the lesbian community. I finally knew that I was a lesbian and had to learn to deal with it.

It was very difficult to deal with those feelings because there was just no place to take them. Although I was separated at the time, people still thought of me as heterosexual and married. That closed down support from friends and people that I knew.

After about six months of counseling, my counselor suggested an encounter group. I joined that and made friends. One of the women in that group took me to a gay bar. I didn't know that gay bars existed. After that, my social life seemed to revolve around the women that I met. I went to parties that were given by lesbians. I went out to the bars with other lesbians. Now, my relationships are with other lesbian women.

I am not currently in a relationship. I am emotionally involved with someone, but we are not in a relationship. This is very difficult for me—because this is a woman who is married. Her husband took a job in another state, and she moved with him. If she had stayed here, I doubt if the relationship would have ended; I think it would have continued in some kind of way. We still have phone conversations, and I'm still trying to get her to see me some time. I can't deal with the idea of ending it completely. I can't not have a connection with this woman.

I should say that this is one of the most difficult positions I have ever been in. I find I call her every two weeks. I can't bring myself to say that I don't want any contact with her. Now, I'm trying to get her to meet me in Arizona later this month.

I don't consider myself really out because I'm not out at work. I think my ex-husband knows. I came out to my dad a few months ago. I have no sisters and have little contact with my brother. My children have known since I knew. I had to tell them because I wanted an open relationship with them. My oldest son was 12 at the time. My sons adjusted to the change really well. We even took trips together. With other people, it's not very difficult to maintain secrecy; I'm pretty closed anyway.

I think one of the most important things that a woman thinking about a change can have is a support system. And, as a black woman who went through this, I think it's just extremely hard to have. There weren't a lot of black women there for me in the lesbian community. I need a space to deal with myself as a whole person—as a black lesbian mother.

Mary

I'd like to take a poll of my straight women friends to see if they have ever been attracted to women, just to see if I am really very different from them.

I was married in 1972 when I was in college working on my bachelor's degree. I was only 20 and it was my declaration of independence from my parents. But I just transferred my dependence to him. It was pretty much a disaster from beginning to end.

We were married for a total of four years, two of which I was still in college. Then I got a teaching job, and it seemed very odd to be acting like a professional during the day and then go home and be treated like a child. So I initiated the divorce. That was one of the biggest steps that I had ever taken on my own behalf. I was single for four years before I remarried.

I went into the service and I met Fred. We did a lot of traveling together and were very good friends. I had a lot of respect for him and I had fun with him. We were married when I was 28. When he finished his tour of duty, he started going to school at a community college, and I found out I was pregnant with Terri. I separated from the military a month before I had Terri, and a year later we moved. He finished his undergrad degree at the university, and things were really rough financially.

Fred got management jobs in restaurants, and I was at a publishing job, but we weren't earning very much money. We tried to make sure that Terri's needs were met and that we were able to spend lots of time with her. We were very stressed.

I have a lot of grief over the whole breakup. We had a big commitment, and it's hard to watch those dreams just disintegrate. We were together for 10 years and have been separated now for two. He lives a couple of blocks from Terri and me. This is intentional so that we can share parenting.

The marriage broke up, but we're not divorced yet. I'm the one who left. I think it wasn't either person's fault. There were some things that combined to make things rough for us. We felt very isolated from family support, had odd work schedules and a lot of financial pressures. The two of us made a lot of intentional sacrifices. We put our child ahead of our relationship. For me there was a lack of spiritual sharing; we basically quit growing. I felt like I was just cheerleading this thing on. We just looked at things so completely differently.

Somewhere along the line, I decided to stop the cheer-leading, and the marriage crumbled. I think he had been wanting this to happen but wasn't going to initiate it. I don't place all the blame on him because he was busy trying to make a living. He had no emotional energy left over for his home life.

He had an affair when Terri was in kindergarten. I was outraged. I felt we had been off to such a good start, and we were such good friends. How could somebody violate that trust? All that did was expose the fact that we had big problems.

One of these problems was that I became very disinterested in sex. I still can't decide whether or not that had to do with the lack of emotional sharing. I think so many women feel that way about men. I don't know how much of that was tied up with my now discovered lesbianism; I have no way of knowing.

That whole year that Terri was in kindergarten, there were a lot of painful things going on. We never fought in front of her; in fact, we hardly fought. We just had a more icy silence. Just nothing going on. I started sleeping out on the couch instead of in our bed. That went on for a very long time. He didn't like it, but we just weren't connecting.

It took me a long time to get to the point where I would admit that the marriage was going to break up. I knew I wanted to leave and live by myself again. I was remembering those years when I did live by myself and fantasizing about having my own apartment and leading my own life again. But, I felt like I had this weight on my shoulders. I wondered how I could afford to live alone.

Anyway, I started seeing a counselor. She told me that if a woman decides to leave a marriage she can usually find a way to make it happen. I kept that in my mind. I had decided that once I was done with my marriage and out of there that I was done with men because, emotionally, there is just nothing there. It would have to be a very special person; I didn't want to have anything more to do with relationships for a long time. I thought I would concentrate on my friendships with women, and my activities, and be celibate if that's what it meant. I just wanted to live life fully. I didn't need to have men anymore.

I had left my marriage emotionally, but I was still married. One day Ellen came into this publishing company to work. We ended up working together, and we immediately became friends. A couple of weeks after she started work, she was talking about a relationship she had just gotten out of and she used the word "she." She told me that I knew something about her that she didn't always talk about to other people. She seemed to want to check my reactions and make sure I was okay with it. That was fine with me.

I had known gay men in the past, but really the only lesbian I had known was someone who wouldn't have interested me anyway. Ellen would talk and I asked her lots of questions about lesbianism. She was ready to tell me her perspective on things. She had been a lesbian ever since her adolescent years. She came out at 19 in college and never looked back.

We had long conversations about sexuality. I said that if all the cultural things were left out of it, we'd all be bisexual. She said that for her part that wasn't so. She said that on a continuum she'd be on the queer side. Finally, she asked me if I had ever been attracted to a woman and I told her that I had been.

I have been attracted to women all along. It was just taboo to talk about those things. I'd like to take a poll of my straight women friends to see if they have ever been attracted to women, just to see if I am really very different from them. I just don't know. If the marriage had not crumbled, I don't know whether I would have explored any of this.

Ellen invited me to a movie that she had known I wanted to see. It was a really powerful spiritually oriented movie. I said that Fred would probably like to come, too—even though I wasn't wild to have him come. I just thought he should come, too. We were sitting there in this movie and I was just a basket case. I was moved to tears with all the things that were going on. Ellen was on my right and Fred was sitting on my left, giving me no feedback at all. I'm sure he was thinking, "There she goes again doing her usual blubbering."

I was deeply moved inside, and all I wanted to do was throw my arms around Ellen and sob. All of a sudden, it just came to me with this great clarity that one could have that really close connection with another woman. All of a sudden, it wasn't theory anymore. I understood how that could be.

I didn't say anything about that to Ellen. As things went on in our friendship, it just became evident that she was interested in me, but cautious because of the fact that I was married. She also knew the status of that marriage. I started keying into her and her body and thinking what it would be like to be with a woman. Things just started developing from there.

So, now I am with her. We have been together two years. This is not what I would have planned. I would have planned that I would be a single person and gotten over all those other wounds first. I wasn't planning to look for a relationship. I was just going to be myself. But that's not how it happened. It is wonderful! She is the only woman I've ever had as a lover. I feel this is going to be a very stable relationship.

My husband knows I'm a lesbian now. He is very hurt that I'm in a relationship, and now he'd like to make our marriage work. What's interesting is that a co-worker where he works who has been helpful to him happens to be lesbian. I've never met her, but my daughter really likes her.

That was how Fred found out about Ellen. My daughter would talk about all the time she was spending with us, and I would not try to make her edit her conversations. She needed to be able to talk about whatever she wanted to. So I figured that sooner or later he was going to want to know. He did want to know, and I had to tell him.

My daughter is 10 now and she knows I'm a lesbian. That has been ongoing, too. She had participated with me in freedom rallies before any of this happened. I believe that one deliberately teaches children that the whole idea of being gay is not something to be shunned, or ashamed of, or spat on. I didn't want her to buy into any prejudices. I explained in sequential stages about Ellen and about our relationship. She finally asked me several months ago if I were a lesbian. I answered by saying I wasn't sure; that things can change. I told her I wasn't quite sure what I would call myself. Since then I had another talk with her and I told her that if a woman loves another woman, and if that's the way things seem to be, that the name for that is "lesbian." I told her that was what I was.

I don't think the subject has come up at her school. I think as far as peer pressure goes, she would think twice before she would let them know that her mom is a lesbian. Even though she is young —kids, they are right there. They follow this stuff. At our church her friends know that I'm with Ellen, and that is fine.

I have not talked to my mother about being a lesbian. I'm just going to have to wait and see how it goes. She's pretty homophobic. Since I don't live close to her, I'll just see.

I try to be discreet. I'm only now beginning to deal with thelegalities of the divorce. It's just been too much to think about emotionally. I am acutely aware of the fact that I have legal binds to this other person. I could jeopardize the custody of my daughter if I got too far out. Once I am divorced, maybe my closetedness will change.

Jane

Aha! So that's it. There isn't anything wrong with me; I was just with the wrong sex!

I eloped when I was not quite 18, in 1965. I did not want to be around my mother, and that seemed to be the way out. I would have my own house and my own husband—and she couldn't tell me what to do.

A few months after the elopement, we had a church wedding. The marriage lasted about two years, and then kind of back and forth for another couple of years and another kid. I have two children, both from that first marriage. The marriage ended because he had lots of affairs and I finally got fed up with it. My children now are 25 and 23.

I married my second husband because he threatened to commit suicide if I didn't. I fell for it! He was scheduled to go for a one-year tour of duty in the Indian Ocean. We got married and he left the next week. He pulled his little schtick and I fell for it, and I married him. That was 1975 or 1976. I don't remember which. It lasted three years.

I initiated the divorce for several reasons. He was a manic-depressive, but I didn't know it at the time I married him. The mood swings were really incredible. There were many, many explosions. During his manic phases, he was really nuts sexually. He would just be out doing his thing all over the place. He finally went into a hospital. Then he got out, and while celebrating New Year's Eve in a bar, he left me. I was dancing with friends, and I came back to the table and he was gone. He took my car. I had to borrow a dime to call him, and he said, "You weren't coming home with me anyway." I said, "Okay, then I shan't." That was the night Janet and I got together. She was my first lover.

I met Janet about a week before the bar episode. I had gone to a friend's house, and she came in. She was five feet, nine inches, 120 pounds of muscle, and 21 years old! I was 34. That was a little over 10 years ago. We were together for four years, and she is still very dear to me. We talk on the phone all the time. She taught me a lot.

When I look back on it, I see why I couldn't make those marriages work, even though one was dysfunctional. I always felt that something was wrong with me. It was just like, "Nope, not that one. Nope, not that one." I wondered how many men I was going to go through. I had very intense and intimate relationships with women, though not sexual. It never occurred to me to be sexual. It simply was not a part of my frame of reference.

My second husband was the one who planted the seed in my mind. He did one of the typical male fantasies, "I want to see you with another woman." When we would go out in public he would say, "Oh, look at that one! Look at that one!" I finally told him that he was not going to pick out the woman I go to bed with; I'll pick her out. I'll find her somewhere.

So I did. I did that a couple of times. I finally said to him that my happiness was not going to lie with a man. I told him that I could feel that I was going to be with a woman. This was probably a year before we got divorced.

Then I met Janet. She walked into the room, and people were all talking about going to The Bar that night. I didn't know what The Bar was. Somebody asked me if I was going to The Bar and I looked at her and asked if she was going to The Bar and she said, "Yes." And I said, "Then I'm going to The Bar."

That relationship ended because we grew apart. She was growing up and had things to do, and I wasn't really ready to go back and do certain things over again. The age difference was too great and we just went our own ways.

I am currently in a relationship. We're not wearing each other's rings and we have been together for about a year and a half. I'm not in a position to live with her right now because I'm helping my children and my granddaughter and all. But my lover and I have fun together. Just living is fun.

I never sought counseling. When I met Janet, I never went back home. That was it. It was like, "Aha! So that's it! There isn't anything wrong with me; I was just with the wrong sex!" Now everything I can possibly do with women, I do. Men—you'd better give me your card because I'll never remember who you are.

Some women have very nice marriages. They have a home and children and a standing in the community. I didn't leave behind anything like that. My children were with me all the time.

I came out to my son. I took him for counseling and I went with him. He told the counselor that if his mom was happy, then so was he. He is now 23 and still sweet, but he is a Dead Head. He follows the Grateful Dead around. He winters at my house. He comes in with nothing but the rags on his back, and we rerobe him and he sleeps and he takes baths and eats lots of food. He gets to go to the dentist and gets physical care, and then the weather warms up and he leaves. He panhandles and works on the sanitation crew of the Grateful Dead. What a way to live! I don't know how long this will go on.

My relationship with my daughter is fine now. Her problems started before I came out. I finally know what caused that sweet little 12-year-old to turn into a banshee; it was sexual abuse by my second husband. I didn't know that at the time. It was a textbook case. He told her, "Don't say anything to your mother because she won't believe you; she'll believe me. She'll throw you out because she loves me." She didn't tell me, but she acted out. It's a wonder one of us didn't kill the other one over that couple of years before she finally just took off.

She is now making progress, but she is very negative and has low self-esteem. She has an over-eating problem. We are taking it one step at a time. She lives with me and has a two-year-old daughter. She actually said, about a week ago, that she was going to check out the counseling center and see what they have available. All those decisions have to come from her, not from me. She is going to the university, and doing well. This is a kid with a genius I.Q. She was invited to join MENSA when she was 11. My children are not closeted about me. My daughter used to use my lesbianism as a weapon, but she doesn't now.

I can't think of anybody I'm not out with. I'm out at work, and it is fine. Right now, I sell copiers because it pays the bills. Earlier, I worked for a company as a customer care rep, which was mostly instructing. I loved that job. Then about a year and a half ago, the company eliminated my position for financial reasons, so I went on unemployment and looked and looked for a job. Finally, after eight months of unemployment, the sales manager called up and asked me if I would like to sell copiers. I said to myself, "No, but I need a job," so I took it.

My mother knows I'm lesbian. I don't know if my father does. My mother lives in California with her fifth husband. My father, to the best of my knowledge, is still living in Atlanta. My mother's reaction was, "Oh my God, we don't discuss that." She refuses to acknowledge her great-granddaughter because she does not approve of the circumstances of her birth: my daughter did not marry the father. This is from a woman who, before she divorced my father, ran away and had two children by other men! She had a very convoluted series of marriages and affairs. My grandmother raised me. One time, my half-brothers and sisters had to be taken away and put in foster homes. So here is this woman not acknowledging my grandchild. I am not speaking to her right now.

My dream would be that I would get a Ph.D. and that I would be teaching women's studies courses at the university. I want to be secure and settled in a job with a retirement plan.

Karen

My god, this is a very different experience than I've ever had with a man. This is like a soul experience. This is not just a sexual experience.

I was quite a tomboy when I was young. As I got older, I noticed that my girlfriends were having crushes on boys and that I was having crushes on girls. I tried not to, but it didn't work. My interest was always in girls. It felt odd—something kind of different. I didn't know what it was. I even had crushes on the women teachers. I didn't understand it and I didn't know if anybody else felt this way. I heard jokes about fags, queers, and homos and I thought that I sure didn't want to be one of those.

I had this huge walk-in closet in my bedroom. My dad hung his suits and sports jackets there so I had easy access to them. I would put on his ties or suit jackets, slick back my hair, and think I was the coolest thing. I felt weird. I felt that there was something wrong with me—really wrong with me. I thought that if I ever got caught in that kind of behavior they would haul me away. So, I kept it a secret.

Girlfriends were way too important to me—desperately important. I was probably asking too much of my friendships. That puts a lot of weight on the friendship. I was often disappointed because the girls that I would choose very often chose other people who were lighter and who just liked to be more playful. I wanted this "relationship" thing. I felt alone and weird. I couldn't talk about it with my family because we didn't talk about feelings in my home.

We moved from Portland to Bremerton, and I was thrown from an eight-year elementary school into a junior high situation. It was very traumatic to me. I found a girlfriend in junior high who was as alone as I was. I don't know whether she was a lesbian but she was needy. That was my first pseudo-sexual relationship. I feel guilty about it to this day. We often stayed overnight at each others' homes. Under the guise of sleep, we snuggled and comforted each other. She thought I was asleep and she probably hoped that she was asleep. We were best friends by day, and more than friends by night. It was very odd. I felt like something was really wrong with me and we never talked about it. There was a little touching and some kissing, but we had no idea what two women could do sexually. The relationship ended because I started feeling a need to get a boyfriend like the other girls. At my first junior high dance they announced that all people with dates should get in line for refreshments. I had decided to go to the dance alone, so I just grabbed a boy and said, "Come on, let's get in line." I was like the other girls.

I dated him until I graduated in 1967. This seemed the "right" way to be intimate, and I got him to get the ring. I still had a lot of interest in women, but I could not be "queer". I just could not be that. What would my parents think? I was their hope for success. I needed to do the nice home, picket fence, children, etc. Someone else's dream was a heavy weight to carry. But I was the oldest; I was the girl. I could do it. I was sure I could do it. We married a year later.

I was determined to keep my feelings for women a part of my past, a phase. I knew that this marriage was my ticket out of a bad home situation. My step-dad was fairly abusive—not directly to me—but to my mother and my three half-brothers. My mom kept me separated from the direct abuse, but I got to see and hear theirs. So, I thought, "I'm going to get out of here. I'll get married and I'll make it work."

Even on the day of our wedding I thought, "What am I doing?

I shouldn't be doing this." But there were a lot of gifts down in the reception hall, two hundred people coming, the white dress, and the whole deal. I wish I could have been honest with my fiance, he deserved that, but from the marriage I got a son whom I dearly love. He came about five years after we were married. If I could have left the marriage right after I had the baby, I would have but I didn't think I could make it on my own. My husband was holding on to the dream as much as I was. I kept all the traditional home fires burning, and then some. He worked long hours trying to be the right kind of provider. We fought over many things: money, sex, use of time, personal priorities. He would say there was something wrong with me and I'd say it was him.

During all this time, I was still attracted to women. I would say to myself, "This has got to stop—something has to stop this feeling." I found myself staying away from home, away from that relationship. But nothing was stopping it and we kept fighting.

One summer I started playing softball. The coach was a very confident woman and knew how to do many things in the world. She was very athletic and I thought this was wonderful. There were lots of other women on the team who were in marriages. I didn't know anything about this woman who was coaching , but I did know that I liked her and was attracted to her. She was very interesting and we would spend a lot of time talking. I came to know that she was a lesbian. I thought that this was my chance to find out a little bit about this "other way". I asked her a lot of questions during many late night talks. Over the course of our conversations, she became attracted to me. I made it clear to her that I was just on a "little investigation", just gathering information. I told her that I really wasn't interested and that I was married. But one night we just "happened" to have the opportunity and it got taken. I thought, "My god, this is a very different experience than I've ever had with a man. This is like a soul experience. This is not just a sexual experience." This was very different and I very much liked it.

It wasn't very long after that that I told my husband that our marriage wasn't going to work. Our way was not to fight about what was really wrong. We pretty much kept stuff shoved under the table. He acted very surprised. The first day I asked for a separation and the next day I asked for a divorce, because that's what I really wanted. It was a wretched, nasty divorce. He said some terrible things to me and I was not honest with him. I didn't say that it was because of my sexuality. I was just sure that if I did I would lose my son. I might have, I don't know. My husband knew that I was really a good mother and that was the saving grace. Looking back, I don't think he would have taken our son away from me; he would have liked me to raise the both of them! He knew a good mom when he saw one. I have since shared my sexuality with my ex-husband and he still loves me. I wish I could have been honest then.

After my divorce, I entered into a relationship with my woman coach. It was wonderful for a while—really wonderful. Finally, I had an opportunity to experience something I'd always wanted. I was loving a woman and being loved in return. But just being with a woman doesn't guarantee that there won't be relationship problems. We weren't any better at solving our relationship troubles than my ex and I had been. We began to drift apart and I started spending more time away from home again. Painfully, that relationship also ended. Perhaps we should have stayed friends from the beginning. But I will always be grateful for the opportunity that allowed my sexuality to have a place in the world.

It seems to me that Jan, my current partner, and I had always been close. We had been friends for a very long time and raised our kids through school together. During the ending of my first lesbian relationship, I got to know Jan even better. Neither of us was looking for more than the friendship we already had, but one night we crossed the line of friendship and we both knew that the energy of our connection was more than we wanted to ignore.

Jan and I are still together after eight years. We have our times when we have to work things out, but what we have is a mutual dedication to figuring it out. I trust her sexually; I trust her emotionally; I trust her spiritually. I *trust* this person and it's a trust that I have never been able to access with a man.

Being is a same-sex relationship has its own problems, but sharing our sexuality with the important people in our lives can be equally challenging. I was terrified to tell my son that I was a lesbian. I thought that he must certainly know, so I expected it to be no surprise. He was sitting on the couch and I held his hand. He was thirteen. I told him that Jan and I were in a relationship. He said he hadn't known, but I knew that I had raised a wonderfully open-minded child when he said, "Mom, it's okay. Who you love isn't anyone else's business." I was in tears, nearly flat out on the floor, because I was so afraid that I wouldn't hear those words.

Telling my son was the hardest, but certain long-time friend-ships were also difficult. I remember when I told my best friend, Sally. She was quite surprised and tried to be supportive, but then we didn't talk for about a week or so. I thought I was going to lose the friendship, but I didn't. She just had to think about it. I've learned that that's some of the process. Sometimes you do lose friends. I didn't lose that one.

I told my mom over the phone and she was great. She didn't even miss a beat. She just said, "It doesn't matter, I love you anyway." It was way better than I thought she could do. But then she said, "We won't tell your dad." What a double message! I told my aunt, who is actually more like a mother to me, and she was wonderful about it.

My dad found out about it the first day Jan and I visited my parents in their home. It was my mom's birthday. My aunt and my brother and his family were there. Jan and I were alone in the dining room and she was standing behind me rubbing my shoulders, not a big deal. My neice, who was about nine at the time, came into the room, looked at Jan and me and asked, "Are you guys gay or something?" The nine-year-old in me who had been waiting half her life to speak responded, "As a matter of fact, we are." She gasped, "Gross! Yuk! You mean like girls kissing girls?" Every homophobic thing in the world came out of her mouth. When my mom re-entered the room my niece exclaimed, "Grandma, did you know they're gay?" And Mom responded in a demanding voice, "Oh, no they're not, dear, they're just good friends." My niece was bewildered. Then my dad came into the house, and she exclaimed again, "Grandpa, did you know they're gay?" Dad just walked over and picked up the paper, sat down with his back to us in his favorite chair, and didn't say a word about the proclamation. Neither he nor I brought it up any time after that. But his behavior has remained open to both Jan and I.

My mom passed away three years ago, but she always stuck to her story that it was just between us. After Mom's death, I shared my sexuality with my brothers, one by one. It was not easy, but somehow easier after Mom's death. My brothers accept Jan and I and we're welcome in their homes. My dad passed away last year. It is so much easier to have my parents gone. They were an absolute block in my life for so much. It is a pity that parents can be that stifling to their children, and it is too bad that kids can't say to their parents, "This is who I am." I would hope I could say to my son that whoever he is is okay with me.

For me personally, being a lesbian means that somewhere inside of me I feel that the deepest relationship that I'm to have will be with women. Being a lesbian means that I can live from that place. It's not a whole lot different than if I were to ask heterosexuals what that means to them. It just means that I can love who I'm supposed to love.

One of the things that I find very significant in being a lesbian is having the opportunity to fully operate from both sides of myself. In relationships with men, there seemed to be very clear roles. But, that isn't who I am. I am confident of both the masculine and feminine sides of me. I haven't experienced that role limitation with women. But a relationship with a woman can come with its own problems, too. When you have two women who both want to drive the nail, then nobody holds the board. You have to work that out. Maybe that's a problem in good, healthy, agreed-upon heterosexual relationships, too. In any case, I feel that I am finally able to lead from any part of me that wants to lead, from my strongest to my weakest. I've found a person who loves the whole of me, and I'm free to love the whole of who she is.

JAN

When you invite somebody into your soul and they are willing to go and you're willing to risk having them there, then doors open that have never been open before.

My parents both worked outside our home; Dad was a mailman, and Mom worked in an ice cream factory. We looked like a typical family of four, but it was a difficult family environment—a lot of anger, and a lot of hurt. I spent a lot of my childhood being pretty insecure and afraid, and believing something was wrong with me.

As a small child, I followed my brother, who was three and a half years older, everywhere I could. He was my hero and I wanted to do everything he could do. But as we got older, he preferred playing with his buddies, and the best I could hope for was to be the "white flag" in a snowball fight between the boys or be allowed to sweep their camp. I wearied of those opportunities.

The other girls in the neighborhood were my cousins. Sometimes we played, but they were either older or younger than I and we often went our separate ways.

I played alone a lot—often with dolls; they were quiet, too. Among us, we decided on the names of all the children that I was going to have. By the time I was in school, I had two more companions. One was my piano, which brought out the spiritual part of myself. The other was a girl named Ellen. We were best friends and played at school, at home, and at camp throughout our elementary years. I looked forward to seeing her everyday and was devastated if she didn't want to play with me. Our friendship stayed strong until we went into junior high. She entered the world of dating boys; I did not. I cried all year long because Ellen didn't want to play any more.

Still, I had my piano, my violin, and my singing. And there was my sewing which grew out of my love for my dolls. I met other friends including Cheryl. We became good friends for a couple of years. We vowed never to wear make-up, or rat our hair, and to always wear bobby socks. Another girl came over to sing on Saturdays, and another inspired me to learn to play the guitar. From another girl I learned about teaching and leadership skills. I didn't date or go to parties.

My father was a square dance caller, and square dancing was part of our family life. A young male friend I had known from kindergarten became my square dancing partner when I was in junior high. We didn't date, but we talked to each other on the phone and saw each other at school and sometimes walked home together. We depended on each other, and my relationship with him took the pressure off about dating. Later, after college, I learned that he was gay. It made sense to me.

I hadn't thought about what I was. I knew I wanted to have children and a home. As my parents' marriage fell apart, I believed that I was supposed to do all of those things better. I also thought being married to a man was the only way to accomplish that.

I went to college at a Catholic university. I grew up around my Quaker grandparents and had never seen a priest or a nun, nor would I have known what they were if I had. I was very simple in my spirituality and going to a Catholic school opened my aware- ness to the multitude of ways in which people worship and connect with their spiritual selves.

In college I dated some, but stayed mostly focused on music, spiritual matters, and school—in that order. Since I lived in a dorm, I also got to know women. I began playing guitar and singing at mass. I met some of my life-long friends and eventually my future sister-in-law. While in college, I added another option to my life's venue, becoming a nun. I didn't do it, but thinking about it opened my mind a little more.

Another experience I had during that time was with a woman. We were talking and she began to wonder what it would be like to be intimate with a woman. So I agreed to try it with her. She ended up in hysterical laughter. We didn't do much, but I liked it. I never told her that because she was on the floor laughing. After that, I began to think that I was bisexual.

I had relationships with different men, some lasting longer than others. I also had close spiritual relationships with some men; these felt way more natural to me. And always I had friends who were women that I looked forward to seeing—time talking, singing, and playing. Still, I continued to believe that I ought to be married and I longed to have children. My college friends were getting married, and match-making energy was all around me.

Then a friend introduced me to her brother. She was sure we would be a wonderful match. At first we were. We both loved making a home, being with family and we liked farming. Everything seemed right. But he was a lot more conservative than I realized and began attending a fundamentalist church. By then, we were going to have a baby. It was a difficult, painful, and confusing time for me. I believed that I loved him and that he loved me. We got married, a simple family wedding in my mom's home, with lots of friends and family and hope for the future. We were waiting for the baby to arrive, we both worked and in the evening he had his church activities.

After our first son was born, my husband's involvement with his church intensified and I stayed home with our baby. Our differences became more distinct. A year later we had a second son. We both tried hard to have a marriage, but the distance between us widened. I began spending more time away from home. Many times, I would take our children and visit friends, not returning until night. The relationship with my husband was agony, and after three and a half years I called it quits and moved out with the children. We've worked hard over the years to mutually raise the two boys we both dearly love and to maintain a friendly relationship.

My next involvement with a man came on the heels of my first marriage. He and I lived together for about three and a half years in a community household. We had a large six bedroon house, that could easily accomodate ten people, including the two of us and my two boys. Mostly he withdrew into himself and I tried to make sure that everything was okay for him. This was not easy since there were so many people there. However, the people camouflaged the difficulties in our relationship. I became more and more financially dependent. I hoped this would be the right relationship, even though I knew deep inside that we were mismatched.

Just before our daughter was born, we moved into a regular house in a regular neighborhood and began to act like a regular heterosexual couple. He worked a lot and I had my hands full raising three childrren. Then we bought our first home, the house I still live in. From that point on, our marriage deteriorated. We had many unresolved issues. I look back at old letters I wrote but never mailed. If I had been willing to look at what I had written back then, perhaps I would not have stayed in that marriage so long. In the end, he moved out and we later divorced.

In that marriage, too, while I regret the pain and turmoil, the gift was another child, this time my daughter. The children are the best part. I wish I had known then that I could have raised them with someone who is like-minded, with someone who loved me for who I am, and who does family in a similar way.

Karen and I first became friends when our sons were in elementary school. We enjoyed talking and sharing a lot of similar interests including the raising of our children, camping, other people and music. Toward the end of my second marriage, we became close friends. Around that time my father died and much of the pain of my childhood surfaced, and I went into therapy. I shared a lot of this process with Karen, allowing her to give me

214

emotional support. I invited her in because my heart was willing and most certainly because she was the right person. When you invite somebody into your soul and they are willing to go, and you're willing to risk having them there, then doors open that have never been opened before.

We helped each other with our children and their activities. We worked together repairing my house, fixing up rooms for the kids, building decks, replacing old doors, and painting rooms. We repaired wiring using diagrams in Time/Life Books. And we talked—about everything. We grew closer to each other and eventually we became intimate.

We've been in a relationship for quite a few years now, and we still talk about everything. Although we don't live in the same house, (my house is small and until recently all of the children still lived at home) we know we are a family. We are working on the logistics of how to live together. Neither of us have a high income and it has been a challenge. I teach music out of my home and my daughter and Karen and I raise goats, so keeping this location has seemed necessary. Besides the home improvements, we've built a kind of mini-farm.

All of the children know that Karen and I are partners, and they all love us. We're the moms. My mother and brother have been quite accepting, and they love Karen. That part has been far easier than I ever dreamed. Sometimes I think too much about the future and get afraid, but I'm learning to stop doing that.

Building a community has been harder than either of us expected. It's a challenge for any couple to build a mutual base of friendships. Most of the people I've known in the past are married couples. While I maintain friendships with some of them individually, I know that I have changed; we don't have as much in common as we once did. A big change for me has been my need to spend a lot of time with my partner. When you love someone it takes time to maintain the quality of the relationship.

We have a group of women with whom we sing on Friday nights. Some of the seeds of community are growing out of this group. We have spent time individually with all of the women and have gone to a cabin with the whole group to sing, laugh and talk. Friendships also take time and patience.

Karen's and my relationship is a very good relationship even though there are stresses within it. It is not easy to go to a park to talk and see only straight families all around; no obvious reflection of gay or lesbian families. It feels as though there isn't anybody else in the world who is a lesbian. We were at the beach the other day and there were all these straight families, and I kept thinking, "When do we find the other picture?" I know it's got to be out there, but where do we find it?

I'm sure there are resources, but we are busy people. At some point we'll have to push aside some of our "busyness" and find a way. Both of us would like to know other women who are in relationships with women; but neither of us want to seek relationships solely on the basis of sexual orientation, but rather on the basis of common interests and compatability.

I have struggled with the term "lesbian." I simply don't like having a label. I'm the same person, but I happen to love a woman. She is a special woman. She is someone who challenges me on many levels. She is a wonderful playmate, a wonderful lover, and we delight in many of the same interests. We do family in the same way. We occasionally have conflicts, but I know we will find our way through them, and learn more about ourselves and each other in the process. It seem less about being a lesbian, and more about being Jan and Karen.

Lynn

There are so many of us who are out, it's not as scary as it used to be. . . It's the best form of love anybody can have.

I was married in 1969 for 16 years. It was a long time. I was 21; he was 24. I lived in Minneapolis.

At the time, I remember having lots of feelings about getting married. Mostly, I had a sense of relief that I would have something to do with my life. My home situation was not abusive or terribly painful, but there were enough tensions there that marriage was an escape. I had no sense of being passionately in love. I remember thinking, "Well, he's not so bad."

It seemed like kind of a fresh start for me. I hadn't had much success in deciding what to do with my life, and it seemed to me that this was my chance to do something that had a chance for success. I had done a little dating of men, and I certainly had no conception of what being a lesbian was about. I just knew I wasn't like that.

I don't think I gave the marriage much thought. I just thought I would do what I had to do and that would be that. There were times during the marriage when I felt very content, but mostly, I felt oppressed. I would say that the years that my kids were little were the most tension-free times of my marriage. The children took up my life and gave me a purpose. But after awhile, I felt like I was in a tomb. I thought that I would die unless I got out. It didn't have to do with sexuality, but rather, with my sense that there was no substance to my life. My religious upbringing said to me that

217

I ought to be doing something more with my life. I had a kind of guilt about that.

At that time, and up until my divorce, I was involved in a very conservative fundamentalist religion. I did a lot of work with women's groups, one of which was a Christian feminist group. As a result of this group, one of the things I was being exposed to in my reading was the whole notion of loving women. That was the turning point for me. I began to see that, to me, the issue in feminism was whether or not you could totally love women. Then the question became was there any point at which you could say, "I won't love women?" And that meant sexual love as well.

Finally, I threw out everything about morality that I had been taught and decided that to be committed as a feminist to women meant *loving women*. I then needed to find some confirmation from some other source. I had heard about this book called, *Is the Homosexual My Neighbor?,* and I remember being afraid of reading that book. I knew it would tell me it was all okay. When I bought it and read it, it dispelled every notion I'd ever had about what the Bible says. At that point, I felt like I was open to anything. However, I didn't make the choice to be a lesbian . . . yet.

When I turned 35 and my youngest went into the first grade, I made the big break and I went back to school. I hadn't been in school more than a week when I promptly fell in love with a teacher—a female, of course. I was mad over her. She was one of the first radical feminists I had ever known. I knew she could teach me a lot, and I was open to a lot of different things. I was aware of my own feelings in a way that I had never been before. So, we developed a friendship. She was very careful not to turn it into a sexual relationship. If she had initiated anything at that time, I would have just been right there.

I went through two years of being totally in love with her—but still married. I was realizing that I couldn't be everything I wanted to be and remain in my marriage. I had the undying hope that this teacher would decide she wanted me. At the same time, there was something that told me that that would never happen. I had to begin to make some decisions based on what I wanted my future to be and where my commitments were. So I began thinking about my own sexuality and what I wanted.

I realized that there was some part of me that just felt totally natural about being a lesbian, and that this was the decision that I had to make. I felt it was a political choice. To me it was the only choice for a feminist. I still can't imagine making any other decision.

I saw a counselor during my divorce—for my divorce. She was a lesbian therapist. I've never had any counseling around my being a lesbian. I wasn't tormented by it. I have never been ashamed or embarrassed or felt like a freak.

In 1984, while still married, I had several close relationships. I had one friend who was going through a divorce and she was exploring different kinds of relationships. We were very close, but she never could deal with a physical relationship. I went to Boston for a conference and met a woman there to whom I was very attracted. We ended up spending a few days together and talking a lot. The opportunity came up for the two of us to be alone and we did have a sexual experience. That was the first sexual intimacy that I had with a woman.

I remember thinking that I didn't know whether I could do it. I didn't know what I would think or whether I would like it. There was a part of me that was just watching to see how it would go. I thought, "Well, I did that pretty well. I could probably make it as a lesbian!"

That was when I told myself that I was going to be a lesbian. I was the one who did everything, and this other woman was grateful. It felt right to me in terms of trying on behaviors. I remember thinking at the time that I knew she and I would not have a relationship. For a few hours I was kind of star-struck and wondered about it, but it became clear to me that it wasn't going anywhere.

When I came back from that conference I sought out my friend—the one who was going through the divorce—and I reported back from this Christian conference. I thought she would think it was funny, but when I told her, she just got these huge eyes and she excused herself and left. When she came back, I asked her where she went, and she told me that she had gone into the bathroom and just screamed. She told me that she couldn't believe that I did that. I had never considered the enormity of it. I just did it, and it was fun. It felt like another step in my own growth. Anyway, she could not deal with it.

A few days went by, and she came around, and we ended up becoming lovers for about four months. Then, she couldn't handle it anymore. She was going through a divorce, and she was also a recovering alcoholic, and she had started drinking again. She was in very bad shape in a lot of ways. I think her husband suspected that there was something going on between the two of us. My husband never did.

I now have a wonderful relationship with Mary. I am very, very happy. I had known Mary since 1982. She lived in Seattle and I lived in Minneapolis. She and I belonged to the same Christian feminist organization. We knew each other because we were on the national board of the organization. One of the first feminist things I ever did was to come here to their national conference. I walked into the area and there was this blatant sign that said, "Any lesbians and friends come to room so-and-so for a get-together." I thought, "Wow, this is really something! They could actually put the word *lesbian* in this message center."

Mary was the coordinator of that conference. It turns out that she was not out, and she had not even admitted the possibility to herself that she was a lesbian. So, we kept meeting at these conferences, but we didn't actually get to know each other until 1984. When I got to know her, I was just totally impressed by her being. She is one of the most wise, compassionate, gracious women I have ever known. I had no conception of ever pursuing a relationship with her.

Mary had told me that she would keep in touch, and she called me every now and then during that year. I remember being totally dumbfounded that she would even think it was important to talk with me. The only time we had even seen each other was once a year for the last four years at these conferences. Then, by the next conference, I had moved out. My ex-husband had seen fit to give me only $200 a month, and I was trying to live on that.

Mary called to see if I was going to the conference coming up in California. I told her I didn't think I could do it because I didn't have any money. She suggested I call someone to get some scholarship help, and she told me on the phone that she was really sorry that I was living in such poverty. She said that she really wanted me to come out to the coast because she wanted to tell me about something. She said, "I am happier now than I have ever been in my whole life, and I want to tell you about it because I want to make some changes." That's all she said, and then we hung up. I said to myself, "Mary is a lesbian!" I just knew that that was what she was talking about.

So, I went out to Fresno to the conference. I was in the airport and someone called my name. I hardly recognized this woman because she was so different. I realized it was Mary, and she looked wonderful to me. We gave each other a big hug. At this point, I had not said anything to her about my being a lesbian. So, when we got to the conference, I just decided that I was going to tell her. When I said that I was a lesbian, she just looked at me and started laughing. She said, "You are? I am, too." We were in this place surrounded by all these women and we just collapsed into each other's arms.

We decided we didn't want to stay there anymore, so we took our food to the room and we just started talking about everything that had happened to both of us. We spent every minute of the conference together—four days.

We drove up to an executive meeting at a private cabin in the mountains after the conference. I remember that I was so calculating about the whole thing. I just knew that I wanted to be with her. When we got there, I dashed into the cabin and found the one room that just had one bed, and staked out that room. We had been together all day, and by that night, we both knew that we wanted to be as close to each other as we could possibly be. I've always wondered how many lesbian couples date their anniversary to the first night they spend together.

I still wasn't sure that that was the beginning of a relationship because we still lived in separate cities. We really got to know each other over the phone. I still wasn't sure I wanted a committed relationship. That seemed oppressive to me coming from a marriage. I was really torn for awhile, and it was hard being so far away.

In the meantime, I was in this four-month relationship when Mary and I got together. I practically lived at Kristen's house, but I was beginning to chafe. I felt it wasn't quite what I wanted. I knew I couldn't stay with her the rest of my life, but I had so many things going on in my life that I didn't want to think of having to end that relationship and start another. Yet, when I got back from being with Mary, that's exactly what happened. I went through the process of ending the relationship with Kristen.

At the same time, there was this other woman, not Mary. I was ending this relationship with Kristen, I was exploring beginning this relationship with Mary, and here this other woman came back in my life. For a few weeks, we had a sexual relationship. I guess I was making sure I didn't leave any stones unturned! I had to be sure about this. I didn't want to wonder what it would have been like. Somehow, being with this other woman didn't seem right to me.

Mary came to Minneapolis to visit, and we talked it all out. I asked all of the questions I had been wanting to ask, one of which was how old she was. That was a real important thing to me. I knew that she was older than I was but I didn't know how much. When she told me, I almost dropped my teeth because I hadn't realized that she was that much older than I. She is another generation older than me—18 years older. It made me pause for a minute. Here was this woman who was almost as old as my mother. I'm just beginning a career and Mary is winding down hers.

It was during that visit that I knew I wanted to be with her. I had started investigating graduate school at that time, and I started making arrangements to apply. One issue I had to work out was leaving my kids. I have two sons. They were with my husband, but I had always lived close to them. But when I thought about wanting to be in a relationship with Mary, there was no other option that I could think of. Mary's career was in the West. She was willing to do anything—to take early retirement and move to Minneapolis—but, somehow, that didn't make any sense at all.

I had been seeing a counselor for support going through the divorce, and I sought short-term counseling for me and my kids around my move. My kids know that I'm a lesbian. When I had first moved out of the house, a friend had me house-sit for her, and my two sons could come to stay with me. One of the times they came over we went for a walk; they were 10 and 13. I told them that I was a lesbian and what that meant about loving women, and they didn't say a word. So I let it lie at that point. My youngest son always takes things in stride. He finally said that he didn't care what other people said, and he didn't care what I was. My other son has always been much more reticent to talk about my being a lesbian. They both have let me know in their own way over the years that it was okay with them. They have met Mary and they like her.

My oldest just turned 19 and he is a freshman in college now. My youngest son is 15. They both live in Minnesota with their father. When we were divorced he got physical custody but we had joint legal custody. That whole custody situation is one that is very painful for me. It's probably the one area in my life where I still feel very powerless and oppressed by the system. My ex-husband got custody because he insisted on it. Basically what he said was that if I didn't agree to that he would fight me with every penny that he had, which was considerably more money than I had. I had no income; I wasn't working then.

My mother knows I am a lesbian. She is a very conservative, "closeted" mother. I am very open about being a lesbian everywhere I've always been, and telling people that I'm a lesbian is not an issue for me. But talking to her was the most frightening thing I ever did. I didn't have any idea what her reaction would be. But it was everything I could have hoped for. She said it was my decision and that she didn't love me any less.

My advice for women who are thinking about lesbianism is, "Go for it!" The decision is not the scary sort of decision that it used to be. There are so many of us who are out. There is a formidable power that has been unleashed. It's the best form of love anybody can have.

Carroll

I believe being a lesbian is a spiritual choice. Part of coming out is a spiritual commitment to being one's true self. It's making a choice for authenticity and growth.

I was a senior in college and I remember going with my mother for a walk in the rain. I told her that I didn't think I would ever get married. She didn't say anything. It never occurred to me that I could be attracted to women. That summer I had a job as a stewardess and I met this man. He started writing me letters and I found out that he was going to the University of Alaska. We started dating and, by the end of the year, he wanted to get married. I said that I didn't want to get married. I wanted to go into the Peace Corps and he said he'd go into the Peace Corps with me. So, we made plans to get married. I wasn't all that excited about it, but I was at a point in my life when I didn't know how to say, "No." Now, I can't believe that I would not say, "No," to something as big as marriage. He went to work in Alaska. I went to work in Boston as a counselor with problem kids. We were supposed to get married the following September. He was going to meet me in the airport when I arrived in Fairbanks, but he didn't show up. It had happened before and it happened afterwards. Did I say, "Forget this wedding?" No. I postponed the wedding one time but nobody told me I didn't have to do it. I had the jitters and was very uncomfortable getting married. But I didn't know what else I was supposed to do. I got married at twenty-three and we went into the Peace Corps. I actually had a miscarriage there and I came back.

I knew there were beginning to be problems. I felt as if he had been charming during the courtship but, once we were married, I found that he wasn't interested in a relationship of any kind. I felt as if he felt that all he had to do was court me and then I was his. He would go places and wouldn't tell me that he was gone. I remember one time when he disappeared and we were living in a compound and didn't have a phone. I went down to the guard and told him that I wanted to call this American who had a phone. The Thai man laughed at me, because in Thailand there was nothing for a man to fear. I called the board room of the American mission. I got hold of Paul and told him that Bob was missing and I didn't know what to do about it. Paul told me Bob was there and that he'd been there since six o'clock that night. "We're just talking," he said. So one of our issues was that he would just disappear. The other issue was the balance of chores. He thought nothing about having me be responsible for everything. He did essentially what the Thai men did, which was go off and play with each other. Right outside the compound there was a little hut where you could get whiskey at ten in the morning. The Thai men would start drinking even before their shift, and my husband fell right in with them.

I liked what I was doing in the Corps. But with him there was no relationship in terms of what I thought a meaningful relationship should be. He seemed to want me just to take care of him. I felt like a misfit. I didn't know how I got myself into that situation. It wasn't where I belonged. I didn't fit. I would say something about my miscarriage and he would say it was because of cultural shock. He thought it would be okay when we got home. But he chose to go and recruit for the Peace Corps for another six months. Even at the time, I told him that I thought we should go home and work on our marriage and that it wouldn't be possible if he were traveling around with the Peace Corps. But I told him that it was his decision, and that I didn't want people to think that it was a mutual decision.

I went to live with my twin sister for six months and he came by every once in a while. In fact, that's how I got pregnant with my son. He would come by and stay for a weekend. I realized that I was much happier when he would go away. When I was with him, it was the worst of my life; when I was without him, it was the best of my life. So, as we were planning to go back to the University of Washington to graduate school, I actually talked to him about a divorce. He said that, as far as he was concerned, the marriage was working for him and, that if I wanted a divorce, I would have to do it myself. He said he wouldn't cooperate. I can't remember when it started, but he was very belittling of me all along. I couldn't understand how he thought there was nothing wrong with the marriage when he acted like I was stupid and couldn't think and nothing I ever did was right.

I was seriously considering divorce, and then I found out I was pregnant. It shifted things. In the first place, he was more attentive and he was enthusiastic about the baby. It brought us together temporarily anyway. He was the nicest to me when I was pregnant. We bought a little house in Seattle. I had the baby and he supported me in the childbirth. I was in graduate school at the time, and he was in law school. Then, he started disappearing again. The baby was mine to take care of. He adored him from a distance but he still left me alone. He would go out with his law school buddies and drink all night. I suspect now that he was an alcoholic. Of course, my father was an alcoholic. It was the family secret. My mother was a Christian Scientist. That didn't fit with having an alcoholic father so it was never discussed.

So, I finished graduate school and got a job. I loved my job and loved my son. I liked being a mother and I adored that little boy. But the marriage didn't get any better. My husband finished law school and got a job in which he traveled for the state. He would be gone, and then he would come back and dump on me. I wasn't the perfect wife. I never did become a very good tradi-tional wife. I wasn't the perfect hostess. I felt I was a misfit and I tried to hide it and figure out how to fit. I didn't have very many friends. I was relatively new to Seattle. There was a woman across the street who was glamorous and into being the perfect wife and she loaned me this book. The premise was that if I did some of these things and be nice, he would be nice in return. What happened was I was nice and he liked that, but he wanted me to be nicer. It was never a two-way street. I couldn't do enough. Marleen, this woman across the street, manipulated her husband. My husband told me that he wished I would be a little more manipulative. I decided that something had to change. I couldn't go on for another thirty or fifty years like this. I actually said, "If this is all there is I don't want to be around." And I seriously considered suicide. But I was such a coward and I had my son to think about. I decided that I would either commit suicide or first try to fix the marriage. That's when I started reading and went to a counselor. We both went in and he was charming. He charmed the counselors. One of the things I said to the counselor was that I wanted him to share responsibility. He said that he would carry out the garbage, for example, if I would remind him to carry out the garbage. Then I had another chore! The counselor thought that that was reasonable. Counseling just left me more frustrated.

I had an opportunity to get a job in Olympia. I suggested that he look for a job there and that we move there and work on our marriage. So, we moved to Olympia and both got good jobs. In theory, we were a family. We were both in the same place. It was supposed to get better.

One of the things I remember happening in Olympia was that there were notices about the National Organization for Women and I would get butterflies in my stomach from reading these notices. I wanted to go so badly, but I was scared to death. One of the things I was scared of was that I would lose my marriage. I let several months go by, then I went to this meeting of NOW. It was in one of the church basements. There were all these women— strong women. There were all these changes that were going on like ERA and abortion issues. I thought, "Wow!" I felt that this was where I belonged. These women were talking about real issues that mattered to me. So I jumped into NOW and became very involved. I got into things that were mostly employment issues. My job in Olympia was director of the state family planning program. I eventually got on the YWCA board. I realized that some of these women weren't married and they were living with other women. It wasn't that I didn't know that lesbians existed. In fact, in Alaska two of my teachers were lesbians.

I realized that some of the women in NOW were lesbians. Then I started doing social things with them. That was really my first realization that that was a possible lifestyle. It never entered my mind that I would get a divorce and then go and be with women. I didn't think I would ever be with anybody since marriage hadn't been a very good thing for me. One of the things that I had told myself during the later part of my marriage was if I didn't have the courage to get a divorce, then I was required to be sexual with my husband. I said to myself once a month—but basically I spent several years being raped. I'm ashamed of that. It was emotionally very painful.

We had a custody battle and he got custody of my son. I had this good friend who was a minister in Monroe and she had gotten a divorce the year before. I had supported her while she went through her divorce. She had agreed to support me during mine. This was in May of 1975. The only problem was that she was going to Africa shortly. So I decided I'd wait until August for the divorce. At the same time, I realized I couldn't have sex with him any more. I couldn't stand to have him touch me. In fact, when he reached to touch me, I told him I was filing for divorce. I subsequently filed. I couldn't stay another minute. I moved into the garage room. He got a very adversarial lawyer. I moved into the house next door and we had joint custody.

My son went back and forth every other week. He would arrive at my house disheveled. Basically, my husband neglected him. He had been a pretty distant father. I would clean him up. For two years I lived next door until the trial. I had a lawyer, a feminist friend of mine, in the community. She always wanted the case to be decided as joint custody. She wanted it to be the first in that county. I wondered about the chance of joint custody if we were not talking to each other. Basically, I ended up losing custody and I think it was because of my lawyer. To lose custody was the hardest thing in my life. For two years, I never mentioned that I was a mother who had lost custody of her child. My son was seven at the time.

The argument that my husband used at that trial was that now that we had the equal rights amendment, women shouldn't automatically get custody. Any man who wants custody has a very likely chance of getting it. The other argument was that it was a male child and the third thing was my over-involvement in women's issues. He never said I was a lesbian because I wasn't, but he did imply that I could be.

I had actually started dating a man before the custody trial. I was with him for two years. He was very nice. It was a very healing relationship for me because he liked me and thought I was a wonderful person. He loved my politics. He was very good to me sexually. One of the interesting things about it was that he had this long-term relationship with this woman in Seattle and they split up because she wanted to get married. I could live with his seeing her, but at the end of six months I got into a relationship with a woman. When he found out about it, he just fell apart. He actually had lesbian friends, but when it came to my being a lesbian, he couldn't handle it.

There was a woman I was attracted to while I was still with my husband. I can remember feeling physically attracted to her and thinking, "Oh, I guess I can be attracted to women!" She was with another woman. That was a revelation to me. Somewhere along the line, I had known that women could be attracted to women.

The first woman that I was involved with was Betty, a person I hired. I called her for an interview and I don't know whether I knew she was a lesbian or not at the time. On the phone we discovered that we lived in the same neighborhood and she suggested we carpool together. She interviewed for the job and she got it. Then, I changed positions so that I was no longer her supervisor. We worked in the same building and we started carpooling to work. She was always doing things for me—like figuring out little things that I needed and dropping them by the house—but she never indicated that she was interested in me. Meanwhile, I was very attracted to her. I didn't know quite what to do about it. One of the things I did was invite her over to my house. I don't drink anymore or smoke marijuana anymore, but at the time I did both. I cooked her a dinner and we had wine, marijuana brownies, and candle-light. I remember afterwards having this conversation with her about bisexuality. I volunteered to give her a neck massage and we ended up kissing and I asked her if she wanted to spend the night. She said she didn't want to, but she did stay over and we made love. I stayed with her for two years.

I left my job and we went to law school together. We said we were going to support each other through law school, but it turned out to be much less than supportive for me. Life was very stressful for both of us. Her way of handling it was to get mad at me. It raised havoc in our relationship, and we split up during our fifth year of law school. What ended my relationship with Betty was that she was secretive about being a lesbian and in law school there was this man who was interested in her and I felt that she led him on. I'm not a secretive person and I don't want to be involved with a person who is. But, I bless her for getting involved with me, a woman who had never had previous experience with women. I've never felt sexually attracted to a man since then. At this point, I fit into my life. Even if my relationship wasn't perfect, this was where I belonged—relating to women.

The following year, I decided I would just focus on law school and not get involved with anybody. Then there was a woman who was also in law school, and she started inviting me to do things with her. It was kind of like she was coming on to me all the time, but she never would initiate making love. I told her that I couldn't handle the trauma of another breakup. But we did get together. I finished law school and went for several years without a relationship.

I have had about five or six relationships with women and I feel like I've gotten something major in my life from each of them. My last relationship was with a woman named Peggy. I met her kayaking and I always liked her. When I first met her, she was in a relationship and I knew her partner. She used to go down to Olympia to visit her mom. She started coming over regularly. Although I liked her a lot, I never considered her as a partner because of our age difference. She used to help me on my house and one time in one of our projects she suggested we go into the hottub. We did and she said she wanted to kiss me and I said, "What about our 20-year age difference?" We ended up going home and going to bed. I told her that this didn't mean we had to get married or anything. We stayed together for almost five years and actually had a very good relationship in lots of ways. She was a live wire at any party and that was fine with me. People liked me, but it wasn't my style to be very extroverted. One of the things I got out of that relationship was how to let a person be exactly where they were. We had our own lives and the life we shared. It might have lasted except that we got involved financially. Neither one of us was a good financial manager. I refinanced my house in Olympia to buy a house in Seattle. I found out that, in order to qualify, I needed her name on the title. I asked her if she was willing to do it and she was. I don't think either one of us knew the ramifications of it. It was really a financial stretch for me. I ended up feeling overwhelmed as I was the one responsible for the paper work. She agreed that she would keep track of the money and it really wasn't something she did well. We ended up falling apart financially. We're still trying to resolve what her share of the equity is. She left the relationship emotionally and eventually she moved out of the house. If we hadn't bought the house together, we might have saved our relationship. She now says she doesn't want to buy a house and be stuck with all that. I wanted someone who would share the responsibility.

One of the things I worked out over the years is that I don't want to be with anybody who doesn't want to be in a relationship. When she said she wanted to leave, I supported her in leaving. One of my commitments was to remain friends with her. I haven't remained friends with my other lovers. I told her that I didn't know how to remain friends and that it may be awkward and uncomfortable, but I wanted her to know my commitment. Actually, we are friends.

The grieving wasn't about the leaving but figuring out how to grow in my own way. I didn't have a community, but I have created one at my church. She had a community because she had a second job and had a lot of younger friends. The age difference could have become an issue at some point.

I am coming out more and more. Last fall, I read *Queer in America*. I really liked what the author said about how people who are homosexual perpetuate homophobia. We keep it secret because we are afraid it might hurt somebody. So last fall Peg and I went down to California to see my sister. I was going to ask her and her boyfriend to come out for me. I wanted them to identify Peggy as my partner when they have conversations about family. My sister started yelling at me that she didn't appreciate my imposing my political beliefs on her. That was a shock. We went on down the road and stopped at two friends of mine. I told them the same thing I had told my sister and they had no problem with it. Then my niece, who is my sister's child, pretty quickly accepted us and would introduce Peggy as my partner. I said the same thing to my son. He said he treated me the same as his dad, but he doesn't introduce Peggy as my partner. On a previous visit I had asked him if he had told his fiancee and he said he would. So this trip I started saying little things in front of her. We never talked about it but it turned out that her favorite brother is gay and she just found this out. So I think it may be helpful to her.

I am asking people at work to do the same thing. If they have a conversation and somebody says I don't know any lesbians, then I've asked them to say, "Well, you know Carroll Boone, don't you?" I think the best way for people to come out is not in big pronouncements, but rather in little situations.

I never came out to my parents and they are both gone now. I'm out to all my sisters. When I first came out to my youngest sister over twenty years ago, she stopped talking to me about the latest men in her life. When I went home to my mom's funeral, I said, " I wish I had come out to Mom before she died," and my sister said, "Oh, it would have killed her!"

I'm not in a relationship now. I am open to the possibility of one and I want to attract to myself a life partner. My preference would be to have a long-term committed relationship to grow in. But that hasn't been the way it has been. I am very happy to have arrived at loving women. One of the things that I do at the church is to lead empowerment groups for women. I helped start a group called Soul Sisters, a lesbian support group, in which we all support each others' growth. I do a lot of things with the larger community, but my own focus is to help lesbians heal and also create my own support community. I believe being a lesbian is a spiritual choice. Part of coming out is a spiritual commitment to being one's true self. It's making a choice for authenticity and growth.

Claudia

*To me, it was an adventure. It was like
coming home. . . . It fit.*

Both of my marriages were to the same childhood friend. It
was just assumed we would get married. We were married about
35 days! I was 19, and I got pregnant. I was stupid, and he trapped
me.

He was thrilled to death, but I hated being married. He was a
wonderful, sweet, and sensitive man. I hated sleeping next to him!
Sex was great, but the emotional part wasn't. I was a kid—
immature, stupid. He was in the Marines, stationed on Whidbey
Island, Washington. I was never there if I could help it. He felt bad
about it not working out, yet I was done. He dropped me off at
my Dad's house and the look on my Dad's face—"What the hell
are you doing here, 35 days later?"

My husband and I tried to talk about it, but things got out of
hand, and I ended up getting a restraining order against him just
so he wouldn't be around me.

After the baby was born, Dwayne came around again, and
then we started to talk. This was 1969. I had gone to see a movie
called *The Fox*, and it was like a light bulb had gone off in my head.
Things started to make sense. I didn't feel that alienation I felt
before. Meanwhile, Dwayne and I had been talking and we had
started dating again. I mentioned that film to him, and he said,
"Oh, if you ever let a lesbian get hold of you, you'll never go back
to men." It was weird. I said, "Really?"

Then, before we remarried, I had my first experience with a woman. That put me into a total state of confusion! We went out one night with his boss and his boss's wife. There was an immediate attraction between her and me. I was blown away at that point. She was older and sophisticated. We went back to their house and the guys were out in the living room drinking and talking. We went back in her bedroom so she could change clothes and she kind of came on to me. She said, "Dwayne is so crazy about you, you guys should be together. Why don't you get married again, and we can carry on and nobody will ever know?"

So, that night I told him that maybe we should get married again. We drove down to Reno that night. I thought it would be perfect. You talk about living in a dream world!

He had no inkling—no idea. The minute I said, "I do," I said, "What the hell did I do?" We tried to work it out, and that lasted about 40 days. I just couldn't deal with it. It was like being a teenager all over again. I was never home, and I finally told him about women. He said that that was okay with him because he loved me. He said, "It's okay as long as you come home."

I still didn't feel right about it, and one night I didn't come home 'til about six in the morning. When I got home, my mom was there with him. He was close to my mom, and he had gone over in the middle of the night all upset and crying and told them everything. They both looked at me and—well, I will love him to this day. He just put his arms around me and said, "I just want you to be happy. If that will make you happy—that's okay."

That was my first understanding of unconditional love. The same with my mom. She just asked me to see a psychiatrist to be sure that I was okay, which I did, and he said I was fine. That's what happened. The boss's wife and I never really got together again. We saw each other for lunch a few times, but we had different schedules. I also sensed that she was an alcoholic and self-destructive; otherwise, I probably would have pursued it. But the world had opened up for me. I discovered women!

My first woman lover was Olivia. This was in 1969, after Dwayne and I had broken up again. I was working for a figure-reducing salon, which was quite popular then. It was run by women. Those were crazy times. Anyway, there was an immediate attraction between Olivia and me. She certainly took the lead, and before I knew it, I had moved in with her. I had only known her a couple of weeks. We split up after about six months. I got involved with other women and so did she. We kind of lost track of each other. It's been about 10 years since I've heard from her. The last I heard she went to Chicago.

Then in 1978, I started a 12-year relationship. I first met her at a party that Olivia and I had. She had moved up here with her lover. Meanwhile, I was living at my parents' home with my daughter. It's not unusual for an Italian family to have four generations in one house.

Anyway, I had known this woman for a couple of years when we ran into each other one night down at one of the clubs. We went out together, and I moved in with her. God, that was a habit! I moved in with her and left my daughter with my folks. That lasted 12 stormy years.

In retrospect, one can understand why. We have motivations that have nothing to do with the other person. At the time, I thought things were fine. But, when I look back, we were smoking dope and drinking some—doing all that stuff. She was out of town two weeks out of each month because she traveled for a company. So, in essence, we only saw each other six months out of the year.

My lover was 20 years older than I was. I can look back now and see issues with my mom that I was acting out with her. It's funny when you hit your forties—things start to happen.

I just didn't feel good about anything. I would have affairs while we were a couple. Even with my ex-husband. He was the only man I felt safe having sex with—both disease-wise and psychologically. The crazy thing was that I never really liked it. It was weird. I can see now that I didn't know what I was doing.

What brought this woman and me together couldn't keep us together any longer. It was painful.

What caused it to end was that my mother died. When my mother got ill, my dad had died and she was living alone. My lover suggested that it would be a great idea for us to get a house and have Mom live with us. I had this relationship with my mom that was love-hate, but I did it anyway, and Mom moved in downstairs. I got the feeling that my lover was manipulating all of this, and I was operating out of guilt.

When my mom died, that did it. I knew my life was going to change. When I finally decided I had to change my life, our relationship changed. I tried to get my lover to go into therapy so she could understand that. I wanted her to understand that we shouldn't be together any longer. That was the coward's way out, and it was pretty stormy. So that was it.

Meanwhile, Dwayne and I would talk about all this a lot. He always wanted to know what was happening. To this day, he is an interesting fellow. I could talk to him about anything. He is still around. He has been married for the last 12 years, but we are all together for family holidays. That may seem strange, but there is no reason for any animosity or jealousy with his wife because she knows I'm gay, and I'm no threat to her.

It was good for my daughter because she never had parents that hated each other. My daughter is 26 now. I told her I was lesbian when she was 12. She told me she had known since she was 10!

I think my daughter has had a pretty good sense of herself. I wanted to do for her what I really didn't get from my mom. I just wanted to nurture her and give her a sense of herself so she could move out on her own and not do what I did. She is a successful Ford model and she's doing just fine. She's had relationships with women, but she's straight. She thinks the soul is the soul. The body's just a vehicle. She says if she meets someone with whom there is a connection, she doesn't care what body it's in. She's not married and is very career oriented.

The change-over was really bizarre in that I had none of the problems that a lot of women have; I mean, I embraced it. I'd even talk about it with all my friends. I never had a problem with the straight world. I think it was because I was comfortable with myself, and I didn't have any hangups about it. To me it was an adventure. That was '69 and '70. Those were the years when the thing to do was to know a gay person! It was all right. It was like coming home for me. It fit.

I have a sister, and we are as different as night and day. I was the wild black sheep of the family. My sister is very conservative—married an FBI man.

I never talked about it with my dad. All my friends would come over and Mom was like a surrogate mom to them. I secretly think my mom was a lesbian; I really do. My grandmother, who was the matriarch, said, "It's not who you are, it's what's inside here that counts." What she said went in the family.

When my mom died, I had to find out what was going on. So I started therapy. It turned out to be a lesbian therapist, although I didn't know it at the time. She has very strong boundaries. It's true—when you are ready the teacher appears; the connection was there. The therapy has been absolutely wonderful, and it's also the hardest thing I've ever done in my life.

My issue was not my lesbianism. It was all the other issues. Just in the past five years, I have recalled that I was abused by uncles and by boys across the street. I was very sexually precocious. You suppress the abuse, I guess. I didn't turn to drugs or alcohol. I was lucky; I think it was the nurturing from my grandma. I always had to be in control and you can't be if you're drunk.

Sex was almost like a drug to me, but I'd feel funny afterwards. I love women, but I don't hate men. I don't consider myself a separatist, but if there were no more men left in the world, it wouldn't bother me. I truly believe that this is what I chose to do this lifetime—this experience. For the past two years I've been single. I did meet somebody a year and a half ago. It was an immediate attraction. We didn't do the same old lesbian thing. Have you heard the joke about how you tell a lesbian on the second date? She drives up in a U-Haul!

There is a lot to be said about the old saying that a long courtship is the best courtship. Two years—hey, that's nothing. It gives you time for the masks to come down. So that's what we've been doing. We have kind of seen other people in between. We have redefined the relationship.

I'm not ready for a marriage. I'm just now discovering what I want in a relationship. I want to be claimed. I want to be treasured. Sex is fine, but I can't have sex just to have sex anymore. I did a lot of that.

When I came out, there must have been 20 bars here in Seattle. Down in the square you could park your car and go all night. Because we were the baby-boomers, we were the largest population of gay women. It was a new phenomenon. It was unbelievable. You didn't have to worry about disease. I met women at bars and parties. You can meet women anywhere. I meet them at Larry's Market, for God's sake, or Nordstrom's make-up counter downtown. That's the best place! The only difference is that you do safe sex now.

I want to have a partner someday. I know exactly what I want—the soul part of it. I want serenity. I want to be a whole person so I can be a whole person with somebody else. I want to explore some of the talents I've discovered that I have. Everybody always thought I had it all together. Now, I believe in more of my talents than I did before.

I'm letting the spirituality happen in me. I have come to a place with my spirituality that I have peace and serenity. I think there will be a balance; I can have spirituality and also make money at the same time.

I've discovered that I can write. I want to get back into the theater, or in the production end of it. Back in high school, I won the best actress award and won a scholarship to the Pasadena

Playhouse, but I never did anything about it because I was too scared. I would really like to get involved in that again.

I manifest what I want. I hope I come back next time as a lesbian, too. I'm having so much fun.

Barbara

I told him that I wanted a divorce. I said, "Jack, you don't know what you had. You had a writer, an artist, a musician, and a hell of a woman."

I was twenty-four years old and had my own car, a forty-seven Studebaker, which I still have. At the time, I had several good female friends, but none of them were gay. We were buddies and we would go places together. We went to California—six thousand and forty-one miles—in sixteen days. This was in '51 or '52.

One friend, Shirley, had a sailboat on Lake Michigan and we would sail in that little eight-foot sailboat and have lots of fun. One night we had a little episode where we all got a little drunk and kissed each other and she said, "Barbara, I know you might feel this way and I don't mind it, but I don't think you should do this until you have sex with a guy." Subsequently, I did have sex with guys. Meanwhile, my parents were pressuring me to get married. My mother kept saying, "Why don't you get married? I don't have any grandchildren and all my friends have grandchildren." But, I couldn't have cared less. I was having a good time.

In October of '54, I was on my way to an air show in Chicago. The car conked out on me and I pulled into a gas station and I lifted up the hood and was fooling around with the carburetor. My dad had showed me how to do theses things. The car would goof up and I would put on a pair of overalls and climb under the car, fix it, and get back in. In the fifties, we were all wearing those long skirts. I was under the hood and along came Jack Lindquist. He was kind of a handsome man and sweet. He said the usual line,

"Are you having trouble? Do you want to go have a drink?" So, we went off and had a drink. Then we went off somewhere in his car and had sex on the first night and for three months that's all we did. We would date and go off and have sex somewhere.

Jack was in construction and drove a dump truck. He was just very masculine and just a real nice guy. He was going off to Florida because he had been laid off over the winters months. I told him if he didn't take me with him, I wouldn't be there when he got back. He said, "Okay." So, we decided to get married. I always said I married Jack because I knew we would breed well. So we went to Naples, Florida and got married. About a year later, I had my first child.

I was twenty-four when we got married, I had only known him for three months. In March of '55 I had my first child and then I had another in "56, '57, and '58. I was a totally faithful wife and a professional parent spending my time raising my kids. I was a den mother for five years and a girl scout leader for three years. I was doing all that kind of stuff and in '65 I started going to a Unitarian Church.

I was a Sunday school teacher and that's where I met Jeanne. We were Sunday school teachers together and she was the head of the religious education committee. I wrote a curriculum for junior high students when Jeanne was the head of that committee. It was called Parapsychology and Religion. I was becoming interested in the fact that miracles could be explained if you looked at them as parapsychological occurrences. Jeanne liked it and we were going to go ahead and do it. Then, somebody on the committee and the minister decided that it wasn't something they wanted to do and they rejected the curriculum. I was pissed. Jeanne had to come and tell me that they had rejected it. So, I was mad at her because I thought she was part of those that had rejected it. After about six more months, I figured the heck with it. I thought that if thechurch didn't value my contribution and the kids and my husband didn't want to go, then I didn't need it any more. So, I quit going.

I was forty in nineteen seventy. I weighed about 160 pounds and was matronly looking. I thought, "I am forty, my kids are all teenagers, and I need to get my act together." I went on a diet, started roller-skating, lost 52 pounds, wrote a novel, and I started back to college to get my degree. I really took charge of my life when I was forty. I was looking around, half-heartedly, for a teaching job. But, Jack wasn't happy about that; he didn't really want me to go to work.

In 1972, I began to think I wouldn't mind going back to the Unitarian Church because I had some friends there and it was intellectually stimulating—home certainly wasn't. My husband not only looked like Archie Bunker, he sounded like him. He was a typical bigot, a wonderful kind-hearted soul, but he would swear at the ethnic groups and that kind of stuff. So, I was beginning to get bored with the whole scene and decided to go back to the Unitarian Church.

I would go to church and Jeanne would invite people over to her house. So, I got reacquainted with Jeanne as well as the Unitarian Church.

Jeanne would invite me over to her house and we would have these talks, and I realized that Jeanne was a very attractive woman. Jeanne, at the time, found herself having feelings for our friend Arlene. She was in love with Arlene but never did anything about it. And, of course, we had to talk about it. We talked about our feelings for other women. First, I told her about mine. Then she said, "Well, I have these feelings for Arlene as well you know." And, that first time we were there, we suddenly realized that we also had feelings for one another. I said, "Jeanne, oh no, we couldn't do this." She said, "What could it hurt, if we just let it happen?" Then, she forgot immediately that she said that.

At the time this was going on in my life, my father had a stroke. By that time, my mother had died and he had a little house that he had bought. This stroke put him first in the hospital and then in a nursing home. I had to sell his house and take care of all the

244

stuff he had because I didn't think he would ever come home. At that time he was seventy-four.

Jeanne came to visit at my dad's house and we moved his stuff. I said something stupid like, "I don't know how women could be in love and how it works." We were really high on our feelings for one another. We realized that something was going on and maybe this was something we could allow to happen. We were both still married and had children.

I was visiting my dad every day at the nursing home. I was meeting with Jeanne every once in a while. Our third or fourth meeting was right after Christmas at Fellowship Hall and we had our first kiss. That was it. Of course, we had to keep it under wraps. We talked on the phone and we wrote poetry to one another. Every time I talked to her on the phone I had to take it out in the back yard or the storage room so no one could hear.

In the meantime, my dad recovered. He decided that he hated the nursing home and wanted to get out. He had a girl friend and she got an apartment for him. It was okay by me. I didn't know he was going to recover. So, he got out and was on his own again.

Jeanne and I continued our relationship, but we both felt that it wasn't right. We would try to stay apart and we would say, "Oh, we've got to quit this." While all this going on, I was having a mini affair with some guy from the university. I had been a faithful wife until I fell in love with Jeanne. The affair didn't seem to bother Jeanne. She and I hadn't gone to bed together and we were savoring the romantic time. I was upset because I didn't know how to handle it. So, Jeanne decided that she would reject me. She figured that would be the end of our relationship. At that time, I had had it with my teenagers and I had had it with the relationship. I told my husband that I was going away for a weekend to a motel to get away from the kids. Of course, he didn't know anything about the relationship with Jeanne or what had transpired. So, I went off to a motel on Lake Michigan and spent two nights there. I was ready to call off the relationship and I could tolerate my kids again, so I came home. Finally, Jeanne and I met again and she had her journal with her. She had some poetry in it and gave it to me to read. I read it and thought that it was good. We had a nice talk and she suddenly said that she couldn't not have me in her life. So, on April first we got back together again.

Jeanne and her husband were going to their place on the peninsula. Jeanne was trying to get everything taken care of before they went. She was writing stuff in her journal. She had a section that said, "Thank you for April" which had all of our adventures in the journal. She left the journal lying on a table and her husband found it and read it. She was standing in the basement washing clothes and he came down with this in his hands. He asked if the writing was true and she said, "Yes." So, he knew from that point on.

At that time, Arlene and I were good buddies and we would drink wine and talk and smoke and stay up late and just talk. Sometimes Jeanne would be there and sometimes not. One time, Arlene went to see Jeanne at her house. Harry turned her away and told her that he and Jeanne had something to talk about. So, Arlene came back and we talked for the rest of the night. She was with us through all the trauma we were going through.

That whole year, Jeanne and I tried to stay apart. She went to counseling, but she just couldn't let Harry control our relationship. So, she would just deliberately meet me; we would just go ahead and do whatever we wanted to do. Meanwhile, my marriage was crumbling around me and our boys were going to join the Army. It was in late '74 when Jack and I decided to get a divorce. We had this kind of truce for several months because we hardly slept together anymore. I was having so much fun with Jeanne that I didn't care. Yes, I did care because he was just not interested anymore. I told him it was important to me. Sex had been part of our marriage that didn't happen; he was just not interested anymore. I told him that I wanted a divorce. I said, "Jack, you don't know what you had. You had a writer, an artist, a musician, and a hell of a woman." He said, "Yeah, but I never wanted any of that; I just wanted a wife and mother for my kids!" I thought, "You ass-hole. You had that and the other besides and you never appreciated it." And, then I thought, "I have someone who really appreciates that; I have Jeanne. We are equal, intellectually equal, and she really appreciates me and my talents." I don't think he was bright enough to know what was going on. He might have suspected a little bit, but I don't think he really got it until later. The official divorce didn't come through until the spring of '75. My two oldest sons had joined the Army by then and my daughter, who was 16, and my son, who was 14, told me they were going to live with their father

When I got divorced in '75, Jeanne was still married. The next year, we went to Europe together. At that time, I was living in an apartment in Racine. I lived alone for three years. Ultimately, the kids and I became friends and we would have family events together. So I wasn't left out, but it was a time when I was very emotional.

In '76, I found out that the school where I was teaching kids with learning disabilities was going to close because they lost their funding and they planned to mainstream all the learning disabled kids. So, I was going to be out of a job in December.

Jeanne was working for St. Luke's Hospital and she decided that she would like to have an assistant and that I would be the perfect assistant because I had all these talents. I had very mixed feelings. We were having this relationship, and she was still married. I thought it was a stupid idea for us to work that closely together. Yet, it was so exciting to be able to do public relations, a lot of photography, writing a newsletter, and put out a bi-monthly magazine. It was just so exciting to think about and I thought it was going to be a lot more interesting than a teaching job. So, I went to work with Jeanne. Our friend, Arlene, was the personnel director there.

By this time, Arlene and I had picked up a lot of guys together because all this time I was trying to prove that I was not a lesbian. I had relationships with 13 men during that period. Those were the days of the sexual revolution. We were in our forties. We had so much fun, but it was Jeanne I really loved. I was just fooling around with the guys. What did she think about the guys? It didn't bother her. Jeanne wasn't jealous because she knew that I loved her. I was having sex with Jeanne at the same period of time. Lots of orgasms! We were always turned on in those days. We were writing things and all that but at work we were sometimes very volatile. In the first place she was also my boss. That irked me sometimes because she would take the boss role instead of the lover role. That's why they don't allow people who are lovers to work together. We just proved the point.

Then, Jeanne told me she was leaving Harry and that she couldn't live with me because she needed her own space for awhile. She got her own apartment. Previously, for about a year, she had rented a little tiny room where she tried to write a novel. We made love there so much she didn't have time to write. Anyway, she was living in this apartment for three months and I was living on the other side of town in my apartment. It wasn't more than three months when she said, "I think we should buy a house together." We were still working at St. Luke's and I was having headaches from all the stress of our relationship and working together. They put me on anti-depressants and I was so zonked from the medication that, when we went around to look at houses, I would sleep in the car. Jeanne would wake me up to go look at these houses. Finally, we found the house we are living in now.

I realized that I needed some kind of counseling or something. I was drinking too much and it was crazy. So, I decided that I would check into a treatment center for a month. While I was there, I got canned because a supervisor and a subordinate could not live together in the same quarters. Our lovely boss knew about our relationship. So, I got laid off in March of '78, and Jeanne was the only one with a job! Now I had a house and unemployment compensation! We wondered what we were going to do.

We thought about opening a bookstore because we each would have the money to put our half into that. Jeanne's dad had the storefront and we had the money. So, in October of '78, after we fixed up the storefront, we opened a bookstore called Mother Courage Bookstore and Art Gallery. We had both read the play by Bertolt Brecht and we were mothers with courage. We thought the title would be catchy. Jeanne's divorce became final and she got her money to invest in the house and the store. I really had to trust her in order to go ahead with those endeavors. It was a lot for me. We called ourselves a full-service general bookstore with an emphasis on books for women. In the late seventies, women's bookstores were wonderful places, and some of them still are, but there are not too many of the originals still left. Jeanne worked at St. Luke's and then she would come and work in the store.

Meanwhile, one of our friends from Milwaukee had written a little book to help children talk about their abuse. It was written in long hand on three sheets of yellow legal paper and she wanted us to publish it. She wanted Jeanne to produce it and me to illustrate it. At first I said, "No." We were losing money in the bookstore and I didn't want to spend any more money. I did not want to publish this book. I wasn't exactly fond of her. She rubbed me the wrong way. But, Jeanne wanted to do it. One of the other reasons I didn't want to do it was that I didn't think I could illustrate it properly. I finally got an idea that I thought would work and it did. We published that under the name Mother Courage Press in 1981 when we were still in the bookstore. We printed a thousand copies and that book found its own market. There was a need for it and Jeanne did a lot of PR and sent it around to lots of places. So, we kept reprinting.

A friend in the Southwest sent us her book on abuse and we published her book as well. We decided, after five years in the book business, that we weren't making any money and that we should close the bookstore, so I could devote my time to something more meaningful. At that time, I took a course in tax preparation and I worked for H & R Block for awhile. Then, I got my insurance license and I tried to be an insurance agent for a day or so and I didn't like having to sell all my friends insurance. So, I decided to concentrate on the press. I was handling all the shipping and stuff on the two books and that was taking up a lot of time. We had rented out the property where we had the bookstore. Then we did two more books in a row. Then we really went for broke on a novel for which we printed 5,000 copies and we probably have 4,000 left! The rest of our books came along. Our returns on the publishing were very uneven. All told, we published twenty-four books and we still have twenty in print.

Jeanne continued working until 1984, when St. Luke's decided she was no longer necessary to their operation. That was a big blow to us because we didn't have any other income. Jeanne sent out all kinds of resumes and went on many interviews. She finally got this job in Milwaukee at a bigger salary. When Jeanne took that job, we thought we would have to sell our house and move there. We actually had it on the market but it didn't sell. Thank the Goddess it didn't. We decided to buy a mobile home. We parked it pretty close to where Jeanne worked. I would go up there part of the time and stay overnight. At that time, I had the press office in the house and I would work there and help her with her job by doing freelance work for her. We did that for ten years. Then, there was another shake-up where she worked and they eliminated the public relations job. Again! After Jeanne left, they closed the hospital altogether. I convinced her that she could retire. We sold the trailer and cut the rent immediately. We had no travel expenses and we got rid of one car. Actually, it seems we have more money now than we had when we were working.

So, that's the story. That makes our love affair at least twenty years in this house. Yes, it has been a love affair. There have been times because of my health that Jeanne has been very seriously upset about the physical part of our relationship. Because of my heart condition and my arthritis I had lost all interest in sex, to tell the truth. After twenty years, why do I need that? I'm an old lady now. But, actually, in the past month or so after I discovered that I had an underactive thyroid and started taking something for it, I think I've regained some of my interest. I think it is going to be okay.

Jeanne

I swear there were times when we were together that sparks actually were between us. It was scary and exciting and wonderful.

I was born to Mildred and Charles in 1931. She had been divorced and had an eight-year-old son when she married my dad. She was five months pregnant with me when her son was killed by a car. When I was born she almost died.

My dad was a good man and he loved us. We had a wonderful extended family on my mother's side. When I was ten, she was admitted to her first hospitalization with a nervous breakdown. She got out of the hospital and then she got sick again, in and out of private hospitals. My father couldn't afford that so she went to a state institution. When she got out of there, it seemed like everything was all right.

My father yearned to go into the service. He was older than most but he felt that he needed to go. He applied for the Navy. He got past the physical and he went off to World War II and left me with my mother. My mother was a wonderful person— very creative, very spontaneous, humorous, and intelligent. She was a real feminist struggling for equal rights and equal pay. I had a good role model for that. Before the war was officially over, she got sick again and living with her was very bad. They diagnosed her as schizophrenic. I was in foster homes or I lived with relatives. Our extended family was there when she was good, but they didn't know how to handle her when she was sick and they backed away. My father was honorably discharged early because of my mother's illness.

I became a 14-year-old tennis champion. There weren't too many kids in Racine who could play tennis, so I was always the girls champion. The park across the street from my house was my home away from home. Later, I became a playground leader so that when my mother came home I was close by to help her.

I left the Lutheran parochial school for public high school. My best girl friend was an Armenian girl. My freshman gym teacher and mentor liked me. I was a good athlete. Her partner taught the the older girls and she let us take over the classes, check off the shower lists and hand out the towels. I had access to the gym any time I wanted, so I skipped out of the boring typing and shorthand classes.

I met my husband-to-be in ninth grade. Throughout high school I was always his girl except for my junior year when I went to a pajama party and met an eighteen- year-old girl who had just graduated. She and I became very close that whole junior year. Her father was a fireman and he would be gone—twenty four hours on and twenty-four hours off. Her mother went overseas after World War II to see her family. We had such a wild summer and year. We were very happy together. We slept together. We necked and fooled around, but we never did anything more sexually. We had a big row when she was ready to get rid of me. We haven't see each other for years and years. I really loved her, more so than any of the boys. I don't think I even had crushes on boys.

I was editor of the paper and top athlete in the school. School was the center of my life. I liked my boyfriend and I went out with some other guys. The boys liked me because I could play tennis with them. I was a good sport and I didn't ask for a whole lot. But we had a good time necking. I really had a very exciting social and emotional life. We had beach parties and we would get home some times at three or four o'clock in the mornings. I have always said that I have a guardian angel that has always watched over me because I always emerged unscathed from all the experiments with the necking and going to dark places. I was blessed. Nothing happened to me that I didn't want to happen.

My journalism teacher and I became good friends. She told me that I had better not let my guy go because he was a good catch. So I started going steady with him. I enjoyed being with him He was quiet and I was outgoing. At dances, I would jitterbug with the girls and he would stand there and wait for the slow dances. Then we would walk home and we would neck.

He was very stable for me in my chaotic family life. He was Armenian, too. I loved the Armenian people. So many took me under their wings and treated me like family.

Harry and I went steady, were engaged to be married for four years, and I was technically still a virgin. My first orgasm was with all of my clothes on. I was very surprised. In those days if you got pregnant, you were shit out of luck. I didn't have any guidance. Although, when I got engaged, my father and I had a talk at the supper table. He told me that sex was one of the most important parts of your life and that there was nothing wrong with trying it out before you marry. I said, "Dad! No, I wouldn't do that. No, no I wouldn't do that." And, I didn't. We were handling our sexual urges in a mutual way that both of us could deal with. It was all right.

I went to two years at the university extension so I could be at home and help my dad. My boyfriend worked for a year because he was a year behind me in college. I never expected to go to college, but one of my homeroom teachers urged me to go. I had a wonderful mentor—the publisher of *The Journal Times*. I baby-sat his kids and then he would drive me home. Once he asked me if I were planning to go to college and I said that I didn't think so. He told me that I could do anything I wanted and if I needed any money to come and see him and he would see if he could get me some help. That was all I needed. My father was a sign painter who didn't have any money and we had all these medical bills with my mother permanently in the mental hospital.

I went to the University of Wisconsin in Madison and I am very proud of that. I even graduated with honors. I got my degree in English, journalism, and education. In those days you could be a nurse, a secretary, or a teacher. I thought a lot about what I would do if I didn't get married. I always wanted to go to New York City. I wanted to be an actress but I knew it wasn't practical. So I settled down. But, as a school teacher, I had an audience. I was a good teacher and the kids liked me.

We got married in February 1953; I graduated in June. We lived in a trailer park that was left over from veterans' housing. The rent was about twenty-five dollars a month. I became a teacher in a town near Madison and he commuted and finished. Then we both became teachers in the same high school in a town up north. We both were very popular.

While he was in college, he was able to qualify for ROTC which gave him officer's status. These life decisions on minor points make all the difference in the world. He could have been in Korea, but instead when it was his turn to go in to the service, he was stationed in Frankfurt, Germany, and I joined him there.

Life in Germany was wonderful. I applied for a substitute teacher's job in the Army high school. They liked my work and made room for me to be a full-time English and journalism teacher. Those were glorious years. We were there for three years and we went all over Europe on our vacations. Frankfurt was a great city. We took all of my money, put it in the bank, and lived off of his. Everything was so cheap there. It was '55 to '58.

We took a vacation and went to the Brussels World's Fair and that's where I got pregnant with my son. We both had signed up to teach in our home town when we were to go home. But, in those days, you couldn't teach if you were pregnant.

We bought a two family flat so we could rent part of it and make money. My husband was teaching but he decided to get into the computer field just when it was starting. It was the right thing to do. He worked hundred-hour weeks and I was home with two babies. I had one miscarriage and later we lost a baby who was born in the seventh month. That was the beginning of the end of our marriage. Losing that baby had a lot to do with it. We were never told how important it was to talk about it and grieve together. I would always write and I wrote how I felt, but he didn't. I never knew until we were in marriage counseling years later that he resented me not doing "the right thing" about his grief over the loss of the baby.

He was making a lot of money compared to teaching. I had always wanted a house on the lake, so when we had the chance we bought one. I devoted myself to two volunteer projects. I helped start our local Montessori School and directed the Unitarian Universalist Church School. He actually let me out of the house two nights a month without him so that I could go to those meetings. I didn't know then what it was that was killing our marriage.

Because of my volunteer work and the fact that I made good impressions on people, I had a chance to work for an important foundation. My husband wouldn't let me take it, not even a part-time job. Then a year or two later there was a part-time opening at *The Journal-Times* and I took it. He didn't like it, but I was not going to be cheated out of this job. My work was a hit right away. I brought in the early feminist views. I saw things from different dimensions. I realized then that my husband was penalizing me for having the job and I was getting angrier and angrier.

The turning point in my life was in 1968 when I heard the word "feminism" and Simone De Beauvoir's book, *The Second Sex,* on a Studs Terkel radio interview.

Then came the Democratic Convention in Chicago and I was outraged at the War in Vietnam and what the police were doing to those protestors. My son and daughter were with me in that election. My 11-year-old son went door-to-door trying to get people to vote Democratic and my nine-year-old daughter baby-sat at our church so people could help get out the vote. My husband told me that he was going to vote for Nixon.

Both Barbara and I were very active in our liberal church school. Barbara became angry at me because the board had rejected the curriculum that she had worked on. Meanwhile, my friend, Arlene, I, and a neighbor of mine went on a trip to New York City and we had a really good time. I realized that my loneliness was driving me crazy. My husband was boring. He was unhappy with me because I was working, going on trips with women, and doing all this feminist stuff. He hated it when I read *Ms* magazine. I realized one day, when I was looking around for an affair with one of the men at *The Journal Times* that none of them were any better than my husband.

Then, I woke up one morning and it was like the top of the box came off and I realized that I didn't have to restrict my love to men. I had an incredible crush on Arlene. I told her and it was the most nervous time I've ever had. She was very calm and accepting, but she said she could not return that kind of love. That was fine for the stage that I was in. We became very good buddies and had a lot of fun. My husband hated her because she was happily divorced and he thought she was a bad role-model for me. He didn't want me to have anything to do with her. Well, we were like sisters and we did a lot, but I couldn't get close to her.

So, here came Barbara back into our circle and she was exciting and we didn't know what to do with her. She was very erratic. She was in the throes of emotional trauma. She was compelling. I was a rescuer and I was going to rescue Barbara and make her feel good. I knew what it was like to love a woman and I knew unrequited love. Who did I think I was? Anyway, she was so intense. She represented all the scary thoughts that I had about my mother. Not that Barb was crazy, but my thoughts were on her all of the time and I never knew what she was going to do. I was afraid that she might commit suicide during that summer. I didn't want to risk myself that much but I could not stop it. It was electric. I swear there were times when we were together that sparks actually flew between us. It was both scary and wonderful. I wrote a journal and she wrote poems and we shared them. When we weren't with each other we were very preoccupied with each other. I was there to counsel her. She remembers one thing and I remember another. I remember hugging her and we kissed. I said, "What could it hurt if we just let things happen?" She said, "Everything—you and me and the children and all." I guess I opened up and it was overwhelming. It was everything I would ever want and yet it took us time before we would sexually touch each other. It was so tantalizingly beautiful.

After the first time we actually made love in my bed, we came downstairs and were having a drink. Barbara was tuning my guitar. For the first time in the history of my marriage, my husband came home from work in the middle of the day. He found the two of us. She was on one chair and I was on another. I couldn't believe it. He had sensed that something was wrong. Barbara and I had a circle of six friends that we put ourselves in so it didn't look like it was just the two of us. We would always go out as a gang. Once my husband sat me down and said that he had the feeling that there might be some homosexual feelings among my women friends. I told him not to worry. I had everything under control. I didn't feel like I lied because it was under control—from my vantage point.

Barbara and I parted in March of '74. But then we called each other on April Fool's Day and we met each other at my front door. My daughter was going out the back door on her way to school and Barb's car was coming around the corner. I met her at the front door and the dog was barking. We embraced and we kissed and that was the day I count as my commitment to her. When I look at my journals and the little diaries Barbara kept, it's amazing how much we saw each other. Barbara was getting divorced and she was very sad and lonely, but she didn't want me to leave my husband and kids. She was going through hell with her kids, and didn't want me to experience the same thing.

258

Six months into our affair, my family was going up north for a vacation. I put all our love notes in an envelope to give to Barbara. I had to go down to the freezer, and while I was there, my husband picked up the envelope. He opened it and read the first line, "I love you, Barbara." He threw it at me and I never went to that party. Arlene came to the house to see what was happening and he wouldn't let her in. He and I lived together for three and a half more years during which he knew that I was having an affair with Barbara. He expected me to get well. He expected me to see the craziness. He expected me to change. He thought the beautiful family that we had and the beautiful home and the stability and everything would bring me to my senses. I suppose it should have, but it didn't. It was chaos and he knew that whenever he would go on a business trip or meeting that Barb and I would be together. The kids had their extended family and friends. I wasn't hovering over them. They had my friends' children and they were all going around together and going to church events. They all watched out for each other.

I took a tiny room of my own for three months, agreeing to come back home after that. I was to write the first half of my novel. I was also working now as the PR person for one of the two local hospitals. At the beginning of a union strike on the hospital, I said at an executive rally that I would put out a newsletter every day the strike went on. The strike lasted six weeks and I published a newsletter every single day while having an affair with Barbara and using whatever was left of my energy for my family. I did it. I don't know how.

Having this room was a big threat to my husband and children, and after I went back home, I kept the room—a continuing threat because I always had a place of my own to go to whenever I chose.

Barbara and I even went to Europe in '76. We had a three-week honeymoon, although I still was married. Our trip was wonderful. I could write a book just on that.

259

I was continuing to do a good job at the holpital after the strike and I was to have an assistant. Meanwhile, Barbara lost her job and came to work for me in that assistant position.

It was a mistake. Barbara is a person who needs to do her own thing. She is so creative and she can do anything, but she doesn't like to take direction, and she knows it.

A year and a half later, Arlene, who was the hospital's person-nel director, and Barbara went to Greece on a hospital cruise. My husband, the kids, and I took my son out west to college. I missed Barbara so much. When we got back home my husband told me that he could no longer stand it. He said, "You will have to get some therapy, Jeanne. I will not be married to somebody for twenty-five years and let this happen." That's all I needed. He had made an ultimatum. He went off on a business trip and I made arrangements for a larger apartment only a block away from my house. I had one day to get my women friends together and we moved the things that I needed.

My daughter took over and took care of her dad. She was free of me. We never got into any teenage bouts. She didn't have anything to fight with me about. Many of my friends were supportive of me, but relatives and others weren't. They were shocked, stunned. One of my neighbors told me that they were so disillusioned by Nixon and Vietnam that if I left my husband what more could they believe in.

Barbara and I either stayed at my apartment or hers. We were never alone. We would come in to work together and we were so thrilled. We were a scandal. We had highly visible jobs, but it became the pits. She was so afraid, and I didn't want to lose her. I didn't want to go through any more madness. But we stuck it out and made it work. When she tried to get a different job, we realized that none of them were appropriate. I asked her what she would like and that's when we opened the bookstore. We didn't have any money to advertise and I would write letters to the editor on issues about feminism and witchcraft and equal rights.

My bosses hated it. My boss gave me such a hard time that I was forced to look for another job. I had to pay the mortgage and I couldn't quit. It was such a struggle; it was so hard on us.

I had to push Barbara into the publishing of *Something Happened To Me.* I pushed her into it and that was the start of Mother Courage Press. We closed the bookstore after five years.

I'm really proud of us. We had no resources to fall back on. We kept getting ourselves together. We could have given up on each other any number of times. We were meant to be partners. There was no question about it. We have loved and supported each other through thick and thin. The women's spirituality movement has been so important to us. She has innovated many circle rituals. I've supported her all the way. When I got a job in Milwaukee, she supported me. I wasn't out much in Milwaukee but when you go to a personnel office and they ask you who your beneficiary is and you give a woman's name, the clerk isn't stupid. All the secretaries knew. I should have just come out right away.

Ironically, our friend, Arlene, married my ex-husband and Barbara's old friend married hers.

I'm looking forward to the future. We've been through some rough times with health issues. We've had different expectations of each other. Retirement issues are with us, but we're successfully working them out. We've had some rough times recently, but I know we have straightened them out and I'm looking forward to growing old together. In fact, I have the wording for our tombstones. Mine will say, "Jeanne, beloved of Barbara" and hers, "Barbara, beloved of Jeanne." I think that would be a wonderful memorial for the both of us.

Audrey

Love of self is the whole key to life.
Too bad it takes so long.

When I met my husband, he was in the Navy. He was a gentle sort of guy. We dated for three years and got married. I thought I loved him. I was eighteen. I had my first child a year later. Three years later I had my daughter, Karen. Because she was born without hip sockets, we were in hospitals a lot. Bud's and my time together was not really quality time.

I had some good friends and I thought it would be good for him to meet them. Well, it was so good that he fell in love with my best friend. I was devastated. But, it didn't work out for them. I left him and went to the East coast to try to run away from him. My doctor had given me three alternatives: divorce, separation, or wait until he grew up. I couldn't wait that long. Divorce was a problem because I was Catholic. So, the only alternative was some kind of separation. I called my mother and told her I was coming home. I went to live with one of my sisters who had three boys. It was kind of rough. I didn't have very much, but I guess because I had two kids I found the strength. I don't know what would have happened to me if I hadn't had them. I didn't really know who I was.

We went back to Michigan after four or five months so the kids could see their grandparents. Then my husband and I got together again saying that we should do this for the kids. He went to the East Coast with me and the marriage was incredible. We were like newlyweds. It was so good that I thought we could all go back to Michigan and everything would be okay. But he just went out with other women again. He just wanted out of the responsibility of marriage. Finally, I did divorce him after thirteen years of marriage.

I met my second husband through his wife. I knew her from a children's organization we both belonged to. She died of cancer and I called him up and went to see him. Then, I saw him in the grocery store where I was cashier, and he asked me out to dinner. He was a nice guy, but I was never really in love with him. At that time, my son was twelve and my daughter was ten and he had two older sons. I moved into his house. Three days after we married I knew that I wasn't going to be married to this man for the rest of my life. He felt that he had to hide his affection for me. I didn't want that. I'd been craving affection since I was a kid! It was on and off for three years with me moving out a couple of times.

Then I met a nun through a friend who had her little girl in a Catholic school. We were having a glass of wine when I asked her why she wanted to become a nun. She said she had wanted to escape because her dad had remarried and they had all these children. She had escaped from that like I wanted to escape. She taught school and was trying to make a decision about taking her final vows. We did a lot of fun things together, which was exactly what I needed in my life.

Then, we became involved. I said, "Whoa! This is not feeling very comfortable." At the same time, she decided that she would not take her final vows. For me, this was a way to get out of my marriage. I divorced Bud, and Carol and I got together and lived in the house with my two kids. I was really discrete because I didn't want to hurt my kids. I think I was also a little bit in denial of what was happening. That was in 1977. I was thirty-seven years old when I actually came out. She was full of affection and like a kid. I thought this might be okay, but it wasn't. She had a lot of anger at her dad for marrying and having all these kids, as well as anger at being a nun and what she had to do and couldn't do. For one year she was just in a terrible rage, but I kept thinking she'd get over it. I lived with her for five and a half years and it was very, very tough. Even though all this was going on, we were so discrete that the kids didn't know.

There was a woman I connected with in the lesbian community whose name was Judy. She wasn't doing great with her partner and neither was I. We clicked as if we had known each other from some other place. We left our partners and got together. Her former partner was also in a rage. I never knew what was going to happen. She carried a gun in the trunk of her car, and we were afraid of her. I was with Judy for five and a half years.

I moved to Seattle in 1989 with two suitcases, two boxes, and a thousand dollars. I moved to Seattle because it was two thousand miles away from Judy. She was a powerful person and I wanted those miles between us. I was running away and it was a good decision. I moved into shared housing with four other women. The woman who lived in the next room from mine, Joy, was going through a divorce. She had run away from her husband after 40 years of marriage. He was going to retire and she didn't want 24 hours, day after day, with him. I tried to connect with her, but she was trying to keep herself occupied so she wouldn't have to think about all her stuff. I needed somebody to communicate with in my life and, after a while, we all became friends and family to each other.

As Joy and I became friends, we started doing things together. I started feeling a little bit easier about getting out there in the world—meeting other women. I began dating Eileen and I noticed that Joy was a little jealous about this. I told Joy that I had great feeling for her. She brought out the little kid in me. She was a lot of fun. One thing I liked about her was her depth—her feelings about things. I had never experienced people like that. I felt it but could never express it. I started having real feelings for her and I thought that it was just because of our living situation. So, I moved out of the house telling Joy why I was leaving.

Even while I was dating Eileen, I didn't want to break ties with Joy.

One evening Joy and I called a restaurant for dinner reservations, but we couldn't get in until nine o'clock so we sat and had some drinks and relaxed. Joy loved it. She had been away from nice places for a long time. We had a wonderful evening. I was going to meet Eileen the next morning at eight o'clock. When we got to Joy's home, we started kissing. She couldn't believe what was happening and neither could I. I stayed overnight and it was so great because we were so comfortable with each other. I must have left about six o'clock in the morning. I met Eileen and went camping. We came back on Sunday and I went to see Joy that night. Eileen and I had been involved. I'm an honest person. I can't have two people in my life. I said, "I can't do this, so what I'm going to do is give up both of you." On Monday, I told the same thing to Eileen when she got home from work. Eileen was a kind of spiritual person who said that she could understand that. Later she got angry about it. But Joy accepted it with unconditional love. It didn't matter. The connection was there. I was with her for seven and a half years. We had a rough road because of her alcoholism. She went to a couple of rehab places. I went to co-dependency classes and found out about my trying to save the world. I learned a lot.

With Joy, it was unconditional love. I never thought I even knew what that word was all about. We got the perfect place and she started getting into alcohol again. I could see that her mind was not always clear. I could see her deteriorating. I told her that if she started drinking again, I would be completely out of her life. Then I found a bottle. I made the decision to move but she moved before I did. She went to Idaho where her nieces lived. I told one niece to keep an eye on her because she wasn't doing too well. She fooled them for a couple of months and then they discovered that she had cancer. Of course, she wasn't speaking to me.

Friends of mine went to see her. When they came home they told me that Joy was not in denial anymore and that she had lung cancer. She was a smoker.

She did come to see me for one week. She'd been on chemo and she needed a break from it. It was great being with her for a week. We just meshed. I was going to go see her at Christmas. I was going to leave on the 23rd. She died on the 22nd.

When Joy died, I took a bus to Idaho for the funeral. A family member took me in and Joy's niece was there. It was a tough experience because I wasn't included as a family member or even recognized. Joy and I had bought this beautiful vase and I asked the niece if we could put flowers in it for the ceremony. When I left, the niece wanted me to take the vase home. I have it now.

Three years later, in '96, I started to let go of the grieving. I had pulled a muscle in my knee, but ignored it and continued to work. Then my other knee went out, and I had to stay home. During that time, I walked into my little den and the TV went on without my touching it. The next night I passed by the room and the TV went on again. The next night I walked in there and the telephone rang. While I was talking, the TV went on. I said to my friend that the TV went on again and it was a program that Joy used to watch. So, I hung up, turned off all the lights, and lit a candle. I sat with the candle and really worked on letting go of Joy. It shook me up. I felt her presence there.

One night I was just sitting meditating and the TV went on. I didn't do anything about it. I just let it be on as long as it had to be. That was Joy's last appearance. It was a very powerful experience for me and I finally finished the grieving.

I decided to have a ceremony to change my last name to my grandparents' name. I had my friends there and it was a wonderful ceremony. We had it in a little chapel and I had a luncheon. I talked about all the people who were there and how I was connected to them. I talked about Joy and took "Joy" as my middle name.

A woman from New York, who had recently moved here helped me with the luncheon. Her name was Jan and we became friends. Jan was married, but she said that she had always felt she was a lesbian. She said that for four years she didn't have a physical relationship with her husband. She had had a connection with another married woman, but when Jan left her husband, the woman just took off. So Jan came out here for a visit. I just kind of looked at her and thought to myself that I never would be interested in her. She was very serious and very intelligent.

I called Jan one day and asked how she was. She told me that she was still waiting for her welcoming to Seattle. I told her I was the welcoming committee. I was looking for a buddy and she needed a buddy. So, we became buddies. Then, I started having feelings for her. I told her and she told me that was very nice and thanks for saying that. The next day she said that she needed to pay attention to what I had said. I was going on vacation and she wanted to meet with me before I left. So, I sat in the chair and she sat on the couch. I had prepared myself for rejection; but, she said that she thought she might have some feelings for me. That was a surprise. There was a connection between us. It was more powerful than we realized until we opened that door a little bit.

I went on vacation for two weeks to see my grandkids. While I was on vacation, I'd call Jan and she was very surprised and very happy that I called. She wrote me many cards and letters. Like I said, she's very intellectual, so her words and cards were spectacular. I am self-taught.

When I came back, her mother was visiting. Jan was so excited that I came back and still had feelings for her. Her mother was so lovely. That evening her mother went to bed early so we could be together. We became very involved and, during the next two and half months, we were so connected that it took over our lives. She didn't want to have a relationship. In fact, when she was with her friends, she wouldn't involve me. She never showed any affection in front of her friends because she always wanted to explore other

267

possibilities even though she was crazy about me. I told her that she had to decide what she wanted. We were both starved for love and we jumped in head first. During the time she was with me, she wrote poetry to me that moved me to tears.

But, Jan didn't want to be partners with me without experiencing the world out there. As hard as it was for me, I had to let her do that. So, I let go. I heard over the grapevine later that Jan met a woman from Australia, and I was very hurt. The problem I'm going to have the rest of my life is knowing the oneness that we had.

Life, for me, has been a great growth experience. I thank God for all I went through. Even though it's been tough, it's really okay. The best thing I can say about Joy's death is that it deepened me spiritually. I don't watch TV. I don't get a newspaper. I live in a very peaceful space. Every morning I see Puget Sound; I see the trees and listen to the birds. Because I'm single other people think I'm free to have another person in my life. Freedom, for me, is inside. I'm not the same person who left Michigan ten years ago. Love of self is the whole key to life. Too bad it takes so long. I think we're on this planet to learn that. I'm really looking forward to seeing what's going to unfold next.

Betty

While I didn't find the initial sexual experience with my husband to be entirely repellent, it did not inspire a closer or warm relationship with the man.

I consider myself a lesbian, and have for almost 40 years. Since my first lesbian experience, it was crystal clear that I was a lesbian.

Prior to that experience, I had, in my youth, dated men consistently, although I was not what you would call roaringly popular.

At the age of 19, I was married to a man I had known for five years. He had been a ranger in World War II. All of this was very romantic and people were getting married all around. I decided that would be the best thing to do.

I was a virgin at the time of my marriage, and if my husband had any experience, I think it was very limited. In any event, while I didn't find the initial sexual experience to be entirely repellent, it did not inspire a closer or warm relationship with the man.

I never found the relationship fulfilling in any sense except that the state of being married offered a certain status among my friends and colleagues. I remained married for approximately a year and a half, and we eventually separated and divorced.

I graduated from nursing school and proceeded to go to another city and to work in a hospital. There I met this senior student who would graduate in not too long, and she became my first female lover.

My friendship with this student had all of the elements of courtship leading up to romantic and sexual love. That included the poems that to the present day are those which are shared by lovers. There was a sensitivity to what was going on in our profession of nursing, a sensitivity and compassion, an empathy which she had for our patients.

We spent a great deal of time together— sharing our mealtimes at the hospital and as much time as possible off duty. I lived outside the hospital, and she lived in a dormitory room shared by two other women who were straight. She was a very beautiful young woman, had been a winner of several beauty contests and was very sought after by young men. She dated regularly.

One day, as we lay across a bed reading a poem, our hands touched in the first physical contact. It was like a pink-backed romantic novel—I might suggest that the veil fell from our eyes. We realized the physical relationship which would follow.

I think it was clear to us that this relationship was not acceptable, but we were very naive about keeping it hidden. Although we both continued to date men and on occasion double dated, it must have been plain to many people that our relationship was more than ordinary friendship.

The most serious thing that happened was when I went on a vacation at the height of this romance. I wrote love letters which my lover's roommate found and delivered, as good Christian girls should, to my lover's sister. We had a confrontation in which I denied steadily that any of this was so. I said I could see how those letters could make it seem otherwise. Nothing came of the confrontation except to heighten my awareness of the unacceptability of the relationship.

Over the years since 1947, there have been a number of times when I thought it would have been a great pleasure and a great relief to come out of the closet. I felt this most in the late sixties and early seventies when the feminist movement was strongest. But at that time I concluded that revealing my lesbianism was a luxury—a self-indulgence—which still in the nineties can put a variety of life values in jeopardy with catharsis being the only advantage. Once a thing is said it can never be taken back, and things are altered for all time. I feel as if I would be shamed in the eyes of some persons. I would be afraid that it would threaten my job security. For me now, I don't know how much there is a real need for hiding and how much is a life-long practice.

My family circle narrows as I grow older. I do not feel alienated from them, yet I feel that I can never be completely close because of this secret. It's part of my personality to have total openness, and here is a basic ingredient of my life about which I cannot feel open. This is especially true with my oldest sister who lives here in the same city. I feel close, and I think she knows I am gay, but we have never discussed it and I see no probability or good reason to do so.

What do I do for fun? I play bridge. I swap video cassettes with friends. I like to play board games. I fish when I can find fishing companions, which is as much a problem as finding a sexual companion.

The world talks of sexual preference. I know it's the only term we can use—it's a kind of generic term. But, you know, I really dislike it. It sounds as though sometime at puberty there was someone who held out two hands and said, "Here is heterosexuality, and here is homosexuality; which do you pick?" Actually, we lesbians know that it isn't like that at all. We are as surely homosexual as straight people are heterosexual.

I am a lesbian and that's just the way it is. I have not wished to live my life differently. I have been privileged to know and love some wonderful women, and I would not have wished to change that.

Diane

Once you've been a lesbian, why would you want to be anything else? I find women much more exciting than men. I find the sex so much more fulfilling.

I got married the first time for the simple reason that I had no idea I had any choice. I was 20 and it was in 1948. It was something that everyone did.

Then, in 1953 while I was working as a key puncher, I worked with this woman. I enjoyed her company very much. I became very interested in her, but I had no idea of what was going on. Looking back on it she was what could be considered very obvious. She was very butch looking. She wore very tailored suits.

I knew about lesbianism, but it never occurred to me that I could be, or that anybody I knew could be. She finally told me she was gay, and since I didn't know what that was, she told me. I knew a woman lived with her. When she told me all that, it made it okay for me to be interested in her. Up until then we had just gone out for coffee and the like. Now, I wanted to go out with her and I wanted her to take me to a gay place. So, we went to a gay bar in the village. I invited her up to my apartment while my husband was at work and I had a holiday.

I had had some really strange ideas about what women did together. I knew very little about sex and I disliked it intensely with my husband. I had had one orgasm in my life. Everything was, very bluntly, penis-oriented. My husband didn't do any fancy stuff or anything. Certainly not any oral sex—though I had read about women doing that and that intrigued me.

Anyway, Denise came over and I answered the door in a red nightgown. She kissed me and I had this crazy idea that women wore dildos and I thought she had forgotten to put it on. I thought that we wouldn't be able to do anything!

In spite of the fact that I hated sex, I was looking forward to doing something. We kissed and she made love to me and I wasn't able to do anything. She thought she hadn't made me happy but I said, "No, I'm able to learn." I wanted to do whatever it would take.

A week later, Denise and I found an apartment. I told my husband that I was leaving the next day. That was in 1953. We moved in together and we visited the gay places and I just loved it. I thought it was the most exciting thing. I liked being with her and I never, never regretted what I did. It was easy for me. I never considered going for therapy. There weren't any books; there weren't any support groups. Only movie stars or people who were really messed up went to shrinks. This you had to do all by yourself.

I thought about the fact that we would never have children. The second thought was what if she dies and I get left all alone. With my husband, I could never buy what I really wanted to buy. Everything we bought had to be because it was on sale or something that he wanted. He was such a penny pincher that I never had what I wanted. So with Denise I thought, "Here are two women and we won't have that penny-pinching." Our tastes were so alike. We thought alike. She was fantastic.

So, we lived together for eight and a half years. She was bright and funny and I just loved being with her. I never got tired of being with her.

She had her little things on the side. Women would get interested in her and she would encourage them. There were times when I thought I couldn't handle it. Then, when push came to shove, she would say, "Okay, I won't see her anymore." She would encourage me to get involved with somebody else, and I actually had a one night stand with a friend of ours who had always been after me. It didn't turn out to be much. I would have never left Denise.

Unfortunately, after about a year together she started to show signs of something and we didn't know what it was. Every year she would have an attack and be sicker. She died of lupus erathematosis at the age of 31 in 1961. It was really very tragic. Even when she died, there wasn't anybody I could talk to. There weren't any support groups or anything.

It took me years to understand about being gay. Denise was very butch and I had to be very femme. That was a no-touch situation, since it was the typical polarized relationship. Of course, women like that always say that women who are not like that don't know who they are. I thought I was femme. It was not as fulfilling as it might have been. She had me brainwashed, thinking this was the way I was. I loved her or I wouldn't have been with her for eight years, but I really didn't want to be with another heavy duty butch again. And, I couldn't see myself with another woman like myself. That left me very confused. I didn't understand and I had nobody to tell me anything different, so I didn't do anything for a long time.

After a few years, I dated men and had a couple of affairs. I went to Puerto Rico for a few weekends to see where Denise came from, and then I moved there in 1963. I stayed down there and I dated men, and didn't think anything about gay life. But, when I was making love, I thought about women.

Eventually, I met this man who was a lot younger than I was. We got married. I told him I had been gay, and it was O.K. with him. He was young and lonely. We married and had a child and everything was pretty good for a while. Then, we went on a trip to the Middle-East and he got it into his head that he really wanted to be with an Oriental girl. He liked anything that was different and liked to prove himself. I was pregnant with my second son at that point.

When we got home, he said he didn't want to be married to me anymore and I said, "That's great because I'm pregnant." So he stayed with me. I really didn't want him to leave me because I was in my late forties and here I was with two kids. We had this arrangement that I would be the wife and he would take me out occasionally, and we would make love every four days.

I thought maybe he would be happy for awhile. But, eventually, he wanted to leave again. I didn't want to stay in Puerto Rico under those circumstances, so we moved to Texas. In '76 he decided he didn't want to be married to me any longer. He just went off one day to the Dominican Republic and got a divorce.

I guess if he had wanted to stay married, I probably would have. I still didn't know that I had a choice. I'm not a dumb person; it has to do with how I was brought up. I felt being gay was something other people could have, but it wouldn't be for me. It just never occurred to me that I could lead a gay life.

After the divorce, he stayed around. He kept wearing his wedding ring and he still slept with me. We bought a house together. We went to Europe together. Nobody knew that we were divorced. He was always telling me not to count on his being around. But the sex got harder for me. I thought that was because I was getting old and dried up and things like that. I would have plugged along anyway because I thought nobody would want me at my age and with two kids.

I was kind of lonely and I met some guy at work. He was a programmer also, and we got involved. When my husband came back from a trip, I told him that I had found somebody else. I went with this man for two and a half years until 1981. It was the last man I went with. He was 20 years younger than I was. It got rocky at the end because he wasn't as sophisticated and was much too young. After that, I went for a number of years with no sex.

Then, one year, I went to Club Med and took my kids. I met this woman and we smoked some pot together. She was so sexy and I seduced her. I thought that was terrific. I was the initiator and the aggressor. I was wondering in the back of my head if I would like it sexually. I had not been with a woman for 20 years.

Finally, I went to therapy and my therapist said that I might be happier with women. I had had it in my head that this was because I couldn't get a man. It took me a few more years after that to accept this.

Then I asked my veterinarian and her lover to take me to a gay bar. I was fascinated with it. I couldn't stay away and I made excuses to go in there. My kids were still young and they were a good excuse for not going out much on weekends.

I finally got myself involved in a conversational group that met on Sunday mornings in '86, and then, I started doing more things. I started going to dances and to the bar on Saturday nights. In a few months, a woman I met really came on to me and asked me out. I knew this would be my opportunity to find out if this was what I really wanted. It turned out I liked the sex a lot with a woman, but I didn't care for her.

I have been in my current relationship eight months. That is not a long time but that is the longest I've been with anybody in years. I enjoy being with her and she loves me very much. I have more things in common with her than I've had with anybody. But, we look at things very differently and I don't have the rapport I'd like to have with her. It bothers me sometimes but I'm trying to not worry about it because we have so many other good things together. As I get older, the sex gets better. I don't have to think of anything else and I can just enjoy it.

My children are 16 and 18 and they are aware that I'm a lesbian. In early '86 when I started to go to the discussion group at a church, I would leave them downstairs in a place for kids. They would stay there until time for lunch, and then I'd take them to lunch with these heavy duty lesbians. I told them about the lesbian dances and I told them what gay was. Then, I told them that I was gay also. They had played with the other lesbians' children. I asked them if they had any questions and one of them said, "Yes, can we go to bed now?"

276

I have asked them since how they felt about it. They said that they'd rather I weren't gay, but that's the way things are. They lived with me up until two years ago. The younger one lives with his father and comes down here once a month. The older lives with another boy. We are all on good terms.

I am not out at work. I have one buddy there who is 30, and he knows and likes my partner. I'm not that friendly with anyone else there. I marched in the gay parade last year and I'll do it this year. I don't care if I get on television. I don't think the straight people give two hoots.

Once you've been a lesbian, why would you want to be anything else? I find women much more exciting than men. I find the sex so much more fulfilling.

ORDER ADDITIONAL BOOKS FROM

SOARING EAGLE PUBLISHING

SPIRIT CALLED MY NAME
A Journey of Deepening into Soul
by
Sally O'Neil
$11.95

AND THEN I MET THIS WOMAN
Expanded Second Edition
by
Barbee Cassingham, M.A.
Sally O'Neil, Ph.D.
$14.95

Fax orders: 360-331-4523
Phone orders: 360-331-4412
email orders: oneilcas@whidbey.com

Sales Tax:
  Please 7.9% for books sent to Washington addresses
Shipping:
  $4.00 for the first book and $2.00 for each
  additional book.
Payment:
  prepayment by check

Soaring Eagle Publishing
PO Box 578
Freeland, WA 98249

... *AND THEN I MET THIS WOMAN*

Now available on **T-SHIRTS AND SWEATSHIRTS**

T-SHIRTS are100% cotton heavyweight. Black or White with
... *AndThen I Met This Woman* embroidered in purple.
Med. thru XL—$24.99each; XX—$25.99;
XXX—$26.99; XXXX—$29.99 each.

SWEATSHIRTS are 9 oz., 50/50. Available in Black only with
... *And Then I Met This Woman* embroidered in purple.
Med. thru XL—$29.99 each; XX—$31.99;
XXX—$33.99; XXXX—$35.99 each.

Qty	Size	Color	Description	Price	Totals

Merchandise Total	
ILL residentsadd 8.25% Tax	
Shipping & Handling*	
TOTAL	

Phone or Fax Orders: 630-894-3210
Email Orders: order@outwear.com
VISA, MASTERCARD, check/money order
*Add $3.00 per t-shirt or $4.00 per sweatshirt for priority mail.

OUT! WEAR
Pridewear and Accessories
664A Meacham Road - Suite 215
Elk Grove Village, IL 60007